THE RESILIENT PRACTITIONER

The Resilient Practitioner, third edition, gives students and practitioners the tools they need to create their own personal balance between caring for themselves and caring for others. This new edition includes a new chapter on resiliency, an updated self-care action plan, self-reflection exercises in each chapter, and a revised resiliency inventory for practitioners. Readers will find, however, that the new edition keeps its strong focus on research and accessible writing style. The new edition also retains its focus on establishing working alliances and charting a hopeful path for practitioners, a path that allows them to work intensely with human suffering and also have a vibrant career in the process.

THE RESILIENT PRACTITIONER

Burnout and compassion fatigue prevention and self-care strategies for the helping professions

Third Edition

Thomas M. Skovholt and
Michelle Trotter-Mathison

Routledge
Taylor & Francis Group

LONDON AND NEW YORK

Third edition published 2016
by Routledge
2 Park Square, Milton Park, Abingdon, Oxon, OX14 4RN

and by Routledge
711 Third Avenue, New York, NY 10017

Routledge is an imprint of the Taylor & Francis Group, an informa business

First edition published by Allyn & Bacon 2000
Second edition published by Routledge 2010

Library of Congress Cataloging-in-Publication Data
Skovholt, Thomas M.
  The resilient practitioner : burnout and compassion fatigue prevention
and self-care strategies for the helping professions / Thomas M. Skovholt
and Michelle Trotter-Mathison. — Third edition.
    pages cm
  Includes bibliographical references and index.
  ISBN 978-1-138-83003-5 (hardback : alk. paper) —
ISBN 978-1-138-83007-3 (pbk. : alk. paper) — ISBN 978-1-315-73744-7
(ebook) 1. Medical personnel—Mental health. 2. Psychotherapists—
Mental health. 3. Teachers—Mental health. 4. Counselors—Mental
health. 5. Medical personnel—Job stress. 6. Psychotherapists—Job
stress. 7. Teachers—Job stress. 8. Counselors—Job stress. 9. Burnout (Psychology)—Prevention. I. Trotter-Mathison, Michelle. II. Title.
  RC451.4.M44S57 2016
  616.89′14—dc23
  2015031296

ISBN: 978-1-138-83003-5 (hbk)
ISBN: 978-1-138-83007-3 (pbk)
ISBN: 978-1-315-73744-7 (ebk)

Typeset in Adobe Caslon
by Apex CoVantage, LLC

MIX
Paper from
responsible sources
FSC
www.fsc.org   FSC® C013056

Printed and bound in Great Britain by
TJ International Ltd, Padstow, Cornwall

For my daughter Rachel whose birth was a beautiful moment
and whose continual presence is a pleasure

– Tom Skovholt

For John, Lars and Elias, my loves who bring so much joy to my life

– Michelle Trotter-Mathison

And to practitioners, including counselors, therapists, teachers,
health professionals, professors and clergy across the world, whose
professional caring for others makes this a better world

PRAISE FOR THE FIRST EDITION

"*The Resilient Practitioner* is a 'must' read for every practitioner. Skovholt gives clear explanations of practitioner stress and provides remedies that can be implemented. I really enjoyed the real-life examples and was impressed by the extensive research that forms the background for the book. Skovholt is a master teacher and practitioner. I recommend that practitioners keep this book close by and reread it throughout their careers."

– Clara Hill, PhD, University of Maryland

"This is a wonderful book that merits careful reading by all helping professionals. Well written, engrossing, and amply documented, *The Resilient Practitioner* is recommended with unqualified enthusiasm."

– Ted Packard, PhD, University of Utah; President, American Board of Professional Psychology

"In this remarkable book, the author is eloquent in his perceptive description of the demands on the practitioner. At several points, I felt like I was reading from the pages of my own personal journal. This is a wonderfully stimulating book!"

– William Parham, PhD, University of California–Los Angeles; Associate Director, Counseling Services

"Over the past ten years, I have been asked by publishers to review hundreds of manuscripts. This is one of the best written! The author has a very engaging writing style and his humanity permeates the content. The book has a solid scholarly foundation yet is very accessible, very alive, and rich with vivid, real-life illustrations. What a wonderful job!"

– Mark Kiselica, PhD, The College of New Jersey

"At all career stages, caring professionals will find this book to be a rich resource of encouragement for professional development. It is a bountiful gift to us all."
    – Jaquie Resnick, PhD, University of Florida

"This visionary work is essential reading for practitioners and students in the helping fields. With poetic wisdom and academic clarity, Tom Skovholt addresses the issues involved in sustaining professional validity."
    – Sally Hage, PhD, State University of New York

"In *The Resilient Practitioner*, Tom Skovholt demonstrates a compassionate appreciation for the complexities of the helping fields. Clearly, he has experienced these development challenges, and has listened and guided well as others have navigated these challenging tasks. Now, in this book, his wisdom can be shared with many other 'high-touch' professionals."
    – Kate F. Hays, PhD, Sport Psychologist; Director, The Performing Edge, Toronto, Canada

"Tom Skovholt has identified precisely the difficult career issues for practitioners in the helping professions. He specifies particular steps in balancing care for others and self, sustaining the professional and personal selves, and preventing burnout. Skovholt stimulated me to consider self-care in a whole new way – not as a narcissistic withdrawal from responsibility, but as a means to sustain intellectual excitement and emotional commitment to those with whom I work."
    – Susan Neufeldt, PhD, Clinical Supervisor, University of California–Santa Barbara

PRAISE FOR THE SECOND EDITION

"Skovholt and Trotter-Mathison have offered well-written observations of profound truth, informed largely by the superlative body of research on counselor development by Skovholt and colleagues. A stimulating and validating read for practitioners across the professional lifespan."
— **Camille DeBell, PhD, Associate Professor of Counseling Psychology, Regis University**

"I welcome this book, as a psychotherapist, with my whole heart. The authors have left no stone unturned in identifying the pitfalls which can lead to burnout in practitioners in the business of 'other-care.'"
— **Ursula Somerville, MEAP, MIAHIP, European Psychotherapist and Clinical Supervision based in Ireland**

"The second edition of *The Resilient Practitioner* is packed with insights and practical tools for mental health professionals. This is a great book for teaching and training, and for periodic self-assessment for the mature professional."
— **Arnold Spokane, PhD, ABPP, Professor of Counseling Psychology, Lehigh University**

"The authors explicitly state the case for help-giving as an extremely complex, dialectical and demanding occupation. I have no doubt that students, novices, and professionals in the helping occupations will find this to be a major contribution to their professionalism and well-being."
— **Moshe Israelashvili, PhD, Tel Aviv University, Israel**

PRAISE FOR THE THIRD EDITION

"This book should be required reading for all in the helping professions. Skovholt and Trotter-Mathison identify struggles with which any one of us might relate. They use powerful examples and provide a structure for reflection that would be a valuable resources to all colleagues in nursing and other professions who routinely cope with the stresses of caring."

— **Lori Brown, PhD, RN, assistant professor at Washington State University**

"My best read this far about the personal in the professional in relationship-intense professions. Relevant across disciplines and cultures. In a warmhearted manner, the authors offer well-founded and thought-provoking insights, benefitting both the novice and the experienced professional. An invaluable companion for any relational worker aiming for the long run!"

— **Kjetil Moen, chaplain, researcher, and lecturer at Stavanger University Hospital, Norway**

"As a practitioner in private practice, I frequently turn to this book for reminders of how to persist despite the demands of psychologically taxing work. As a professor and supervisor, I frequently refer students to this book so that they can learn how to engage in self-care in a systematic, thoughtful way. *The Resilient Practitioner* should be required reading for students and should be on the bookshelf of all practitioners in the helping fields such as health care, education, and social work."

— **Julie Koch, PhD, associate professor and training director in the counseling psychology doctoral program at Oklahoma State University**

CONTENTS

ABOUT THE AUTHORS

© Libby Benedict

Tom Skovholt, PhD, LP, ABPP, is professor at the University of Minnesota, a psychologist in part-time private practice, and author or coauthor of thirteen books. He has received awards for writing, teaching, and professional practice and has taught and given workshops around the world.

©Anna Wachter

Michelle Trotter-Mathison, PhD, LP, is a psychologist and the assistant director of the mental health clinic at the University of Minnesota's Boynton Health Service. She also maintains a private practice in St. Paul, Minnesota, and is coeditor of *Voices From the Field: Defining Moments in Counselor and Therapist Development.*

PROFESSIONS UNDER THE RESILIENT PRACTITIONER UMBRELLA

The following list enumerates some of the many who are in relevant professions, broadly defined. All involve the intense giving of oneself to enhance the lives of others. This book is for all.

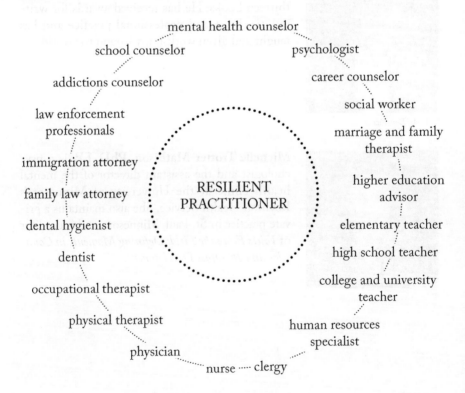

mental health counselor
school counselor
psychologist
addictions counselor
career counselor
law enforcement professionals
social worker
immigration attorney
marriage and family therapist
family law attorney
RESILIENT PRACTITIONER
higher education advisor
dental hygienist
elementary teacher
dentist
high school teacher
occupational therapist
college and university teacher
physical therapist
human resources specialist
physician
nurse ···· clergy

PREFACE

How does the opera singer take care of the voice?

The baseball pitcher, the arm?
The woodcutter, the axe?
The photographer, the eyes?
The ballerina, the legs and feet?
The practitioner in a helping, caring, relationship-intense profession, the self?

In this book, we address the intense giving of oneself to enhance the lives of others. It is the importance of the intense giving, and the fragility of it, that has been the central focus of this book in its first edition in 2001, its second edition in 2011, and now the third edition in 2016. We have spent many months rewriting the book for this third edition. The inventory has been revised; there are new chapters on "What Is Human Resilience?" and "The Eye of the Storm Model of Practitioner Resiliency," and existing chapters have been rewritten. For us, Tom and Michelle, it has been a very engaging, difficult, and highly meaningful project. We have been so encouraged by the response we have received from readers of this book and those in our workshops.

We have written this book for people in a broad group of career fields: the helping professions, education, health occupations, and the clergy. Some readers may not identify with this broad occupational group (counselors, therapists, teachers, professors, social workers, clergy, nurses, doctors, physical therapists, other health professionals and more) because each profession seems so different from the others. For example, a public school teacher may think that her work is very different from that of a nurse or a counselor. Yes, there are differences. Novices in training are often taught about the differences and the uniqueness of their own field. We know these can be important for career identity, role, and function. On the other hand, our own experience in counseling, education, and health services has helped us to see that there are great commonalities among counseling, teaching, and healing. We feel that there are many work concerns that are shared among these professional groups. We view all of these as caring professions because of common work ingredients.

A leading career development inventory, the Campbell Interest and Skill Survey, combines "helping others through teaching, healing and counseling" into one of seven work orientations (Campbell, Hyne, & Nilsen, 1992, p. 2), providing evidence for similarity among these fields. When reading this material, we invite you to consider the commonalities rather than the differences among the careers. If the commonalities can be understood, then this material may be of use to a variety of individuals working in different caring professions.

The questions to be asked by all are: How do those in the helping-caring, relationship-intense professions, who use their own self as a method of change, prevent burnout and maintain professional vitality? How does one establish balance between other-care and self-care? What are the keys to practitioner resiliency? In this book, we ask these questions and hope to provide the reader with useful ways to address these questions and find valuable answers.

SKOVHOLT PRACTITIONER PROFESSIONAL RESILIENCY AND SELF-CARE INVENTORY

2014 VERSION

The purpose of the inventory is to provide self-reflection for practitioners and students in the helping, health, and caring professions, broadly defined. All of these fields are relationship-intense fields in which the welfare of the Other (client, patient, student, advisee, mentee, etc.) is primary. *Practitioner* here refers to individuals in these professions. All of these professions are distinct, with specialized areas of knowledge and techniques. However, they are united by the enormous amount of emotional investment needed for the I-Thou relationship with the Other, who is often experiencing suffering or human need of one kind or another.

Questions are addressed to both active practitioners and also students in training programs across a broad range of the caring/relationship-intense professions. Some of the questions are more relevant to some professionals or students in some training programs than others.

The checklist consists of four sub-scales: Professional Vitality, Personal Vitality, Professional Stress, and Personal Stress.

1 = Strongly Disagree, **2** = Disagree, **3** = Undecided, **4** = Agree, **5** = Strongly Agree

Circle your responses.

Professional Vitality

1. I find my work as a practitioner or as a student to be meaningful.	1 2 3 4 5
2. I view self-care as an ongoing part of my professional work/student life.	1 2 3 4 5
3. I am interested in making positive attachments with my clients/students/patients.	1 2 3 4 5
4. I have the energy to make these positive attachments with my clients/students/patients.	1 2 3 4 5
5. The director/chair at my site/school is dedicated to practitioner welfare.	1 2 3 4 5
6. On the dimension of control of my work/schooling, I am closer to high control than low control.	1 2 3 4 5
7. On the dimension of demands at my work/schooling, I have reasonable demands rather than excessive demands from others.	1 2 3 4 5
8. My work environment is like a greenhouse – where everything grows – because the conditions are such that I feel supported in my professional work.	1 2 3 4 5

Subscale Score for Professional Vitality (Possible score is 8–40) _____

Personal Vitality

9. I have plenty of humor and laughter in my life.	1 2 3 4 5
10. I have a strong code of values/ethics that gives me a sense of direction and integrity.	1 2 3 4 5
11. I feel loved by intimate others.	1 2 3 4 5
12. I have positive/close friendships.	1 2 3 4 5
13. I am physically active and receive the benefits of exercise.	1 2 3 4 5
14. My financial life (expenses, savings, and spending) is in balance.	1 2 3 4 5
15. I have a lot of fun in my life.	1 2 3 4 5
16. I have one or more abundant sources of high energy for my life (e.g., friends and family, pleasurable hobby, enjoyable pet, the natural world, a favorite activity).	1 2 3 4 5
17. To balance the ambiguity of work in the caring professions, I have some concrete activities that I enjoy where results are clear cut (e.g., gardening; a fantasy sports team; a craft, such as weaving or knitting; remodeling and painting; fixing up a car; a collection, such as coins/rocks).	1 2 3 4 5
18. My eating habits are good for my body.	1 2 3 4 5
19. My sleep pattern is restorative.	1 2 3 4 5

Subscale Score for Personal Vitality (Possible score is 11–55) _____

Professional Stress

20. There are many contradictory messages about both practicing self-care *and* meeting expectations of being a highly competent practitioner/ student. I am working to find a way through these contradictory messages.   1 2 3 4 5

21. Overall, I have been able to find a satisfactory level of "boundaried generosity" (defined as having both limits and giving of oneself) in my work with clients/students/patients.   1 2 3 4 5

22. Witnessing human suffering is central in the caring professions (e.g., client grief, student failure, patient physical pain). I am able to be very present to this suffering, but not be overwhelmed by it or experience too much of what is called 'sadness of the soul.'   1 2 3 4 5

23. I have found a way to have high standards for my work yet avoid unreachable perfectionism.   1 2 3 4 5

24. My work is intrinsically pleasurable most of the time.   1 2 3 4 5

25. Although judging success in the caring professions is often confusing, I have been able to find useful ways to judge my own professional success.   1 2 3 4 5

26. I have at least one very positive relationship with a clinical supervisor/ mentor/teacher.   1 2 3 4 5

27. I am excited to learn new ideas, methods, theories, and techniques in my field.   1 2 3 4 5

28. The level of conflict among staff/faculty at my organization is low.   1 2 3 4 5

Subscale Score for Professional Stress (Possible score is 9–45) _____

Personal Stress

29. There are different ways that I can get away from stress and relax (e.g., television shows or movies, meditating, reading, social media, watching sports).   1 2 3 4 5

30. My personal life does not have an excessive number of one-way caring relationships in which I am the caring one.   1 2 3 4 5

31. My level of physical pain/disability is tolerable.   1 2 3 4 5

32. My family relations are satisfying.   1 2 3 4 5

33. I derive strength from my personal values and/or my spiritual or religious practices and beliefs.   1 2 3 4 5

34. I am not facing major betrayal in my personal life.   1 2 3 4 5

35. I have one or more supportive communities where I feel connected.   1 2 3 4 5

36. I am able to cope with significant losses in my life.   1 2 3 4 5

37. I have time for reflective activities (journaling, expressive writing, or thinking in solitude; or talking through one's concerns with others).   1 2 3 4 5

38. When I feel the need, I am able to get help for myself.   1 2 3 4 5

Subscale Score for Personal Stress (Possible score is 10–50) _____

Total Score for the Four Subscales (Possible score is 38–190) _____

There are a total of 38 questions in the Skovholt Professional Resiliency and Self-Care Inventory. All are scored in a positive direction, with 0 low and 5 high. As stated earlier, the scoring system is a method for self-reflection by practitioners and students in the caring professions. There is no total number that is considered best.

As a way to consider professional resiliency and self-care in your career work, consider these questions.

First, scan the questions and focus on your high answers, those with 4 and 5 responses. What do you conclude? Write here.

_____

_____

_____

_____

Then focus on your low answers, those with 1 and 2 responses. What do you conclude? Write here.

_____

_____

_____

Then look across the four categories of Professional Vitality, Personal Vitality, Professional Stress, and Personal Stress. Are they in balance? If not in balance, what remedies could you consider? Write here.

_____

_____

_____

_____

Finally, consider the different topics covered in the inventory, your answers, and the comments you made for future self-reflection, clinical supervision, and discussion with others. Best wishes!

Tom Skovholt, PhD, LP

Part I

1
CARING FOR OTHERS VERSUS SELF-CARE: THE GREAT HUMAN DRAMA

I have always been better at caring for and looking after others than I have been at caring for myself. But in these later years, I have made progress.
– Carl Rogers at age 75 (Rogers, 1995, p. 80)

As a hospital chaplain, Walter Pitt once helped a little girl gather the strength to share parting words with her grandmother. Later, he received a letter saying it was one of the most important moments of the girl's life.
– Ampel, 2013, p. B4

Teaching school is like having jumper cables hooked to your brain, draining all the juice out of you.
– Former teacher, now novelist Stephen King, (as cited by Grothe, 2008, p. 15)

Too often, we therapists neglect our personal relationships. Our work becomes our life. At the end of our workday, having given so much of ourselves, we feel drained of desire for more relationship.
– I. D. Yalom (2002, p. 252)

I tend to give my time away to others before I take it for myself.
– Junior high school teacher, 1996

R*esilience*, a word that is being used more and more during recent years, refers to a person's ability to adapt in a positive way to difficult and trying situations. If you want to read in depth about the concept of resilience, Luthar et al. (2000) have written a scholarly review of the topic, one with

169 references! Or, as a short cut, you can just think of the term *resilience* in this way: The capacity to bounce back from a negative force – like a fishing bobber, pushed under water, pops back up.

Laura Hillenbrand (2010) describes Louie Zamperini this way in her bestseller book *Unbroken: A World War II Story of Survival, Resilience, and Redemption*. It is a story of a man who went through enormous suffering and pain, described in page after page of this book, and kept coming back. In the first page of the preface, we read of 1943. Louie was in the Pacific Ocean, where he ". . . lay across a small raft drifting westward . . . The men had been adrift for twenty-seven days . . . deep into Japanese controlled waters" (p. xvii). Louie was captured and spent many months in concentration camps where he was the special victim of a brutal guard . . . but, like the resilient bobber, he kept physically and emotionally bouncing back in the camp, and in the decades after, too. Then in 1998, fifty–five years later, he returned to the site of a concentration camp where he had been held in a cage decades before. Now in triumph, eighty-one-year-old Louie carried the Olympic torch while the local people watched in respect as they saw "the old and joyful man, running" (p. 398). The title *Unbroken* captures the life story of Louie Zamperini so well. Resilience and more resilience in action.

So many heroic stories of altruism reveal examples of balancing of other-care and self-care: Rosa Parks on the bus comes to mind, as do the Protestant reformer Martin Luther, social worker Jane Addams at Hull House in Chicago, Captain Chesley Sullenberger landing his plane on the Hudson and checking to see again and again that all were out as the plane filled with water. We will finish this section with one more example, this time about the Japanese civil servant who saved hundreds of Jews. Working as a Japanese civil servant in Lithuania in 1940, without asking for authorization, Chiune Sugihara spent 20 hours a day filling out exit visas for desperate Jews (Levine, 1996). In the teeter-totter of other-care vs. self-care, he swung to other-care because, he said, it was the right thing to do.

The resilience demanded of the helping professional is of another dimension; there is not the intensity where basic physical survival is the axis that one's life revolves around. Yet, the helping professional often expresses the agonizing pull between other-care and self-care: There is a continual pull, constant strain, a tautness. It may not be intense. The common form is subtle, felt as body tension. Usually it doesn't knock one over. It is more like a small wave rippling through – maybe a wave going in two directions or waves pulling in three directions. Or is it four? Sometimes it is a skirmish that quickly becomes war.

Exhausted when saying yes, guilty when saying no – this tension is between giving and taking, between other-care and self-care. This is a universal dilemma in the human drama. It is just more intense for those who are, by nature and inclination, emotionally attuned to the needs of others. It gets highly illuminated when intense human interaction – helping, teaching, guiding, advising, or healing – is the occupational core. Here, giving of oneself is the constant requirement for success. Caring for others is the precious commodity. It is caring for the Other, when by nature we are, as a species, geared to meet the needs of the self, that provides much of the strength of these caring fields.

The best ones who enter these helping fields have this natural lean toward the needs of others. They see, feel, smell, touch, and hear human need all around them and want to respond.

The best ones struggle the most and figure it out; or leave; or burn, from the inside to the outside, while hope dies. It is not natural to put the Other before the self. The human senses – smell, sight, taste, touch, hearing – are there to protect the me, to promote the me. To know the world through the senses of the Other is like swimming upstream, hard to do and easy to resist. How much should one work for the Other – this moment, this hour, this day, this week, this month, this year, this decade, this career? How much to give this hour to the one I am trying to help when there will be another day of many hours, and another week of many more hours, and another month of even more hours? How much to give of the self for the Other this hour?

In these three paragraphs, we are not talking about dipping into one's own well of fortitude for Louie Zamperini-type resilience. However, to see human suffering and need all around oneself and to constantly be on the teeter-totter of other-care vs. self-care – do I give or pull back – demands its own kind of resilience. Hence, this book.

To be successful in the helping professions, we must continually maintain professional vitality and avoid depleted caring. For counselors, therapists, teachers, clergy, and health professionals, this can be a very difficult task. Since Freudenberger (1974) first used the term *burnout*, many authors have discussed the difficulty of professional vitality in the helping and related fields (Baker, 2003; Canfield, 2005; Larson, 1993; Linley & Joseph, 2007; Maslach, 1982; Mathieu, 2012; Papastylianou, Kaila, & Polychronopoulos, 2009; Robinson, 1992; Rothschild, 2006; Shirom, Oliver, & Stein, 2009; Sussman, 1995; van Dernoot Lipsky & Burk, 2009).

A central occupational strength in the caring professions – perspective taking – makes the boundary regulation between the needs of others and the needs of self a difficult task. Occupationally, we are trained to see life from the perspective of the Other, and perhaps we do this naturally by personality, as well. L. King (personal communication, February 1996) suggests that we often have a personal history of active caring for others: "We are often the great friend who listens, the 'fixer' in a relationship, the diplomatic person in a disagreement, and/or the 'helper' within the family of origin." In another place, Skovholt (1988) wrote:

> One of the most distinguished characteristics of our profession is our intense focusing on highly skilled perspective taking: a combination of empathy, perceptual flexibility, tolerance for ambiguity and affective

sensitivity. When successful, all of this translates into a profound ability to understand the world as other people understand it. This well-honed ability, one of our occupational strengths, is not possessed by many people in other occupations.

(p. 283)

In the theater of life, the Other becomes the illuminated part of the stage; our I is often outside the illumination. The lives of others – their hopes, ideas, goals, aspirations, pains, fears, despair, anger – are in focus. Like a leaf under a microscope, we see all of this in highly illuminated detail. As a counselor, therapist, educator, clergy member, or health practitioner, the Other gets our attention. Out of the illuminated microscope, we can easily lose sight of our own needs. We even lose sight of the need to not respond to all needs around us.

In addition to perspective taking that focuses on the needs of the Other, we often are pulled to see things from multiple perspectives. That way we can naturally engage in activities such as family counseling in which we can see the issues from the viewpoint of each family member, as, for example, the mother, father, daughter, and son. Some people would hear of the Wallace Stevens (1923) poem, "Thirteen Ways of Looking at a Blackbird," and say, "Wow, there are thirteen ways?" Those in the helping professions often use multiple lenses at the same time to understand others.

Being able to see the world of human need through multiple viewpoints can be valuable. Sometimes, though, those in the caring professions lose touch with their own viewpoint and their own needs.

Settings of intense human need can be very unsettling for those in the helping, teaching, and caring professions. This occurs because we are taught to assess, experience, and respond to human need at a much more intense level than the public. That is the goal of training. Nursing homes are an example of a difficult arena. With a honed ability to do perspective taking, one can easily feel the loneliness, fear, and despair of the residents. One practitioner struggled mightily to visit her client in such a place without being overwhelmed by all the other human need. She was caught in the option of exhaustion versus guilt while searching for boundaries of when to reach out and when to pull back. Here, the "shoemaker has no shoes" problem of low self-care can easily occur. Sussman (1995) comments:

Many therapists, for example, grew up playing the role of caretaker, go-between, parentified child or burden-bearer within their families of origin. Having learned at an early age to attune themselves to others, therapists often have great difficulty attending to their own emotional needs.

(p. 4)

Where in the practitioner's life is self-preservation and self-care held and nurtured? Perhaps the answer can be found in the struggle between altruism and self-preservation within the bigger human drama. As a species, we have been remarkably able to increase our numbers. In recent years, it has been at an astonishing rate, from 2.5 billion in 1950 to 7.2 billion in 2014 (U.S. Census Bureau, 2014). We have accomplished this growth and domination of all other living species with an acute sense of species self-preservation.

Biologically, each of us is wired to preserve the self. The senses continually warn us of danger. The physical defense system fights disease and threat with white blood cells, energy pouring from the adrenal glands, and other miraculous processes. The desire to have children is often thought of as a biological self-preservation. The psychological defenses keep us from harm through the use of denial, rationalization, and projection.

Just as self-preservation seems to be an urgent human drive, we can also find evidence that altruism and self-sacrifice are central. In the winter of 2012 in Newtown, Connecticut, Sandy Hook Elementary School was tragically attacked by an armed gunman (Associated Press, 2012). While the school was under siege, teachers and administrators put the schoolchildren's lives ahead of their own. Several accounts of heroism were reported in the aftermath of the shooting. Teacher Victoria Soto was said to have physically shielded the children in her first-grade class. Principal Dawn Hochsprung and psychologist Mary Sherlach literally put themselves between their students and the gunman by attempting to intervene, rushing toward the shooter. All three died in the shooting, offering the ultimate sacrifice as they worked to do what came naturally to them as individuals and as helping professionals: to protect and care for the children they served.

Books such as *Man's Search for Meaning* (Frankl, 1946/1959) and *Do Unto Others: Extraordinary Acts of Ordinary People* (Oliner, 2003) tell of ordinary people who have made extraordinary sacrifices of the self. Kohlberg (1979), a leading scholar in moral development, measures morality with the famous case of Heinz, a boy caught in the dilemma of either stealing medications to keep his mother alive or not stealing – caring for others versus self-preservation.

The dilemma of Heinz is a sample of the larger human drama of altruism versus self-care. Within this larger human stage, counselors, therapists, teachers, clergy, and health professionals do their work, attempting to live on the balance beam between too much other-care and too much self-care. For example, how much sleep deprivation should the practitioner endure to adequately prepare to help the client, student, parishioner, or patient the next day? This is just one example of many dilemmas continually faced by practitioners in the high-touch fields.

Exploration of the practitioner's world begins in the next chapter. There, we explore the deep satisfaction of the work. We are speaking of the deep, and often subtle, pleasure that comes when enveloped by work that aims to make life better for others.

SELF-REFLECTION EXERCISES

In this chapter, we attempted to describe a major human theme: Should one's energies go toward the well-being of others or of the self? Or a combination? Of what? When?

1. What kind of reaction did you have to the ideas of Chapter 1?

_____

_____

_____

_____

_____

_____

_____

_____

2. How accurate is the description in this chapter of the "pull between Other-care and self-care" for you?

_____

_____

_____

_____

_____

_____

_____

_____

2
JOYS, REWARDS, AND GIFTS OF PRACTICE

Life need not be easy, provided only that it is not empty.
                                    – **Lisa Meitner cited by Maggio (1997, p. 12)**

In teaching others, we teach ourselves.
                                                            – **Proverb**

There is no greater pleasure than knowing that you made a real, lasting difference in the life of another human being – a common experience for the effective psychotherapist, one that never loses its special meaning.
                                    – **J. C. Norcross and J. D. Guy (2007, p. 21)**

This is the true joy in life, the being used for a purpose recognized by yourself
as a mighty one; the being thoroughly worn out before you are thrown on the
scrap heap; the being a force of Nature instead of a feverish selfish little clod
of ailments and grievances complaining that the world will not devote itself to
making you happy.
                                    – **George Bernard Shaw (Larson, 1993, p. 2)**

A teacher affects eternity; he can never tell where his influence stops.
                                                – **H. Adams (1918, p. 300)**

For the most part, it was wonderful to treat children. Usually they were resilient and recovered from their illnesses, and all of the time they were responsive
to a caring approach.
                                    – **Pediatrician T. Berry Brazelton (2013, p. 35)**

A person who saves one life, is as if he saved a whole world.
                                              – The Talmud (Danby, 1933, p. 388)

The reward of teaching is knowing that your life made a difference.
                                              – W. Ayers (1993, p. 24)

Most readers of this book are nurturers of human development. This can be very rewarding. Making a positive difference in human life – in the growth and health of the Other – is a central career interest for counselors, therapists, teachers, clergy, health professionals, and other practitioners, too. The close connection to others and the opportunity to help, teach, guide, advise, and heal people brings the joys, rewards, and gifts of practice. Being successful in helping relationships can produce a profound sense of satisfaction.

People have asked us why we did not choose a research career in a lab or a technical field such as software design. We have a variety of answers, such as experiencing a wonderful sense of satisfaction in working with people struggling with life's difficulties. Interacting closely with the most complex of all species is so enriching. The opportunity to try to make human life better for others is a great privilege. And to get a salary for often deeply satisfying work adds to the privilege of having such work. What are some of the specific joys, rewards, and gifts of practice?

JOYS OF PRACTICE

The focus of the work is on positively affecting human need. This goal can be elusive and difficult to achieve, a reality quite familiar to veteran practitioners. Consequently, when the practitioner hits a bull's-eye of success, there is a joy-of-practice reaction. Witness these joy-of-practice reactions.

Michelle recalls a practitioner joy that drew her into the professional helping field:

> As a lay helper right out of college, I worked at a summer residential camp for adolescents who were struggling with emotional and behavioral issues. I worked with one young woman who I will call Mary. Slowly, through my work with Mary, I was seeing small indications that Mary liked setting goals and making changes in her life. After a special outing celebrating Mary's birthday, she came to me and said: "I had a really fun day today. All my other birthdays I was gone – drunk or high – but today I had a lot of fun. Thank you, thank you for today." Hearing this from this young woman helped me to know that the caring professions were for me. I wanted to be

there to help others, like Mary, connect to themselves and their capacity for growth.

Tom recalls a practitioner joy, a bolt of appreciation that felt like the nurturing warmth of a summer sun.

I received a phone message long after the counseling work was over. The former client said, "Thank you, Tom, for the fantastic work you did in the counseling and consulting; it was so valuable. May come back but everything is good now."

Good, very good, excellent, helpful, feel much better, fantastic, am more hopeful – these are reassuring, kind, and encouraging words from clients about our work together. These words get our hearts pumping and corpuscles jumping. We are reminded of Frank McCourt, who taught adolescents for 30 years in the New York Public Schools and later wrote *Teacher Man* (2005), and his words: "Sometimes they will tell you that was a pretty good lesson and you're on top of the world. That somehow gives you energy and makes you want to sing on the way home" (p. 77).

Larson (1993) asked nurses to describe "the most positive moment he or she ever had as a helper." Three of them said:

When a wife of a patient whose case I just opened called the office after I left their home and told my supervisor, "Thank you for sending us such a wonderful nurse."

When a patient said to me, "I'm so glad you're my nurse today because I wanted you to be the one to be with me on the day I die." She died at the end of my shift that day.

A mother of a child with leukemia once said, "We come to this clinic every week and know that you care for many, many children, but when you come to see us, I feel like we are the only people you have seen that day."

(pp. 6–7)

A senior psychologist at a Southern university described to Tom a joy in his practice:

I had a very nice phone message when I checked in yesterday (on my birthday); a client who I worked with about four years ago had called to tell me that she is doing very well, is about to be married, and feels that the only reason she is alive and living so happily now is because of the work we did together. She had been clinically depressed and suicidal for months, and I had worked my butt off with her; such a nice result!

For a member of the clergy, the pleasure of helping came in this way:

> One day he went to visit a woman who was very ill. As he started to leave the room, the woman spoke to him: "You have been such an important person in my life. I want you to know that I have great love for you." These kind words sailed straight into the minister's heart.
>
> (Rupp, 1994, p. 17)

An elementary school teacher experienced a similar "practitioner joy":

> This past fall I received in the mail two letters from two former students, then beginning fifth grade. They were asked by their teacher to write a letter to their favorite elementary teacher. These two girls each wrote to me, telling me that I had been their favorite, and they each had their reasons why . . . The letters brought tears to my eyes, and I know I will save them forever. I kept them at my desk this whole past year, as a reminder that I'm a good teacher and that I am positively influencing children's lives. Receiving those letters was one of the happiest moments during my teaching career.
>
> (S. McNeill, personal communication, 1996)

Can you think of anything better than to have a ringside seat in the human drama and, at times, assist in making the drama turn out well? We are fortunate to be in the helping professions. We acknowledge this with happy memories of past practitioner experiences, enjoyable present work, and positive anticipation of the future in this field.

REWARDS OF PRACTICE

> I do not try to help the other grow in order to actualize myself, but by helping the other grow I do actualize myself.
>
> – M. Mayeroff (1990, p. 40)

> There is richness to the experience of relating on an intimate level with many people.
>
> – P. P. Heppner (1989, p. 74)

As described in the Mayeroff and Heppner quotations, the relationship-intense fields can provide many "psychic income" rewards. Radeke and Mahoney (2000) describe some of the rewards in the high-touch field of psychotherapy (see Table 2.1). In comparing the experience of research psychologists and psychotherapists, the therapists were significantly higher on important dimensions.

Table 2.1 Rewards of psychotherapy

	Percentage Agreement	
Dimensions	*Psychological Researchers*	*Psychotherapists*
Made me a better person	78	94**
Made me a wiser person	81	92**
Increased my self-awareness	69	92**
Appreciation for human relationships	56	90**
Accelerated psychological development	69	89**
Increased tolerance for ambiguity	58	81**
Increased capacity to enjoy life	51	75**
Felt like a form of spiritual service	25	74**
Resulted in changes in my value system	68	61**

Source: Items taken from "Comparing the Personal Lives of Psychotherapists and Research Psychologists," by J. T. Radeke and M. J. Mahoney, 2000, *Professional Psychology: Research and Practice, 31,* pp. 82–84.

** $p < .001$.

In their book, *Leaving It at the Office*, Norcross and Guy (2007) cite the following as some of the rewards of practice: satisfaction of helping, freedom and independence, variety of experiences, intellectual stimulation, emotional growth, reinforcement for personality qualities, and life meaning.

Some rewards are related to the "helper therapy principle," an idea first described by Reissman in a classic 1965 article. Essentially, the idea is that the giver in a human exchange gets a lot from giving. An example is the sponsor role in Alcoholics Anonymous (AA). In an article, Tom elaborated on Reissman's idea by suggesting four ways that giving is rewarding (Skovholt, 1974):

1 *Identity development* – The idea here is that the giving role gives the practitioner a sense of identity. Also, the need for effectance motivation (the joy of being a cause) and competence motivation (the innate desire to be competent) is met through the practitioner's work. Last, a close connection with others reduces a sense of loneliness. In recent years, much professional literature in psychology has documented the importance of social connections for wellness. For example, Rupert, Stevanovic, and Hunley (2009) found that when surveying psychologists, family support was an important ingredient for well-being, whereas conflict between work and family were associated with burnout.

2 *Social exchange theory* – Theories of social exchange attempt to explain the human rules used in resource exchange. Foa (1971) developed a six-resource model: love, status, information, money, goods, and services. In essence, by giving one or more professional resources – information and services – the practitioner receives versions of love, status, and money. People, including practitioners, treasure receiving these resources.

3   *Modeling* – The modeling literature is rich with examples of how we learn by observation. Examples are learning to teach by watching one's teacher and learning to parent by watching one's parent. This is a powerful human development method. Practitioners closely observe those they work with when attempting to make positive changes in an emotional, intellectual, spiritual, or physical area.

Much of the interaction and observation occurs in private space, although some is public (i.e., the classroom). Like a cultural anthropologist in these encounters, the high-touch practitioner is able to closely observe human behavior and learn from it. Of course, this must be done in a way that is both ethical and in which the needs of the other are primary. Yet, these encounters do provide rich opportunities to learn via modeling. Often the learning is about deeper human themes, such as the impact of motivation on change, the ingredients of success, ways to encounter pain, and how friends and family affect goals. If done in an ethical way, this modeling can be instructive for the practitioner.

Here is an example. A few years ago, Tom attended a ceremony for winners of teaching awards. Eight awards were given out. All eight of the award winners spoke passionately about how much they learned from their students. Ironic, in a way. These were distinguished professors. Aren't they supposed to be the givers of knowledge to the unenlightened? No, they spoke of how their students were their teachers and how grateful they were for what they had learned.

4   *Direct reinforcement* – The practitioner's work can lead to direct social reinforcement, such as forms described by Skinner (1953) of attention, approval, and affection. Certainly, getting reactions like these can help make the practitioner's work satisfying.

GIFTS OF PRACTICE

One great gift of practice is species immortality. This is a term that we use to describe the connection that we, as practitioners, have to the ongoing evolution of our species, *Homo sapiens*. Through helping, teaching, religious and spiritual ministry, and health care, practitioners are connected to the great human life chain that stretches from the far past into the far future. Like sharing one's DNA with others in a biological chain, practitioners, through their acts of empowering human growth, are connected in a positive way to the ongoing human story.

Connecting oneself to the growth and development of other people can provide enormous meaning, sometimes clearly felt and sometimes unconscious, for the practitioner. When the search for meaning is elusive for so many in contemporary society, finding a source of meaning is a great gift to the relationship-intense practitioner. Conversely, meaning burnout, a concept explored in Chapter 6, can be very distressing for the practitioner because the gift of meaning seems to be gone.

A master therapist quoted in Norcross and Guy (2007) expresses this sentiment about the value of meaningful work:

> I have learned so much about life through the experiences of my clients. They have changed me, and I'm a better person for having been a part of their struggles and pain. I've lived several lifetimes and viewed life through the eyes of literally hundreds of people. This can't help but improve my own chances for a happy life.
>
> (p. 30)

Another gift of practice relates to how we grow at a deep and profound level through our work with our partners – such as our clients, patients, students – in the helping relationship. Van Dernoot Lipsky describes her work in a hospital as a practitioner:

> Even at the most devastating moments of their lives, people somehow called up their highest selves. They were suffering on a level I could relate to, and yet despite their anguish, they didn't give up. I received an infusion of awe and hope with each and every shift . . . I felt my old isolation melt. Because I had an opportunity to bear witness to others' pain while helping them to know they could be loved and taken care of as they suffered, I experienced a profound healing. My work at Harborview gave me a gift.
>
> (van Dernoot Lipsky and Burk, 2009, pp. 118–119, reprinted with permission)

In summary, there can be great joys, rewards, and gifts for the practitioner. They can combine in unique forms at different times during a practitioner's life. They can vary in form and intensity across different practitioners and different caring career fields. Yet, although differences exist, the positive qualities of the work – the joys, rewards, and gifts – can be very real and sustaining.

SELF-REFLECTION EXERCISES

In this chapter, we have described moments of intense satisfaction for practitioners. Nurses, teachers, and counselors were quoted about special times when their work felt very helpful to others. This significant helping of others has been called the "psychic income" of the work. It can make it all worthwhile.

1. While preserving the privacy of clients, students, and patients, describe one to three specific joy-of-practice experiences (moments of intense work satisfaction) for you in your life as a practitioner. What was the specific

positive impact on the other person? What did you find most meaningful about this work?

_____

_____

_____

_____

_____

_____

_____

2.   Perhaps one or more joy-of-practice experiences were powerful critical incidents or defining moments, which are events that often serve as turning points in our professional lives. We suddenly see ourselves in a new way because the event leads us to view ourselves differently. Sometimes, critical incidents/defining moments lead us to understand theory or practice with sudden insight. Here, describe a joy-of-practice critical incident/defining moment. What happened? How did it impact your life?

_____

_____

_____

_____

_____

_____

_____

3.   If you are a seasoned practitioner, address these questions. Do you judge situations as joy-of-practice experiences in a different way than you did in the past? If so, what has changed? Are you pleased or disappointed with the impact of time and experience on your satisfaction with the work?

_____

_____

_____

_____

_____

_____

_____

4. It is important for those of us in the caring professions to have meaningful, positive work experiences. Some practitioners do not have them on a daily basis. However, on a random and intermittent basis, they can be very reinforcing for us. Write below in response to these questions: Are you having a high ratio of positive work experiences in your work life? If not, what is missing? What can you do to increase the ratio of positive experiences in your life as a practitioner?

_____

_____

_____

_____

_____

_____

_____

_____

3
THE CYCLE OF CARING: CORE OF THE HELPING PROFESSIONS

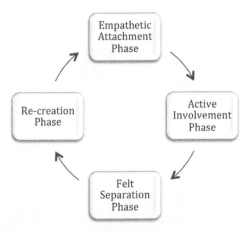

Figure 3.1

Psychotherapy researcher Jerome Frank produced evidence that many different helping methods are similarly effective because of their common factors. The most important common factor, he said, was the presence of "an emotionally charged, confiding relationship with a helping person" (Wampold & Weinberger, 2010, p. 34). Recently, four prominent counseling researchers stated the same conclusion: "some therapists consistently achieve better outcomes than others . . . more effective therapists appear to be able to form working alliances across a range of clients . . . and have a greater level of facilitation skills" (Tracey et al., 2014, p. 225).

These are very compelling words from prominent researchers in the helping professions. They have sifted through hundreds of research studies with this question: What is effective professional helping? The helping relationship is key. For them and many other researchers and practitioners, much of it boils down, as you can see from the quotes above, to the relationship-intense work of the working alliance. We call it the Cycle of Caring, which we originally described in the first edition of this book in 2001 and in article form in 2005.

One of the significant findings in the research comparing different counseling/therapy approaches is how they all seem to produce positive results. This equivalence of outcome is vexing for those who believe method is the deciding factor.

CARING: A PRECONDITION FOR AN EFFECTIVE HELPING RELATIONSHIP

Much of our urgency in writing this book about the importance of being a resilient practitioner relates to the concept of caring. If we cannot feel – want – think – express caring for the Other, we are less useful in the helping professions. In Chapter 6, "Hemorrhaging of the Caring Self," we describe ways the helper's attachment ability is drained by: burnout, compassion fatigue, vicarious traumatization, and ambiguous professional loss and uncertainty. The ability to care is fundamental for the Cycle of Caring.

It is better to know the patient who has the disease than it is to know the disease which the patient has.
                                                    – Hippocrates (460 BC–377 BC)

Care is a state composed of the recognition of another, a fellow human being like one's self: identification of one's self with the pain or joy of the other; of guilt, pity and the awareness that we all stand on the base of a common humanity from which we all stem.
                                                    – R. May (1969, p. 284)

People who have had a great teacher almost always say, "That teacher saw something in me that I was unable to see in myself."
                                                    – P. J. Palmer (2004, p. 82)

When the therapist's intention is being with and for the client, he or she may experience feelings of awe, wonder, warmth, compassion, and love. The therapists interviewed used terms such as "compassion," "caring," "profound respect," "awe," and "admiration" to describe their feelings toward the client.

– Geller & Greenberg (2012, p. 128)

In a world where technological innovation is illuminated in splendor and applause, it seems much too simple to say that something more basic is more important. Yet, in the counseling, therapy, teaching, health, and religious fields, the research evidence overwhelmingly points to the power of human caring as the essential among essentials.

Skovholt and D'Rozario (2000) asked people to describe in two words the teacher they *most liked* in their experience as students. Others were asked to describe their *best* teacher. Each person in this sample of 171 individuals gave two words for a total of 342 words. The favorite word chosen did not describe how brilliant or well-educated the teacher was, the prestige of the teacher's university training, the methods of teacher education that the teacher learned or practiced, or the teacher's physical attractiveness. The most popular word described whether the person as a student felt cherished by the teacher in a personal way. The overwhelmingly popular word used to describe the most liked or best teacher was *caring*. Themes were created from the words in this study, with the strongest theme being *caring and understanding*. For this theme, the following words – *caring, understanding, kind, patient, concerned, helpful*, and *loving* – were stitched together to highlight the importance of the connection that the teacher makes with a student.

Since this study in 2000, both of us, Tom and Michelle, have asked others in resiliency workshops and classes about their favorite teacher and have come up with similar results. For example, in September 2008, 14 doctoral students in a Midwest program in professional psychology were asked to use three words to describe their favorite teacher. Their answers were consistent with other results, and again *caring* was the most popular word. Related words were *patient, supportive, kind, invested, engaged*, and *positive*. Another dimension was *humorous*. They also mentioned ideas like *knowledgeable, recognized my abilities*, and *high expectations*.

Right now, we ask that you think about your favorite teacher. What were her or his most amazing traits? Your results may not be consistent with the results presented earlier. Your answer is your answer. In a fundamental way, your favorite teacher probably altered you. It may have been in your own view of your ability. Maybe your favorite teacher opened up a new field of study or way of understanding the world. Most people have some feeling of connection with their favorite teacher. Most describe the person as knowing about them personally and being concerned about them as a student. When there is a combination of your teacher being very knowledgeable in the content area, highly skilled in teaching the content, deeply committed to your welfare, and passionately caring for you as a person – there is a favorite teacher! Without the personal caring, the other factors usually lose their powerful effect.

Reflecting on your favorite teacher: What were his or her most amazing traits? (Use the following oval to list your responses.)

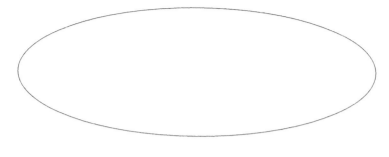

How did these traits help you succeed in school?

_____

_____

_____

_____

_____

_____

_____

_____

_____

_____

Examining factors in student achievement, Klem and Connell (2004) found that teachers' support and caring were central to student success and participation: "Teacher support is important to student engagement in school as reported by students and teachers. Students who perceive teachers as creating a caring, well-structured learning environment in which expectations are high, clear, and fair are more likely to report engagement in school" (p. 270).

Mayeroff (1990) describes the benefits of caring this way: "Perhaps few things are more encouraging to another than to realize that his growth evokes admiration, a spontaneous delight or joy, in the one who cares for him" (p. 56).

The process seems to work as described by psychiatrist Scott Peck (1978) when illuminating the crucial importance of parental love for the child. He wrote: "For when children know that they are valued, when they truly feel valued in the deepest parts of themselves, then they feel valuable. The feeling of being valuable – 'I am a valuable person' – is essential to mental health and is a cornerstone of self-discipline" (p. 24).

Here, this idea of the capacity for self-discipline, an essential skill for student success, may help us understand why teacher caring is valued so highly by students. As additional evidence, let us mention how caring, defined as love, is the bedrock, central element in the parent–child bond. And think of popular songs on the radio. No matter what song, singer, country, year, or decade, they often speak of one kind of caring – romantic love – usually found or broken.

Our premise is that caring is the essential quality that must be *maintained* in the relationship-intense career fields, where there are high levels of need and high levels of personal connection. Here, the inability to care is the most dangerous signal of burnout, ineffectiveness, and incompetence. The inability to care, therefore, must be strongly guarded against during one's career in these relationship-intense career fields. Bohart et al. (2002), in research on helping relationships, use the word *empathy* when describing the power of caring.

THE CYCLE OF CARING

To consider the Cycle of Caring as similar to seasons, we ask you to think of changes in the seasons, especially in places like our state of Minnesota, where there are great seasonal weather changes.

> Spring is the beginning, with rain and new warmth touching the soil.
> Summer radiance bursts forth with all its green growth.
> Fall unfolds with gorgeous colors but a slowing of growth and preparation
> for the next season.
> Winter has a quiet, slower beauty with its snows.
> And the cycle starts again, when Winter gives way to the burst of Spring.

This cycle of the seasons, its beauty and its energy and its excitement, is reflected in the life of the practitioner in the Cycle of Caring (shown earlier in Figure 3.1). Empathetic Attachment is like Spring, Active Involvement like Summer, Felt Separation like Fall, and Re-creation like Winter.

Over and over again – with client, student, patient, advisee, parishioner – the practitioner must engage in a minicycle of closeness and then some level of grief, with the ending of an often intense, professional connection. In the relationship-intense fields, the cycle is ongoing, with empathetic attachment, active involvement, felt separation, and re-creation. In many ways, in counseling, therapy, teaching, spiritual guidance, advising, and healing, we constantly must first care for the Other, be involved, then separate – being able to feel for, be involved with, and then separate from person after person in a highly effective, competent, useful way.

One essence of practice in the helping, teaching, and healing fields is to be a highly skilled relationship maker who constantly attaches, is involved, separates well, steps away from the professional intensity, then does it again with a new person. We could, in fact, say this is the essence of the work; it is a very concise summary of a 40-year helping-professions career.

In a major contribution in understanding human development, Bowlby described these processes in the classic books *Attachment* (1969), *Separation* (1973), and *Loss* (1980). This practitioner's work mirrors the larger human drama of connection and disconnection between people.

This process continues over and over in interaction with those we try to counsel, teach, guide, or heal: empathetic attachment phase → active involvement phase → felt separation phase → re-creation phase → empathetic attachment phase, then repeat. Making positive attachments, being engaged, and making positive separations with others in need of counseling, therapy, learning, or healing is the core professional skill for practitioners in the caring professions.

How many children does the preschool teacher greet as another week starts Monday morning? How many student–teacher–parent consults does the school counselor have each day? How many therapy clients does the marriage and family therapist see each week? How many helping contacts does the social worker have each month? How many patients does the physical therapist work with every six months? How many students does the schoolteacher instruct per year? How many suddenly fired clients does the outplacement counselor have per decade? How many funeral services does the minister have during a career?

How does one do this over and over again? How is this done well? Person after person – attach, be involved, then separate, re-create, attach, be involved, separate, re-create – day after day, week after week, month after month, year after year. Long-term social workers, counselors, therapists, teachers, clergy, and health professionals work 30 to 40 years. They make attachments, involvements, and separations over and over again. Hundreds of them. Thousands of them.

It is the endless Cycle of Caring, with distinct phases, that makes up the life of the practitioner. Each of the phases – attachment, involvement, separation, re-creation – is important in itself, and each will be discussed separately. However, it is also important to focus on the Cycle of Caring as a whole and the need for competent practitioners to be skilled at all phases of the cycle. It is not easy to be skilled at each phase because they are distinct and call for different practitioner attributes. Attachment demands an emotional connection and openness to the experience of the Other. Involvement demands the content skills of the practitioner and the energy to do the work. Separation paradoxically demands the opposite of attachment. To remove one's self is the opposite of connecting one's self. It reminds us of the saying about the tasks of parenting: "roots and wings." Parents who make roots often find it hard to give wings because of the emotional connection to their sons and daughters. Giving wings is easy for the parent who never develops deep roots, although the child usually suffers in such a situation. The same dilemma confronts the practitioner, yet, as with good parenting, the challenge is to be good at both attachment (roots) and separation (wings). The last stage of re-creation can be hard for a variety of reasons. We want extremely responsible and conscientious individuals to enter the caring professions because of the ethics of caring for vulnerable people. Yet, being highly meticulous and diligent as a person does not easily translate to the re-creation phase. This is the letting go, resting, having fun part of the cycle, in order to attach again.

Some individuals are extremely good at involvement but less skilled at attachment or separation. Teachers who focus on specialized content may have this orientation. The specialized content or skills may be the focus for the individual's work (e.g., teaching high school physics, critical care nursing, psychological assessment), and the emotional connection–disconnection may be less of a focus. The emotional dimension at the active involvement phase, however, is also important for ideal results in the counseling, therapy, teaching, and health professions. Now, for a discussion of each phase.

Empathetic attachment phase

The therapeutic value of empathy continues to receive strong support.
— A. Bachelor and A. Horvath (1999, p. 142)

Attaching, connecting, bonding – these are key terms that describe the emotional oxygen-giving link between the counselor, social worker, therapist, teacher, clergy, or health professional and the Other. Attachment theory, described by Bowlby (1988), is considered the most important conceptual work in understanding how a child becomes emotionally secure and able to be close to others. Pistole (2003) and Pistole and Fitch (2008) have provided rich applications of attachment theory to the caring professions.

The literature in the counseling and psychotherapy field supports the power of the human relationship dimensions in this work. In a 72-page literature review on the counseling relationship, Sexton and Whiston (1994) state in the *first* line of their abstract: "The quality of the counseling relationship has consistently been found to have the most significant impact on successful client outcome" (p. 6). They go on to say:

The success of any therapeutic endeavor depends on the participants establishing an open, trusting, collaborative relationship or alliance . . . Research has shown that failure to form such an alliance is strongly associated with client noncompliance with treatment plans . . . premature termination . . . as well as poor outcome.

(p. 7)

Further, the importance of the therapeutic alliance is emphasized by Strauss et al. (2006). They assert:

The strength of the alliance early in therapy is one factor that influences treatment engagement, retention, and outcomes. Ruptures in the alliance also occur and can be therapeutic or can be associated with early dropouts and worse outcomes, if not handled properly.

(p. 337)

In a review of the literature on the working alliance, Castonguay, Constantino, and Grosse Holtforth (2006) report that one of the most notable findings that emerged from their review of the research was that the "alliance correlates positively with therapeutic change across a variety of treatment modalities and clinical issues" (p. 272). Lambert, Garfield, and Bergin (2004) speak to common factors; basic therapeutic factors have been identified as promoting positive change regardless of the theoretical underpinnings of a particular therapist's counseling style:

The humanistic, phenomenological perspective, suggests that the common factor is a caring relationship characterized by warmth, support, attention, understanding, and acceptance. These ingredients are said to have direct healing properties somewhat like the effects of good nutrition or solar radiation, which strengthen the organism and stimulate growth.

(p. 809)

Attaching with our "underside of the turtle" side, yet also . . .

. . . as it became increasingly evident as I continued working with Peter, both sides of the turtle are necessary in our work. I learned how important it was to provide a consistent caring presence with Peter to let him know that I would be present with him unconditionally, no matter what pain or hurt he shared with me. I also learned as time progressed that I needed to keep a certain level of emotional distance, to maintain a separate space for reflection and self-care, to be effective in my work as a counselor.

(Hage, 2010, p. 183–84)

What is the nature of this attachment process? How is this important but difficult task done well? To do this well, we often need to attach with our caring side; we call it the underside of the turtle versus the hard shell. With the hard shell, we cannot get hurt, but we cannot attach very well either. So we must continually present our soft side and attach with it. And, as Sally Hage notes above, we must balance this with our need to be separate too. We must do this with individuals who are often struggling with emotional, intellectual, spiritual, or physical needs. Learning an optimal level of attachment – in which the practitioner experiences the world of the Other, but is not overwhelmed – is an essential professional skill and a complex one. Learning how to regulate and modulate the level of emotional attachment in the curative relational process takes time. It is a paradoxical skill – learning how to be emotionally involved yet emotionally distant, united but separate. Baker (2003) described this as self-other differentiation and discussed how this is an important part of practitioner self-care.

Often, the job of the counselor, social worker, therapist, teacher, clergy, or health professional is to establish a good relationship with individuals who cannot relate well or are highly distressed. Children who are socially rejected often believe that others with good intentions actually want to harm them (Dodge & Feldman, 1990). The helper must often relate to people who have psychological or physical complaints and want things to be figured out for them, or want answers to their questions, or are confused or lacking in confidence, or are hostile or depressed. Often the person is highly distressed, in pain, or feels unsuccessful. There may be a loss or struggle of some kind. For example, Harmon, Hawkins, Lambert, Slade, and Whipple (2005) presume that "some clients, because of their interpersonal histories, find it difficult to establish a trusting relationship with a therapist (or any person), and that these clients are especially sensitive to therapist characteristics and actions that spark memories of past painful experiences" (p. 177).

Mallinckrodt and Wei (2005) suggest that "continuing struggle [by the practitioner] to build a more secure therapeutic attachment and productive working alliance results in a corrective emotional experience that the client, equipped with new social competencies, can generalize to other relationships" (p. 358). To be effective, Other-care givers are expected to be able to attach successfully with these highly distressed individuals. Being highly skilled at creating positive human relationships is, as shown by Mallinckrodt's research, an essential occupational trait for counselors, therapists, teachers, and health professionals.

The responsibility for competent, ethical, professional relationship making is with the practitioner, not the client, student, parishioner, or patient. The client may be very depressed or angry; the student may feel very stupid and ashamed about academic challenges; the church member may be struggling with the sacred; the patient may have a serious physical illness. The practitioner must step forward and create a positive human connection so that counseling, advocacy, therapy, teaching, or healing can occur. To do the job well, the practitioner must absorb much from the Other, especially in the more emotionally demanding fields within the caring professions, such as psychotherapy.

Learning how to attach with the caring side – the underside of the turtle versus just the hard shell – is a part of all degree-training programs in the caring professions. For example, school counselors, social workers, elementary teachers, nurses, physicians, priests, and physical therapists are all taught professional relationship skills and how to be empathetic with their clients, students, parish members, and patients. Practitioners spend hours trying to learn the attachment skills of attending, intense listening, emotional sensitivity, and nonverbal understanding. Accurately absorbing the reality of the Other, caring about the Other, and feeling the feelings of the Other are essential in this skill of empathetic attachment. They learn metaphors for helping, such as "the ocean," a visual way of thinking about immersing oneself in the world of the Other, an empathetic immersion. For some individuals in the caring professions, learning to be empathetic is difficult. These individuals often leave this work while in training, voluntarily or upon request, because of an inadequate ability to connect and, just as likely, because of a lack of interest in committing such a huge amount of one's emotional energy to the work.

Optimal attachment

What do clients and patients recall when they look back, years later, on their experience in therapy? More often than not, they remember the positive support. The focus in training in the caring professions is on teaching the student practitioner to care enough by use of verbal and nonverbal attending behavior. Often, in reality, the problem for many in the helping fields is caring too much – excessively feeling the distress emotions of the Other, such as sadness, fear, shame, anxiety, and despair, and replaying the "movie" of the Other's life repeatedly in one's own mind. The practitioner can be engulfed by the Other's pain and even experience vicarious traumatization, a process described in Chapter 6. Learning an optimal level of attachment, in which the practitioner experiences the world of the Other but is not overwhelmed, takes years of training, practice, and supervision. It is an essential professional skill and a complex one. Learning how to regulate and modulate the level of emotional attachment takes time. It is a paradoxical skill – learning how to be emotionally involved yet emotionally distant, united but separate. The demand to be attuned, to be interested, to be energetic for the Other – the Other who is often in misery, anger, defiance, or hopelessness – and to continue to do it over and over again with client after client is taxing, as well as deeply rewarding, work.

Novices in the caring professions are especially vulnerable to being overwhelmed by the realities of others. We describe this problem under the term *emotional boundaries* in Chapter 4 about stress experienced by novices. Learning physical boundaries, such as with touching, between practitioner and client/student/patient is important. Learning the skills involving emotional boundaries can be even more difficult. For example, a school social worker asked, "When a student or family is really upset and there are no easy answers, I keep trying, and then I take it home with me. How can I leave it at the office?" (I. Smith, personal communication, February 21, 1996). Is this optimal attachment? Being able to know an optimal level and artfully perform the sequence of attach–involve–separate–re-create is a characteristic of a skilled practitioner.

Larson (1993), writing about emotional demands in the helping fields, describes "the helper's pit" where the practitioner becomes overinvolved emotionally and then experiences the pain in a way that puts him or her in a pit of distress feelings. Reflecting an earlier idea by Lief and Fox (1963) about detached concern as ideal for physicians, Larson suggests "detached concern" as an optimal style of involvement and writes that it is "the state of being emotionally involved while simultaneously maintaining a certain emotional distance" (p. 38). Writing about family functioning, Olson (2000) describes the optimal level of family functioning as a midpoint between enmeshed and disengaged on one dimension and chaotic and rigid on another dimension. This can also be a guide to practitioner attachment.

Difficulty in attaching

The task of attaching to the Other is especially hard when the client, for example, does not have the skills for positive attachment. Repeatedly forming optimal, positive professional attachments is often especially difficult for practitioners or those in training who have had serious attachment distress in their personal lives. If the practitioner had intense stress in his or her primary attachments in childhood or adolescence, such as a very distressed relationship with a parent, then forming consistent, optimal professional attachments in later life can be difficult. To paraphrase Freud, sometimes the child is the parent of the adult, which means that childhood events can profoundly affect adult life. Other attachment distress examples include losses, such as major geographic moves, and their effects, such as culture shock.

In *Fear of Intimacy,* Firestone and Catlett (1999) make a compelling case for the impact of early life experiences on later life capacity for intimacy. For example, the authors argue that the child can be strongly affected by the same-sex parent's modeling of intimacy and non-intimacy behavior. Unless the child, when an adult, consciously addresses a fear of closeness, the internalized early life messages can overwhelm any other reality and produce an extreme reaction of fear and avoidance.

As an extension, personal life attachment behavior can have a direct bearing on the practitioner's professional attachment style. The effect on professional attachment may mean that the practitioner attaches too deeply; is unable to attach sufficiently to understand clients, students, or patients or make them feel cared about; or expresses an inconsistent attachment style with one person or across a number of clients, students, or patients. The inconsistency can seriously affect the quality of the professional relationship and, therefore, the possible benefits for the Other. As mentioned earlier, Pistole and Fitch (2008) provide a valuable perspective in their application of attachment theory to counseling work.

The skill of professional attachment is complex. It is more than just trying to help. For optimal effectiveness, there must be a profound understanding of the Other. The helper-healer in the following short story was aiming for skilled professional attachment but missed a key element.

Some Other Day

Preserve me from the occupational therapist, God.
She means well, but I'm too busy to make baskets.
I want to relive a day in July when Sam and I went berrying.
I was eighteen,
 My hair was long and thick
 And I braided it and wound it round my head so it wouldn't get caught on the briars.
But when we sat in the shade to rest I unpinned it and it came tumbling down.
And Sam proposed.
I suppose it wasn't fair to use my hair to make him fall in love with me,
But it turned out to be a good marriage.
Oh, here she comes, the therapist with scissors and paste.
Would I like to try decoupage?
"No," I say, "I haven't got time."
"Nonsense," she says, "you're going to live a long, long time."
That's not what I mean,
 I mean that all my life I've been doing things
 For people, with people. I have to catch up
 On my thinking and feeling.
About Sam's death, for one thing.
Close to the end, I asked if there was anything I could do . . .
He said, "Yes, unpin your hair."
I said, "Oh, Sam, it's so thin now and gray."
"Please," he said, "unpin it anyway."
I did and he reached out his hand – the skin transparent, I could see the blue veins –
 And stroked my hair.
If I close my eyes, I can feel it. Sam
"Please open your eyes," the therapist says;
"You don't want to sleep the day away."
She wants to know what I used to do.
Knit? Crochet?
Yes, I did those things,

And cooked and cleaned
And raised five children
And had things happen to me.
Beautiful things, terrible things.
I need to think about them,
    Arrange them on the shelves of my mind.
The therapist is showing me glittery beads.
She asks if I like to make jewelry.
She's a dear child and means well.
So I tell her I might
Some other day.

**– E. Maclay (1977, pp. 46–48)
Reprinted with permission by Sanford J.
Greenburger Associates, Inc.**

Active involvement phase

By far the most common and important way in which we can exercise our attention is by listening . . . How difficult it is to listen well. Listening well is an exercise of attention and by necessity hard work . . . There are times when I shudder at the enormity of what I am doing when I accept another patient.

– M. S. Peck (1978, pp. 121, 141)

Trust in the other to grow and in my own ability to care gives me courage to go into the unknown . . . And clearly, the greater the sense of going into the unknown, the more courage is called for in caring.

– M. Mayeroff (1990, pp. 34–35)

This is the work phase for the practitioner. One's content area expertise in the relationship-intense professions varies greatly and this content expertise makes these professions dramatically different from each other. So while the process parts of the work may be similar, the content part demands great knowledge and specific skill for different career fields. Think of how these differ so much: teaching adults to read, explaining the Bible by being able to read old Greek, repairing teeth, helping patients maintain adequate blood sugar levels, assessing whether there is child abuse, helping an adult cope with sudden unemployment. This content work rises as a dominant part of this phase. A central question becomes: Does the practitioner know how to assess the problem and make things better? However, the focus of this book is not about the content areas of the caring professions. These fields vary greatly (e.g., from psychotherapy to physical therapy), and covering all the specific content skills here would remove us from the focus of this book – the wear and tear of emotional giving in one's professional work.

The active involvement phase demands the continuous attachment of the practitioner to the other person in need. The consistent, sustained work for the Other makes this phase of the cycle. An analogy is with the work of parenting, in which the long phase of active involvement follows the early days of birthing and attachment. The consistent caring for one's child over the days, weeks, months, and decades is one indicator of positive parenting.

The practitioner's consistent emotional caring is part of the active involvement phase. This time period may be the mental health counselor's contract for 10 sessions, the teacher's rhythm of an academic year, or the physician's following of an elderly patient's long, slow decline. The active involvement phase can also be the majority minutes of a one-session meeting, the time between attachment and separation. This could be, for example, a one-time advising appointment, tutoring session, or home nurse visit.

Felt separation phase

With every hello there is a goodbye.
– S. Larson, junior high school teacher

Parting is such sweet sorrow.
– William Shakespeare (Romeo and Juliet, Act 2, Scene 2)

All counseling relationships must eventually end.
– R. Goodyear (1981, p. 347)

From terminations that are highly satisfying to those that are downright disturbing, the provider's emotional experience receives scant, if any, attention.
– D. D. Davis (2008, p. 173)

We know much less about the practitioner's experience with professional separations than experiences with the empathetic attachment phase. In personal life, attachments and separations are connected, as in the widely accepted thesis that the quality of previous attachments and separations predicts future attachments and separations. If so, do professional separations take on as much importance as professional attachments? Perhaps the ability to separate well, to be energized paradoxically by the professional loss process, may be a key attribute for the relationship-building elements of long-term professional vitality in the helping and related professions.

How then do highly competent practitioners separate? Teachers of children give hints of their attachment when they speak of their students as "my kids." Are there, in fact, elements of loss and grief in this professional separation process? Are there elements of a grief process that operate positively and enable the practitioner to attach again to another client, student, parishioner, or patient? Some examples of the dynamics of professional attachment and separation follow.

When Tom taught undergraduate courses, each course was one academic quarter of 10 weeks. He would often have a group of 30 students – living, feeling, thinking, acting human beings with names, faces, hopes, fears, and dreams. He would struggle to learn their names, and they may have thought that he was indifferent to them for one reason or another. He realized in time that, each quarter, he was still struggling with the loss of the classes that he had the quarter before and that he was still possessed by those classes. It was a kind of emotional, retroactive inhibition. A class can, after all, be a living group, a living organism that, all of a sudden with the final test, disappears and dies forever. It would usually take until the sixth or seventh week of the new quarter for his grief (Is that the right word for this loss? Do we even have language to describe the loss of professional attachments?) to wane and his embarrassment at not knowing names to grow. Then he would learn the names, only to have the whole process repeat itself the following quarter. He did not understand this attachment, involvement, and separation process for a number of years. He is sure most of the undergraduates knew nothing of it. They just hoped to be treated well, learn something, get a good grade, and move on.

A colleague working as a residence hall director in the past spoke of a similar loss reaction. For years, he experienced a three-week depression in June when the resident assistants and students left the dorm. The dormitory, teeming with people to whom he was professionally attached, suddenly was empty. He expected to be relieved and elated. Instead, he felt lost. For years, he did not really understand his reaction.

An internship training director described her struggles, when she was a student in training, with professional separation (S. Renninger, personal communication, February 1995):

> The more clients that I see, and the more clients that I terminate with, the more I am aware that this is a process of loss. I believe it is currently affecting my professional work as I am increasingly having difficulty getting close to my clients. I find myself hardening and retreating behind my "expertise." . . . I believe that this year I feel the losses more than ever before, and I think it is connected to the brief therapy I am providing. I saw most of my clients at my past therapy site for the entire year. We had time to connect and time to terminate over a period of several sessions.

Do highly experienced, highly competent practitioners – experts in attachment, involvement, separation, and re-creation – experience the separation process in a way that permits them to attach again? Is there a way to do this that distinguishes positive professional separations from negative professional separations in terms of the ability to attach again? Is there a pattern of attachment, involvement, and separation that continues, cycle after cycle, and produces good, ongoing professional attachments, involvements, and separations for proficient practitioners? Our suggestion is that an optimal level of other-care versus self-care highly correlates with proficient professional attachments for experts in the relationship-intense fields.

The concepts of "anticipating grief" and "honoring the loss" can facilitate the separation. Anticipating grief means the internal preparation a person does, often without much conscious awareness, in preparing psychologically for change in one's life. Examples include the death of a loved one after a long, slow illness; the end of school and graduation; or a long-planned geographic move. Practitioners know that the cycle of empathetic attachment → active involvement → felt separation → re-creation with clients, students, parishioners, and patients is contained within very specific limits, and they can internally prepare for the change.

Davis (2008) discusses five kinds of termination in mental health work with clients: prospective, flexible, complex, oblique, and unprofessional. She also says "termination may be likened to a pilot's task of landing an aircraft" (p. 1).

Using her metaphor of landing a plane, we will provide some examples. Prospective termination consists of a long planning process by practitioner and client, talking about the trip during the descent, and a really smooth landing. The plane stops and they both get out and go their own ways. This is a positive process for the practitioner and tends to energize the practitioner to enter the Cycle of Caring again.

Flexible termination lacks the long planning process. Suddenly, it is time to land the plane as, for example, the client announces midsession, "I think this will be my last visit." The practitioner as pilot then shifts the focus to termination and together they do the separating well phase work together. Again, this is an ending that gives energy to the practitioner.

Complex termination does not have a smooth landing. The plane gets to the runway and stops, but it is often a harrowing event for both practitioner as pilot and client as passenger. External events may force termination, such as a college internship training site where both graduate-student clinician and student client stop when the school year ends. Other examples involve a conflicted therapy relationship that slowly gets worse or a stalled therapy process with either practitioner or client not satisfied with the work. Then it ends perhaps by the client not returning for the next appointment. Complex termination can deplete the practitioner for the next Cycle of Caring.

Oblique termination can be likened to the client as passenger jumping from the rear of the plane via a parachute while the pilot is guiding the plane unaware that the passenger left. This happens when the client cancels an appointment and disappears while the practitioner had been thinking that the work was going well and that they were in midstream.

This lack of closure for the practitioner is a stressful experience we call ambiguous professional loss. Ambiguous loss (Boss, 1999) is often stressful for a person because the factors of loss are unclear – is a MIA soldier returning or not? For us in the caring fields, ambiguous professional loss occurs during all those times when things end without an ending in our work with clients, students, parishioners, and patients. We will discuss the stress of ambiguous professional loss and remedies for it in later chapters of this book.

Back to the pilot metaphor and the last kind of termination in the group of five by Davis (2008): Unprofessional termination occurs when the practitioner acts in an unprofessional manner and the helping relationship ends. The metaphor is that the plane crashes because of pilot error. There are many reasons for pilot error, but none are acceptable for the passenger, just as unprofessional conduct by the practitioner, for whatever reason, is never acceptable.

The varieties of termination offered by Davis are all part of the ending process in helping relationships; all human relationships have a beginning and an end. A good termination is positive for both parties. Honoring the loss means building in a time and energy commitment for the separation. This is not idle practitioner work. Practitioners need to do professional attachments again and soon. Doing separations well permits new attachments to emerge.

Grief work is not about dying. Grief work is for living; it makes intensity in living possible. That is why it is so important. Do not misunderstand. We are not suggesting that every practitioner, after only a short contact with a client, for example, engage in a long mourning ceremony. Professional grieving of the loss reflects the depth of the attachment and involvement, just as in one's personal life; therefore, more contact with the Other leads to more time and energy for honoring the loss. For example, a nursing home nurse may go to the funeral of a resident that she cared for over a long period. An elementary teacher may devote the last days of the school year to honoring the loss of her students and of the class as a living, breathing group that will never reappear in the same way. She may engage in a series of goodbye and transition activities to help the children and herself. A counselor or therapist may spend all of a last session with a client reviewing progress made, talking about goals for the client, and saying goodbye.

Some practitioners develop separation rituals for themselves. These may involve internal thought processes (i.e., thinking about the work with the individual in a certain way) or external events (e.g., a ritualistic walk within one's office area). Using one's own creativity and imagination can be fruitful for doing this. One academic advisor, writing about her ritual, said:

> It is helpful to think of ways I can say goodbye and separate in ways that leave me feeling renewed and ready for new connections with clients. My own ritual is to picture each client as a great novel, one that I have the pleasure of reading as I become engrossed in the character's life. But always I know that I am merely a page-turner, a facilitator, an active reader who both affects and is affected by the humanness of the words on the page.

Upon termination, I envision closing "the book," my access to the client's life, and place it on an important shelf in my mind.

(J. Langer, personal communication, July 1998)

Re-creation phase

Re-creation is the fourth phase of the Cycle of Caring. It is the getting away from the work phase. It is the "off button" phase as opposed to the three previous "on button" phases. It is as important as the three on-button phases (empathetic attachment, active involvement, and felt separation) because, without an off button, eventually there will not be any on-button phases.

The light switch in a room symbolizes this. Let us imagine that the light switch is attached to a solar panel that collects energy from the sun only when the light is off. When the light is off, energy is generated. Then when the light switch is turned on, there is illumination. And not just dim illumination. A rather, strong, intense illumination. It is the illumination of the highly caring practitioner deeply devoted to the Other, the one in need of help, assistance, guidance, teaching, or healing.

The re-creation phase can be understood using many different words that start with the letter r. These include renewal, rest, refurbishment, repair, restoration, renovation, restitution, and return. Other terms include having a break, time out, and goof off. We like to use the word re-creation because it communicates the paradox of the seriousness of the fun; recreation is about the re-creation of the self. And that is important.

Practitioners vary in the quality and quantity of their time off, their restoration. Some are good at this activity, a kind of self-care. Others never seem to get to it. And that eventually is dangerous, for restoration is necessary to begin the cycle again.

THE CYCLE IN SUMMARY

I have learned one important thing in my life – how to begin again.
– Sam Keen (As cited in Goodyear, 1981, p. 347)

All phases are important just as the great seasonal differences in northern climates depend on one another. The bursting of spring leads to the radiance of summer, which unfolds into the gorgeous colors of fall, which bring on the quiet beauty of the snows of winter . . . and then in time spring arrives.

Sustaining one's self, being vital, and being active in the caring professions means being fully present for the Other. But how does the practitioner maintain such a presence for person after person? How does the practitioner empathetically attach with the "underside of the turtle" side, get involved in working with the other person, end the work in a felt and positive way, then take a break only to start again with another and then another? Being able to do this well is a central focus of this book. The exact nature of the cycle differs across occupations and the nature of the contact within occupations. Yet, whatever the differences, the principle of proficiency with the endless caring cycle remains a measure of a successful practitioner.

The Cycle of Caring is one definition of the essence of the helping professions. It is what practitioners do over and over again, thousands of times over a 40-year career. This is noble and courageous work and so valuable, too, when it is done well. May you learn to be highly talented and skilled at the art form of the Cycle of Caring.

SELF-REFLECTION EXERCISES

We have described the four engagement phases within the Cycle of Caring as empathetic attachment, active involvement, felt separation, and re-creation. We have also said that the most successful work in the relationship-intense fields involves a connection with the practitioner's "underside of the turtle." Considering the cycle, let us ask you some questions.

1. Describe how you feel about your skill level at each of these engagement phases.

   Empathetic attachment: _____

   _____

   _____

   _____

   Active involvement: _____

   _____

   _____

   _____

   Felt separation: _____

   _____

   _____

   _____

   Re-creation: _____

   _____

   _____

   _____

2. Which of the four engagement phases is most satisfying for you? Most exhausting for you? Why?

_____

_____

_____

_____

_____

_____

_____

_____

_____

_____

3. What is your rhythm like in connecting and then disconnecting with your clients, students, or patients?

_____

_____

_____

_____

_____

_____

_____

_____

_____

_____

4

THE ELEVATED STRESSORS OF THE NOVICE PRACTITIONER

The formation of a professional self can be and often is quite frightening.

— **M. J. Adolson (1995, p. 35)**

Praemonitus, praemunitas – forewarned, forearmed.

— **Latin proverb**

Articles connected to students' [and novices'] experiences serve an important function. If only for a moment, they provide validation, clarity, and hope in the midst of great anxiety, discomfort and uncertainty.

— **M. Pica (1998, p. 362)**

Life is easier than you think; all that is necessary is to accept the impossible, do without the indispensable, and bear the intolerable.

— **K. Norris (cited by Maggio, 1997, p. 13)**

There is no gathering the rose, without being pricked by the thorns.

— **Pilpay (1872, p. 67)**

Over many years, Tom has felt distressed when he has listened to a new counseling student talk about the stress of practicum, the confusion, and the uncertainty, as it all hits the student like a sudden heat wave. As he listens, Tom wishes for the ability to give the student a pain-free injection of a secret serum. The serum would be a liquid mixture of the knowledge acquired by thousands of practitioners in the relationship-intense career fields after they have gone through hours and hours of the agony of learning from experience. The quote cited above, "There is no gathering the rose, without being pricked by the thorns," was stated 143 years ago; it is a wise saying that has met the test of time, but it is still about human agony. An agony we often try to avoid – just because a lot of people get the flu doesn't mean it is something to welcome!

Looking from a big picture perspective, it is the difficulties in life that often provide the great lessons for each of us. This is the premise of Gladwell's (2013) book: *David and Goliath: Underdogs, Misfits and the Art of Battling Giants*. A great example in the helping professions of the value of adversity is the life story of Gerald Corey. He is the most successful author of books in the helping professions, with 15 books in press, many with multiple editions. Thousands of students in the helping professions have loved the clarity that he brings to his writing and have rated the Corey books highly. Students feel empowered by being able to understand theories, techniques, and methods as they read his writing. They feel smart, they tell their instructor they love the book, and then the instructor orders the book again. And Corey writes another book and another edition.

Where did Gerald Corey get the drive and skill to write about human complexity with such clarity that beginning counseling students feel empowered by their own understanding? In his autobiographical essay, Gerald Corey (2005) tells us the root of his success was his own school failure. Growing up, he received F and D grades in classes and was absolutely confused and miserable. Often, he did not understand what the teacher was teaching. Gradually he emerged from his dark days of school and started to excel. Years later, after earning graduate degrees, Corey became a community college instructor. There, he was very motivated to make his classes have clear and understandable content. Then his career evolved to teaching students in the helping professions. Then gradually he turned his course content into textbooks for students in the helping professions who were enrolled at other colleges and universities. And after decades, former students at schools all over the US will say they still have their Corey books.

The Gerald Corey success story is an example of what Gladwell discusses in *David and Goliath*: Adversity can bring strength. In this chapter, we present nine factors often contributing to the adversity that the novice practitioner encounters. The innocence of the novice hitting the fog of early practice helps produce an assortment of elevated stressors. So here we go – we will present nine different factors that together produce the elevated stressors of the novice practitioner.

THE CORE NOVICE STRESSOR – SO MUCH AMBIGUITY

Over and over, graduate student Pica (1998) expresses surprise at his lack of preparation for all the ambiguity of practice: "Struggling with ambiguity is one of those unspoken aspects of clinical training that students do not comprehend until they begin their graduate programs" (p. 361). Yes, we are all surprised and unprepared while on our own Lewis and Clark exploration through the wilderness of professional preparation for the helping professions. Perhaps Emily Dickinson said it best: "To live is so startling, it leaves but little room" (as cited in Johnson & Ward, 1958, p. 380). The new practitioner, when first grappling with the confusing uncertainty of the work, deserves one chapter in the life journey of surprises.

Students are usually accepted into graduate training in the helping professions because they have excelled in school. They are hard working, conscientious, excel in learning class material, and develop mastery of assigned tasks. They are good at taking on an assignment and completing it at a high level. In fact, they are often nearly perfect in doing what is required. They feel a sense of control as students. This is expressed by getting high grades in classes. Then they decide to be trained in a high-touch human field such as counseling, teaching, therapy, nursing, the ministry, medicine, or other related field – in part because people are interesting. If only each of us knew when entering this work how interesting the most evolved of all species really is; if only each of us knew how hard it is to control ambiguity. For each of us, when taking our turn as a novice, this is when innocence hits reality.

Recently, Tom wrote about the struggle with ambiguity for new medical doctors in Australia (Skovholt, 2014, p. 9):

> For the physician-to-be, mastery in science and math is central. The pursuit of perfection brings levels of mastery. Knowledge development and mastery in science and math at the school level involves using increasingly complex logical, linear, sequential thinking patterns. There are correct answers and incorrect answers at the university level and mastering the correct answers involves study, memorizing, more study, thinking and more thinking. There are right answers! Like Matt Napier or others who have made the cross-Australia trek, finally the ocean, or the end of formal medical classes, is within view. And the person becomes a junior doctor.
>
> Then the ambiguities of medical practice emerge! Anxiety for the perfectionist medical student who always got the answers right if he or she studied hard enough and long enough. The ambiguity – labelled the art of medicine – emerges and roars because there is now the human world of infinite variety (patient and family members and doctor and nurses and other staff members). They call it practice, as in medical practice, because it is imprecise. It can be so stressful for the junior doctor who is being evaluated on unclear, seemingly shifting criteria. No wonder that the authors of the newly released *The National Mental Health Survey of Doctors and Medical Students* (2013) found that: ". . . the transition from study to work appears to be a particularly stressful period with higher rates of distress and burnout in younger doctors compared to more experienced and older doctors."
>
> (p. 6, www.Beyondblue.org.au)

This core novice stress of so much ambiguity hits new doctors as well as others in the helping professions. Our work involves close contact with this highly evolved species. The good and bad news, mostly bad for the novice, is that human beings – *Homo sapiens* – are very complicated. After many centuries of effort, the world's playwrights, head doctors, and spiritual leaders are still trying to figure us out. The kinds of problems we attempt to solve are full of complexity and ambiguity (e.g., What is human competence, and how do we get there? What is effective counseling? What is the genesis or cure for either depression or anxiety?). To understand this complexity and ambiguity, as practitioners we often use thinking patterns that are not logical, linear, or sequential. Expertise within these webs takes years to develop because complexity and ambiguity are difficult to master.

TREKKING WITH A CRUDE MAP

I didn't teach long enough to know what I was doing.
–J. Smiley (1991, p. 384)

Experience is a good teacher, but she sends in terrific bills.
–Antrim (quoted in Anonymous, 1982, p. 317)

The requirements for the novice to access, integrate, synthesize and adapt information are exhausting.
–M. Mullenbach (personal communication, March 1999)

The novice enters practice as a new canoeist enters white water – with anxiety, some instruction, a crude map, and some previous life experience. All of a sudden, for example, there is the client in front of the counselor, telling a very personal, real story. The story often comes in an incomplete form. The experience is like the sudden rush of water, rocks, and rapids, demanding instant understanding and reaction. The novice often has the urge to both call 911 and appear calm, collected, and professional – whatever that is. In a study of novices in the related practitioner field of medicine, the most stressful situation was the white water experience – having to make clinical decisions while very confused (Zeigler, Kanas, Strull, & Bennet, 1984).

The map is, most of all, a cognitive plan in one's head. It is based on a combination of ideas and information used by the novice (Skovholt & Starkey, 2012), including theories learned in class or procedures and techniques acquired in a practice lab. There is also the intense psychologizing and introspection of the new helping professional, such as medical or nursing students wondering about any relationships between diseases they study and their own bodies. There is modeling, too, of advanced practitioners, which is an age-old method, like how the apprentice bricklayer learns by watching the senior craftsman. One's personal life enters the cognitive map regarding how to react to human situations. With more age, one may also have had a parallel career or two (e.g., being a mom before becoming a psychotherapist) that provides part of the map.

The map learned in classes is not part of an internal cognitive schema but rather is external to the novice and comes in the form of theories and techniques from others. These are outside of the novice's professional experience. For the novice in the white water, this is not good enough. The status of novice equals an inadequate cognitive map.

Lack of professional experience makes everything more difficult. Inexperience creates a host of problems, and "I didn't know what I was doing" summarizes them. But what does not knowing really mean? It means many things. The novice teacher, for example, does not have a professional, internal cognitive map to navigate the task at hand, such as managing a classroom of bored students. Like much of the work in counseling, therapy, teaching, and health care, confronting this ambiguity requires multiple well-timed reactions in the right dose. It is a difficult dance that all beginners struggle to perform. There is that bear of a stressor again: the core novice stressor of so much ambiguity.

The theory and research map used by the inexperienced practitioner comes from others, be they writers of theories, supervisors, teachers, or mentors. This is the classic gap between theory and practice that hits all novices in fields such as counseling, therapy, teaching, and health. All of this happens after the practitioner in training has worked hard while attending numerous classes, reading countless books and articles, writing many papers, and taking scores of tests. All of a sudden, what one has learned seems irrelevant in practice. Why?

This happens because the cognitive map was developed by someone else as a *broad* guide to cover a *variety* of situations, not the particular situation the novice has now encountered. Also, the roadmap gleaned from one's personal life is often not adequate for the specific challenge. It is like comparing virtual reality to actual reality or learning a foreign language and then going where they speak that language. All of a sudden, the book learning hits the practical world; language is used differently than in the text in terms of usage, style, and syntax. Another problem is that one must continually try to access the expert's cognitive map, the theory of another, and *spontaneously* use it. So the combination of the theory of experts as a broad guide, the fact that it is the theory of others or personal self-theory and not professional self-theory, and that it must be applied spontaneously in novel situations means that the novice will often have limited success. It is a cumbersome process. For example, the new therapist sits with a new client who is highly self-critical. The therapist decides that this data fits with a cognitive therapy approach and then tries to apply the theory to the problem; however, the unique elements of the client's presentation puzzle the novice, who struggles to find a useful approach.

After realizing that the practice world of unique situations is different from the academic models that often seemed adequate while a student, the novice searches for an explanation for this distressing reality. This searching often coincides with a sense of frustration or disillusionment with one's training. In fact, there is often an intense disappointment with one's educational program, whether an undergraduate or graduate program. We suggest that, in the posttraining exploration in professional development, a phase of disillusionment follows a phase of confirmation and confidence regarding the adequacy and worth of one's training (see Chapter 11 of this book). Most often, the novice, whether in training or soon after, while searching for an explanation for this often overwhelming sense of inadequacy, focuses on the inadequacy of the training program. There is almost universal criticism by individuals at this point, with either specific or general criticism directed to the courses, the professors, or the entire program. It is as if the novice is saying, "If I were better trained, I wouldn't feel so lost and so incompetent just when I need to perform well."

The novice often points a finger of blame also toward the self. When directed toward the self, the novice is saying, "It is me. I am no good at this and just an imposter in this field. Nothing I try seems to work." Pointing the finger at these two fault lines – the inadequacy of one's education and the inadequacy of the self – is captured in a heart-felt description by new school counselor Brent Bandhauer:

> Even after having graduated from an accredited master's program, I didn't learn nearly enough to actually be a school counselor. I sometimes wonder if I really paid enough attention in class or if I read my textbooks too casually. Maybe I just forgot the important concepts that I need to be a helper of children. Yet if I'm asked, I can glibly explain the core conditions necessary for change. I can give a mini-lecture on irrational beliefs and how they impair daily functioning. I can even describe outcome research studies that begin to pinpoint the actual reasons clients do change. Perhaps I studied the theories with the assumption I would be helping insightful clients who know what changes they want. Does the source of this problem lie in my personal shortcomings or in my training?
>
> (Bandhauer, 1997, p. 7)

With extensive experience, one shifts from external expertise to internal expertise, from the theories of others to one's own complex, experience-based rules, procedures, and guidelines for situations. Benner and Wrubel (1982), studying nurses, describe the expert nurse who examines a patient and knows that he is in danger, not because theory says so but because extensive experience says so. Since Benner and Wrubel described this concept over 30 years ago, much of the nursing literature has explored the role of intuition in nursing practice. Through hundreds of hours of experience, internalized theory has developed. The nurse uses these experience-based generalizations to quickly assess the needed approach.

The problem is that there is just too much to know, and one does not really know what will be needed at what point. An analogy is that of a traveler to a foreign country. One packs the suitcases before traveling, hoping to bring the right clothes and articles. Inevitably, necessary items are omitted. The traveler gets anxious and has to compensate in some way. The novice often feels the same. One novice therapist in a study of turning points in therapist development reflected: "I feel like I am on a roller coaster in terms of confidence . . . One day I think, I can do this well, and the next day I am scared to death that I will mess up somebody's life" (Howard, Inman, & Altman, 2006, p. 96). Orlinsky and Rønnestad (2005) also found elevated anxiety for the novice. How does the novice helper learn how to handle these very specific situations? Bandhauer (1997), who we quoted above, responds to this question when describing his development as a counselor:

> I remember someone once telling me that good judgment comes from those experiences brought on by bad judgment. I'm seeking to become a part of the fraternity of wise people who consistently make confident, appropriate decisions. Since wisdom comes from experience, perhaps the confidence I seek must slowly develop over time. To find my way, I must promise to examine my feelings and reactions to my experiences. When I feel overwhelmed, I must attempt to figure out why. I must try to figure out who owns the problem I'm being asked to solve. I must delve into my experiences to identify what or whom I'm reminded of from the past. Maybe in 10 years wisdom will have arrived.
>
> (p. 9)

The professional journey for all means studying long and hard and also attending the "school of hard knocks." This school is necessary but difficult. Sanger (2010), in her ominous-sounding essay about her experience as a novice, "How to Fail," gives an example:

> When my group supervisor at the community mental health center where I was completing my master's practicum presented Grace's (pseudonym) case for disposition, she prefaced it by saying that none of the staff were available to work with this client. What she didn't say outright, but was clear about in her description, was that none of the staff wanted to work with this client. Grace had a long history of bipolar disorder and substance abuse. Her drug of choice was heroin. She had seen the revolving door of inpatient drug treatment more than once and was holding tenuously onto a few weeks of sobriety. In this sense, she didn't necessarily stand out from many of the clients we served at the clinic. But, as I would learn over time, Grace also had a history of burning bridges, with family members and therapists alike. She was quick to lash out in anger and just as quick to apologize beseechingly. She seemed to feel like the world owed her

something, and she was determined to exact whatever that was from those around her.

Looking around the room at my peers, it was evident that no one was jumping to work with Grace. It sounded like a lot of work. With only a little reluctance, I allowed my desire to please my supervisor and my novice "I'm gonna save the world one client at a time" attitude to prevail. I agreed to work with Grace. I didn't know at the time that I was bound for failure . . . When we met for the first time, after a volley of back and forth phone calls and multiple initial appointment no-shows, I already knew that I was in over my head. Grace presented her life as one ongoing crisis; she recounted failed relationships, urges to use heroin, and recurrent thoughts of suicide in a voice that pitched up into a startling crescendo while tears streamed down her face. She spoke so quickly that I was amazed she wasn't constantly tripping over her words. "Breathe," I told her gently. "Breathe!" I told myself, a little more urgently, as I tried to sort out in my head where to begin. I had next to no experience working with dually diagnosed clients and felt nervous about figuring out how to best support Grace's recent sobriety while also attending to her mood disorder and relationship instabilities. The fact that she had uttered the "s" word (suicide) so many times only elevated my pulse further into the aerobic activity zone.

After our first session ended and I had time to regroup and consult, I decided on what seemed like reasonable therapy goals: safety planning, relapse prevention, mood and affect management, bolstering interpersonal skills. As it turned out, it didn't really matter what treatment goals I had chosen, since I don't recall ever having had the chance to really discuss them with Grace. Each time we met there was a new crisis that needed attending to. Not knowing much better at the time, I faithfully followed Grace down the path of each crisis, helping her to put out fires but failing to help her prevent new ones . . .

Despite all of this, we eventually managed to forge what felt like a workable therapeutic relationship. She seemed to trust me. I admired her repeated efforts to engage in a life that had kicked her down so many times in the past. I imagine that, from Grace's perspective, my dogged and naïve persistence to be there for her in whatever way she needed was comforting and relationship enhancing. But it also contributed to growing resentment and emotional exhaustion on my part. It took me awhile to learn that when I feel like I'm doing more work than my client, it's time to co-examine the therapy process. At the time, I couldn't disentangle myself enough to see that my work with Grace had "over-involvement" written all over it.

Grace taught me as a beginner that progress in therapy can be slow, sporadic, and difficult to define. At times, it's imperceptible. It's like one of those flip books that, when paged through rapidly, shows a horse fluidly galloping across the landscape. But, sometimes, the pages catch on your thumb, and the horse stops and starts with a jerk. If you stop on each individual page, the change from one page to the next is almost impossible to discern. Doing therapy with Grace was like flipping through the pages one at a time. Even when I strained, I could barely see any forward movement, even though there was some evidence of change. Over time, she started opening up more in therapy to discuss the big picture – her relationship with her mother, her view of herself, her disappointments and regrets – even while her crises continued. These disclosures, together with our developing therapeutic bond, were progress, but I didn't realize it until much later because it wasn't what I was looking for initially.

When Grace relapsed during the final week of my practicum, my thumb slipped entirely off the edge of the pages of the book. She landed in the hospital, manic, and it seemed as if we hadn't made any forward movement at all. Our last meeting took place on the haphazardly arranged, threadbare couches on the inpatient unit. Grace thanked me for our work together and then asked if I had brought her new underwear like she had asked. I had not. She hugged me. That was it. I walked out feeling devastated. I felt like I had failed.

At times in my work with Grace it felt as if I were trying to balance on a narrow precipice between two deep chasms. On one side was a well of boundless and naïve optimism that, given enough time and effort, I could help anyone. On the other side was a pit of cynicism and hopelessness, into which I sometimes tumbled after losing my footing. When I was in the pit, I felt powerless to do anything. In the middle was that elusive middle ground called reality, in which both extremes had a hint of truth to them.

This sort of non-dualism was a new concept for me. Erich Fromm (1968) described a version of it in The Revolution of Hope when he said, "To hope means to be ready at every moment for that which is not yet born, and yet not become desperate if there is no birth in our lifetime" (p. 9). I had a lot of hopes for Grace – too many, in fact – and this left me vulnerable to feelings of desperation when those hopes weren't realized.

(pp. 72–74, reprinted with permission)

Here, Sanger is writing, for the rest of us, about one of her "There is no gathering the rose, without being pricked by the thorns" novice experiences. Sanger is gradually building her experience base. It is a long, slow, erratic process (see Chapter 11 of this book for an elaboration on practitioner development) that the novice often wants to speed up to reach the safety of competence.

Is it the same wish we ask for in our personal lives? Wouldn't it be wonderful to know the lessons of the last decade without going through the 10 years? Tom is reminded of the Norwegian saying, "Too soon old, too late smart," which describes this very human dilemma. The novice can feel like the youngest child in the family who wants desperately to be as old and mature as his or her siblings but can do nothing to speed up the process.

Experience and lots of it is necessary to make the shift to an internal base (Skovholt, Rønnestad, & Jennings, 1997). In *Outliers: The Story of Success*, Gladwell (2008) discusses the often-used maxim that 10,000 hours in a domain is necessary to excel. The experience must also be of a certain quality, as described by Benner and Wrubel (1982):

> Experience is necessary for moving from one level of expertise to another, but experience is not the equivalent of longevity, seniority, or the simple passage of time. Experience means living through actual situations in such a way that it informs the practitioner's perception and understanding of all subsequent situations.
>
> (p. 28)

Until experience gives one the internal cognitive map, the novice experiences the elevated stress of inexperience. Being lost and confused in the fog of early practice is part of a painful rite of passage for all new practitioners who attempt to counsel, teach, or heal. The ambiguity of so many practitioner interactions makes the life of the novice, like the teen years in one's personal life, a folder for memories in later years. Some accept their own rookie mistakes. Others, like the now-experienced college teacher from Tennessee, suffer from guilt and regret:

> I vividly remember thinking of the song title, "If it wasn't for my bad luck, I'd have no luck at all," when I was told that I'd be teaching 47 undergraduates . . . The hundreds of unsuspecting college freshmen who endured my initial teaching . . . should receive a coupon redeemable for three hours of instruction.
>
> (Eison, 1985, p. 3)

ACUTE NEED FOR POSITIVE MENTORING VS. ORPHAN STRESS – CRITICAL MENTOR – NOVICE NEGLECT

> Mentors and apprentices are partners in an ancient human dance . . . It is the dance of the spiraling generations, in which the old empower the young with their experience and the young empower the old with new life, reweaving the fabric of the human community as they touch and turn.
> – **P. J. Palmer (1998, p. 25)**

Thrown into the tumultuous sea of professional practice, the novice eagerly seeks safety from the unpredictable, powerful, and frightening forces that seem to quickly envelop the self. Seeking safety while on the high rolling seas, the novice hopes desperately for a mentor who will quell the danger and let the novice practice steering the ship. Practice here translates to conducting a 50-minute counseling session, teaching a class of lively children, or doing an important health procedure – and then doing it again and again. Ward and House (1998) describe the rough seas for the novice as "increased levels of emotional and cognitive dissonance" (p. 23), which can be translated as the novice not knowing what he or she is doing – the inexperience factor. Help is sought from a wise elder – a supervisor, teacher/professor, or even a more experienced peer who knows the ropes and has developed expertise.

At this point, the novice badly needs and wants this supportive relationship with a mentor, just as in life, a person at times really needs a parent. Yet, we do not choose our parents, and we do not have the power to have them be what we want when we want it. The saying "the teacher will appear when the student is ready" is a truism that, unfortunately, is only sometimes true. The novice wants and needs the mentor to be a certain way – supportive, positive, helpful in specific ways of managing the voyage, and available (Rønnestad & Skovholt, 2013). The absence of a mentor leaves the novice with orphan distress, searching for his or her way on the high seas without experience. Equally distressing is the novice's disillusionment with a mentor who has failed to provide what is desperately needed. Examples include the absent mentor, the critical mentor, and the confusing and convoluted (while giving instructions) mentor. The terms *orphan stress, critical mentor,* and *novice neglect* summarize the fear.

The most effective mentors seem to operate by a structure similar to what we have called the uncertainty/certainty principle of practitioner development (Rønnestad & Skovholt, 2003). Here, the mentor, perhaps as teacher or supervisor, introduces the novice to the process of searching through the uncertainty. Searching through uncertainty via reflection has been described as the best method of novice professional growth (Neufeldt, 2007). The novice is taught to proceed on the voyage within a framework of there being more than one right way to counsel, teach, or heal the Other. Yet, within uncertainty, the mentor also introduces certainty, as in specific techniques, methods, and procedures that can be very helpful to the confused novice. This mentor blend of giving answers and providing questions is sometimes hard to find. This increases the difficulty that the novice has in finding the best growth-producing mentoring at the time of great need.

A key to development is the "holding environment" created by the mentor. A strong holding environment comforts the novice against negative forces within and outside the self and acts to promote originality and creativity. Torrence (1996), a leading scholar of creativity, said, "The mentor protects the mentee from the reactions of their peers long enough for the mentee to try out some of their ideas and modify them. The mentor can keep the structure open enough so that originality can occur" (p. ii).

The importance of the mentor, at this point of high vulnerability, can be assessed by asking veteran practitioners of counseling and therapy, teaching, and health services to describe the quality of the mentoring that they received during the critical period of their lives as novices. Through the emotional intensity, either positive or negative, and the acute memory recall of events decades earlier, one can ascertain the importance of mentoring for the novice. Specific situations are described, and strong emotions of affection, appreciation, and adoration, or anger, criticism, and disappointment are expressed. Here are three retrospective stories. First, Brinson (1997) writes:

> When I catapulted out of the womb of graduate school . . . it seemed as if I spent much of my time babbling, drooling, crawling and falling on my rear end.
>
> Still wet behind the ears and suffering the after-effects of that traumatic birth experience, I longed for the support and nurturing of a trusted confidant to help me adjust to this new and exciting profession. This guidance became increasingly necessary for me the more I realized that my graduate experience had not prepared me for the "political" dimensions of the profession. . . .
>
> Obviously, anyone who is just starting out in a profession would value the support of individuals who lend their knowledge and expertise toward helping him or her achieve success. While this was certainly true in my situation, I did, however, approach this relationship with a degree of skepticism. Although there was nothing about the behavior or attitude of the individual that gave me reason for pause, the fact that he was a member of a different ethnic group presented a dilemma for me. Since the historical relationship between our ethnic groups has been strained, I was inclined to ask myself, "Why is this person interested in seeing me succeed?" Yet, through spending time and getting to know him as a person, I eventually rid myself of the stereotypes that otherwise would have made it impossible to foster a productive mentoring relationship.
>
> Having a mentor made a world of difference in my growth. . . . Not only did I find someone who could provide me with the wisdom, knowledge and experience of many years in the profession, but I found someone who was willing to serve as an advocate on my behalf when I faced certain crossroads in my career.
>
> I also found someone to confide in about my fears and concerns of being a novice in the profession, without feeling as if I would be judged as incompetent . . . I am grateful for several other ways in which my mentor helped me, especially during times of professional and personal crises when I felt discouraged and dispirited. It made all the difference to have someone in my corner. . . .

Years later, I now share my experiences with you in hopes of reaching other beginning professionals who are trying to find their way and don't know where to turn.

(pp. 165–166, reprinted with permission by the ACA)

In this next retrospective account, Osachuk (2010) describes the emotional intensity of a positive mentoring experience years earlier, in the context of being a beginning student therapist and the impact of David, his professor and clinical supervisor:

It came time to begin my second practicum, and I again requested and hoped to have David as my supervisor. My request was granted. David remembered me from his psychotherapy course. Early in my practicum, during videotape review of my therapy with clients, he was pleased to see the improvement of my skills since the course. Being a new therapist, I was still learning and feeling clumsy and awkward, and I hung on every word of his feedback in supervision, as I was in awe of the depth of his skills and continually wanting to improve. Developmentally I also really needed external affirmation and confirmation of my potential to become a skilled therapist and was hoping at some point to receive this from David in supervision. It was as if David saw the potential in me, believed in me, that I would be all right.

The affirmation and confirmation I was hoping to receive came during a subsequent clinical supervision session. It seems like such a small thing, but it was so important to me at the time. David had shared with me that he had spoken about my growth in a telephone conversation with one of his adult daughters. In essence he shared that initially he was uncertain about how I would do based on his memory of me from the time I was in his psychotherapy course, and he was pleased, actually pleasantly surprised, about the development of my skills since that time. He further shared with me what he anticipated he might experience with me in supervision. He was initially dreading my being his supervisee. He shared his memory of my forced intensity and anxiety while in his psychotherapy course and that it was difficult to be in my presence. He said he was not looking forward to having to work through this with me in supervision. While he did not elaborate, I had the sense that he anticipated that supervising me would personally be very taxing.

The reason he was now pleased was that these qualities were largely absent and that my interactions were no longer forced. He said I had made great strides in being present, hearing my clients, and making empathetic reflections. I was thrilled to hear that. Of course I was still very much a beginner, and that's why I was being supervised. This conversation was a defining moment for me. I was finally able to relax and accept that I was going to be a therapist, that I had made the right choice. This experience would be the first of many further affirming experiences of my chosen profession, my craft.

(pp. 65–66, reprinted with permission)

Conversely, Weis (2010) describes a negative experience vividly recalled years later. The example again is within the context of clinical supervision, but it could be from any of many new skill areas confronted by practitioners in the caring professions.

> I had just explained to my peers and supervisor how I had started my most recent therapy session. My seasoned supervisor chided, "This is the stupidest thing I have ever heard."
>
> What had I done in therapy that seemed so stupid? I had sat side by side with a client, who had long struggled with bulimia, and had reviewed a list of treatment approaches. She and I compared and contrasted the underlying theories and technical elements of her therapy options. That therapy session helped set a tone for an intentional, transparent, and open-minded collaboration. Reflecting on my supervisor's disdain, I concluded that my supervisor expected me to be the authority on matters such as selecting a treatment option.

(p. 52)

The novice seeks a person senior in experience, credentials, position, or expertise. Someone with all of these would work fine. This acute need for positive mentoring is an elevated stressor for the novice practitioner because it often does not happen in the measured-out degree and intensity desired by the novice exactly when needed. The difficulty is often related to the narrow match needed by the novice and the lack of structural or financial considerations built into this novice need. The orphaned novice or the novice with an indifferent, incompetent, or hostile mentor suffers an elevated level of stress. Other novices are more fortunate because they have terrific mentor relationships at this point in their development.

In Australia, as mentioned earlier, new physicians have reported very high levels of stress (see www.Beyondblue.org.au). In order to ensure good mentoring and stop the effects of orphan stress, a critical mentor, or novice neglect, Australian psychologist Dianne Salvador and physician Rachel Collins have written a 2014 guidebook – *Mentoring Doctors* – that is being implemented in hospitals across Australia. Now there is progress!

GLAMORIZED EXPECTATIONS

A vast deal may be done by those who dare to act.
– **Jane Austen (as cited in Maggio, 1997, p. 176)**

One of the classic distinctions in career decision making is the separation between being interested in "people" and in "things," with things related to jobs like engineering and people related to jobs like counseling. Being drawn to working with people often involves the daydream of making a difference in the lives of others. Tom remembers reading as a child about the work of doctors in developing countries – Albert Schweitzer in Africa and Tom Dooley in Southeast Asia – and also hearing stories of his Uncle Erling, a doctor in rural India. All of these stories, in his mind, were about heroic efforts to dramatically reduce the suffering of impoverished people. They were inspiring. As a young child, Michelle was inspired by stories of people making a difference in the world. Both Tom and Michelle wanted someday to work hard and make the world better.

The people ahead of us in a career field, who we idolize and dream of being, seem to be everything we wish to be. When starting in the helping professions, who have been your inspirations? It may be a teacher who cared so much and taught so much, a nurse who seemed so exceptional, an addictions counselor who helped us or a family member stop an addiction, a physical therapist who brought the legs of a loved one back to full use, or a professor who was so good at the work. Idealized, highly competent models can really motivate us. They also help us to see that idealistic may be reachable and realistic. They feed the idea of glamorized expectations as realistic.

It is natural, when drawn to helping people, to want to enter a career where one's efforts produce wondrous results. It propels the individual to study the content of a specific helping profession and persist in an endurance contest of tests, papers, and reports, and to read hundreds of pages of textbooks, listen to many presentations, and do multiple group projects. In the helping professions, novices are highly motivated to find a way through all the academic and practicum demands.

Without full awareness, the novice often is more hopeful about the impact of one's efforts to counsel, teach, or heal than is warranted. This overoptimism coexists with fear about one's skill level. They connect in the goal of magnificent change. If this occurs, the work is impactful, and the novice is a successful practitioner. The novice may reason: If I am able enough, skilled enough, warm enough, intelligent enough, powerful enough, knowledgeable enough, caring enough, present enough, then the Other will improve. If the Other does not improve, then I am not these things, and my entrance into this career field is precarious.

The unclear expectations for the work occur in part because the change process is occurring with the most complex of all species. Remember we started this chapter with the core novice stressor: So Much Ambiguity. This means the question "What is success?" just dangles out there. The beginner often hinges practitioner competence to obvious client improvement such as less anxiety, depression, or anger. Success is mostly measured by direct change of the client, student, or patient in the equation: Improvement of the Other equals practitioner competence. The novice is often not fully aware of this self-focus strand in the unrealistic expectations: "If the client really gets better, expresses appreciation, or likes me, I'm really good at helping."

The following first-person account illustrates the tie between practitioner self-evaluation and client reaction within the vulnerable world of the novice:

Pam was my first client as a professional counselor. I looked forward to meeting her with such unbridled anticipation that I didn't even notice that the air conditioner was broken and the temperature had climbed into the 90s. I fantasized about sitting quietly and listening to Pam with great understanding and much compassion. I just couldn't wait to hear her story.

Pam was already in my office when I arrived. As I stepped through the door she frowned at me, shaking her head. "Excuse me," she said, "nothing against you, but I'm not talking to anyone but Florence." Florence was her previous counselor who had left our clinic for another job.

I was stunned by Pam's rejection of me. Although I attempted to squelch my feelings, it did not work. I was lost. . . . We sat quietly as I looked at her, waiting for her to make sense of her feelings. I, too, had to come to terms with my own feelings. I was ill-prepared to deal with the assault of my emotions. Despite the pain, I almost wanted to thank Pam for creating this experience for me. If I was going to grow in this field, to find my own way, I had to learn to recognize my interfering feelings and deal with them.

The silence felt more oppressive than the weather. I began to feel anxious, almost faint. . . . My relationship with Pam began to grow. She was speaking to me, even though she was singing the praises of another counselor, and I no longer felt devalued or rejected.

I continued to see Pam for a while, though somewhat sporadically. Many of our sessions focused on Pam's mother. She told me how her mother gave her to foster care when she was very little because her new stepfather was so abusive. I could see the anguish in Pam's face as she talked about her foster home. Often I wanted to take her in my arms to comfort her. "No one should have had to go through your kind of torment," I said.

"You know," she said, "I like you better than Florence."

"Why is that?" I asked.

"Because you seem to understand me better than she did."

I wanted to hug her.

(S. Pincus, 1997, pp. 59–60, reprinted with permission by the ACA)

A crash occurs and the stress level goes up for the novice when the expectations, often unarticulated, are battered and broken. This occurs when the Other does not show much improvement. At this point, the human change process, directed by the novice, often seems bland and unspectacular. The result seems to be that no client, student, or patient growth equals practitioner incompetence.

In time, the novice becomes more experienced, in part through a "series of humiliations" while doing the work, and develops much clearer, more realistic and precise, and less glamorous expectations, which tend to lower stress. A feeling of humiliation can occur for the beginner when she is trying as hard as possible using methods and techniques taught in class and practicum and little positive seems to be happening. No longer is one able to cure the other quickly and easily. Rather, human change is, in time, seen as a complex, often slow process in which the practitioner plays only a part. This helps to reduce practitioner stress. But it takes time to get to a place where "realistic" replaces "idealistic."

Only later will the novice really comprehend how so many factors, such as readiness of the Other, play such a role in client – student – patient success. Lange (1988) describes her emerging understanding of readiness:

> [Growth] in my professional development has increased my sensitivity in several areas. First is my appreciation of client readiness to change. No matter how brilliant my insights and strategies, the ability to change rests with clients, who will hear what they need to hear and know what they need to know. What may seem insignificant to me may be the critical incident for a particular client. I am a facilitator and an encourager, but the client decides how and when to create a new identity.
>
> (p. 109)

This "What is success?" question is a difficult one. For example, is a doctor successful if the patient lives? Then how about those doctors who work with high-risk patients with deadly diseases? Right away, with just a few sentences about one occupation, we can see that measuring success within each of the caring professions can be difficult. When it is hard to measure something, expectations can get glamorized without the novice realizing it.

Another factor is the confusion in the literature regarding professional experience and practitioner success. For example, Ericsson (2007) argues that experience does not ensure expertise. Yes, there is no clear connection between more professional experience and more expertise. In fact, high expectations fueled by enthusiasm can produce impressive results by novices. Every year, thousands of counselors, therapists, teachers, clergy, and health professionals in training, individuals still in school, help many people. In an analogous study of helping, college professors did as well as trained counselors (Strupp & Hadley, 1978). These results fuel an element of enhanced hope, a trace of glamour attached to the work, and a sense that if one is really good at the work, then big, magical client, student, or patient improvement will occur. For the veteran practitioner, the paradoxical reality is that significant change is possible when one is not so grandiose and unrealistic.

Our own personal experience leads us to evaluate some counselors, teachers, and doctors as better than others. And others say the same thing: "Good teachers matter more than anything; they are astonishingly important. It turns out that having a great teacher is far more important than being in a small class, or going to a good school with a mediocre teacher" (Kristof, 2009, p. 11).

For the novice, the problem with glamorized expectations is that it is not possible to always have a major impact each of the thousands of times that one meets with the other during a career. When the novice thinks, "I need to have a big impact in every session, every class, every health consultation," then there is pressure and stress. Wanting to do really good work is one thing. Using the client, student, or patient as the only criteria for success is different.

INTENSE EVALUATION AND ILLUMINATED SCRUTINY BY PROFESSIONAL GATEKEEPERS

You supervisors dance on the rim of this machine certain of your power, your values clear and calm in your purpose. I trainee am tumbled and tossed caught in the spin jerked about by the hierarchy's agitation my vision clouded by products that whiten and soften the dark edge of reality. And you and I know that the spinning always stops when you open the lid to check.

– L. Moreland (1993, p. 13, reprinted with permission by the publisher)

For trainees, acceptable levels of practitioner skill seem like a "moving target with an elusive criteria."

– W. N. Robiner, M. Fuhrman, and S. Ristvedt (1993, p. 5)

In all the helping professions, practitioners work with human vulnerability. To contain and hopefully eliminate any harm by practitioners, senior members of each helping field are ethically obligated to regulate their own practitioners. Even after passing through numerous gates, a small percentage of incompetent and unethical practitioners damage clients, students, or patients. The profession responds to these events by building more barriers to entrance, such as only admitting qualified candidates. However, because intensive professional work with human beings is, at the core, complex and ambiguous in nature, the process of selection is quite complicated, confusing, and convoluted.

Enter the novice who must pass through numerous gates. Evaluation is a large factor in the elevated stressors of the novice practitioner. For example, teaching researchers Morton and colleagues (1997) state, "It is clear that evaluation anxiety is paramount for student teachers" (p. 85).

Some of the evaluation stress develops from a lack of task clarity. For example, there is no clear formula for the exact performance of expert practitioners in counseling and psychotherapy. Theoretical differences wash out, and common factors seem to emerge in outcome research (Ogles & Hayes, 2010). Yet, there can be murkiness as well as clarity when defining expertise (Skovholt et al., 1997, Tracey et al., 2014). A classic quote from Raimy (1950) illustrates this: "Psychotherapy is an undefined technique applied to unspecified problems with unpredictable outcome. For this we recommend rigorous training" (p. 150). Similarly, we have heard thoughtful teachers lament the lack of clarity in defining good teaching.

How then can the field evaluate novices when the road to expertise is unknown? Evaluation happens anyway, and must, because the public and the profession demand it. So the novice, often with a supervisor of unknown quality and with ambiguous standards to meet, lives under illuminated scrutiny. The difficulty is magnified by the following reality: "Supervisors are not only admired teachers but feared judges who have real power" (Doehrman, 1976, p. 11). Now, that's stress!

Evaluation is often provided by a senior member of the field, who may be a seasoned professional but may not be adequately trained in supervision. For example, a senior member of the profession may find it more difficult to be the supervisor rather than the practitioner. She or he may be more comfortable with practitioner tasks. Here are examples: the academic advisor helping a student move toward increased clarity about a major, the teacher aiming for increased student fluency in a second language, or the physician helping a patient move toward reduced blood-pressure readings. In contrast to these process goals, supervision involves other skills, such as evaluation.

Borders and Brown (2005) offer remedies to move beyond the natural role, such as counseling, to the supervision role. One conflict is between the helping self and the gatekeeper self. Supervision has more of a pass–fail mindset, one that practitioners often do not use in their regular work. The supervisor is often ambivalent about the grading demands in the supervisor's role (Bernard & Goodyear, 2008). In addition, evaluation by a supervisor may be an added responsibility given, without choice, to the senior practitioner. All of these factors contribute to possible difficulties in the evaluation process and may heighten the evaluation stress experienced by the novice.

POROUS EMOTIONAL BOUNDARIES

The pain stayed with me residually when returning home.
— A novice counselor

When I first taught, I thought constantly about my classes.
— An experienced high school teacher

Rather than stay in touch with the heart that was breaking [when hearing of the suffering and trauma of clients], again and again as a result of what I was witnessing, I had started building up walls.

　　　　　　　　　　　– van Dernoot Lipsky, L. & Burk, C. (2009, p. 3)

What passes in the world for tragedies . . . I hear about them, I see them. I can't be knocked against the wall by each one. I have to construct a coping technique that allows me to survive.

　　　　　　　　　　　– C. Kleinmaier (as cited in Garfield, 1995, p. 6)

The word *boundaries* has entered the lexicon of the contemporary helping professions and is used mostly to describe the not-to-be-crossed line between proper and improper human contact between the practitioner and the other person. In the shifting sands of culture and the historic times, it is a valuable term in defining the difference between "appropriate" and "inappropriate."

Although the novice is often helped in training and supervision to develop clarity for appropriate physical boundaries (i.e., to touch or not to touch), less attention is paid to emotional boundaries. The term *emotional boundaries* refers to the internal feelings and accompanying thinking of the helper. The ability to strategically detach and reattach is a difficult, advanced skill. Novice teachers often think constantly about their classes while not at work; novice nurses wonder if they did the right thing when working with a patient; novice counselors and therapists can be very preoccupied with the emotional pain of the client. This "off-duty" penetration of the emotional boundaries is one more elevated stress factor for the beginner.

This emotional and cognitive preoccupation can be educational. It serves, in fact, to provide the material for reflection, a central method of professional development (Neufeldt et al., 1996; Rønnestad & Skovholt, 2013; Schön, 1987). The task here, however, is to learn how to establish and regulate useful emotional boundaries. The novice, flooded with impressions, images, feelings, ideas, worries, and hopes, often has no established dike to withhold all of this.

In studies of practitioner stress, less experienced practitioners report more stress (Ackerley, Burnell, Holder, & Kurdek, 1988; Farber & Heifetz, 1981; Rodolfa, Kraft, & Reilley, 1988; Rønnestad & Skovholt, 2003). One caution with some of these results is a possible cohort effect. It may be that the most stressed practitioners leave the field so that, at the senior level, the stress profile is lowered, in part, for this reason. Ackerley and colleagues (1988), for example, reported more stress for less experienced practitioners in their psychologist sample. Results were measured by the emotional exhaustion and depersonalization subscales of the Maslach Burnout Inventory (Maslach & Jackson, 1981). Overinvolvement was a variable that accounted for some of the variance on both emotional exhaustion and depersonalization.

Overinvolvement produces porous emotional boundaries that result in elevated stress.

Novice practitioners working with acute human problems, such as trauma, experience difficulty with porous emotional boundaries. Pearlman and MacIan (1995) found that sexual assault counselors with less than two years of trauma experience had higher overall general distress and more disrupted cognitive schemas on issues such as interpersonal trust and safety. Perhaps most intense of all is the flood of emotions that hits the novice trauma therapist who has a personal history of trauma, such as the female therapist at a sexual assault center who was a victim of such assault herself (Pearlman & MacIan, 1995). This is an extreme example of porous emotional boundaries, one of the factors contributing to the elevated stress of the novice practitioner.

Developing a variety of boundaries takes time. This skill involves learning to constantly monitor the self, like the car owner monitors the fluid levels of the car: oil, power steering, transmission, brakes. Mindfulness, for example, teaches us to be present with our experience, bringing attention to the automatic responses we have and may not notice. For example, the novice may tend to become overinvolved with the life of the Other, without realizing this is happening or noticing the impact on the self or other. One looks for a positive interplay between empathetic attachment to the Other and one's own very important self-care needs. It takes time and experience, something the novice does not have.

ETHICAL AND LEGAL CONFUSION

The novice practitioner is focused on being competent in a professional role. Depending on the career field, this activity focuses on an emotional, intellectual, spiritual, or physical domain. The goal is to be helpful to the Other, to be therapeutic in the broadest sense of that term – that is, to help the client, student, parishioner, or patient. At the same time as the therapeutic route is being pursued by the novice, there is another route that is important but often out of the novice practitioner's awareness. It is the ethical and legal route. Of course, the goal is to be ethical and legal when following the therapeutic route. With the ethical–legal route, we are talking about a very explicit focus on ethical rules and legal procedures.

The therapeutic and the ethical and legal routes are, in fact, quite different and must be thought about differently. The ethical and legal route has a strong dose of self-protection, yet this is not the illuminated part of the stage for the novice. The helping professions – counseling, therapy, teaching, and health careers – all socialize beginners, while in training, to care for the Other. The caring is expressed by focusing on increasing the competence of the client, student, or patient. The ethical and legal route asks the novice to be self-protective. Along this route, the concern must also be for others, such as potential victims of a client's anger. This, too, is not part of the therapeutic route.

The two-route dilemma is stressful because it makes difficult work even more difficult. Here is an example. In Tom's supervision of a novice counselor, he was listening to her self-report about a session. The supervisee was describing the interaction between herself and a teenage client, telling elements of the client's story, which consisted of struggles with self, friends, and family. She told how she worked so hard to fully understand the client and of trying so hard to help by using the right method at the right time in the right dose. She was motivated to help, especially when sensing the client's anguish.

Midstream in a sentence, she told how the client wanted to kill her stepfather. Without pause, she told how she processed this angry feeling with the client. The goal was to help the client feel less anger and to find a more constructive approach to the problem. The counselor was fully engaged in driving down the therapeutic route. When Tom heard "wants to kill her stepfather," he jumped the median and immediately started driving on another road, the ethical and legal route. The client's anguish and the counselor's intense efforts were no longer dancing in Tom's head; Tarasoff was (*Tarasoff v. Regents of the University of California*, 1974).* Suddenly, the task was "duty to warn."

The route mindsets are different. The legal–ethical focus is on rules and procedures, not therapy. The practitioner changes from being an engaged therapeutic presence to a person of action. No longer is the client, student, patient everything; now the welfare of others, including the practitioner, takes center stage. Knowing and using the two routes adds complexity to the work of the novice. This is an unwelcome addition because things are already complex. Analogies are being bicultural or being a switch-hitter in baseball. One of the two is hard enough; doing both well and switching back and forth quickly and with grace are more difficult. Yet, competent practice demands both. This adds another stress factor for the novice.

In addition, legal and ethical road signs are often fuzzy because there is so much confusion within the practitioner professions about many important ethical and legal issues. For example, the communication technologies are quickly being used before we have clear ethical principles about their use (e.g., texting, e-mail, voice mail, and various social media platforms). One wants to act in an ethical and legal manner but often does not know what that means in certain situations. That is when the practitioner goes to conferences on ethics or consults with colleagues; however, often this input increases one's anxiety rather than decreases it.

Together, the need to integrate the two routes into one profession and the fuzzy and changing nature of many ethical and legal issues makes for novice confusion. As if the novice is not already confused enough.

ACUTE PERFORMANCE ANXIETY AND FEAR

> As a young teacher, I yearned for the day when I would know my craft so well, be so competent, so experienced, and so powerful, that I would walk into any classroom without feeling afraid.
>
> – P. J. Palmer (1998, p. 57)

> Fear stops all forward movement.
>
> – Axiom

Anxiety about the unknown and fear about the known are like a one-two punch. The novice can feel so inadequate when stepping into the professional role. The result can be acute anxiety cascading upon the person. These moments can be unforgettable. As if it were yesterday, although it was decades ago, Tom remembers entering a college classroom with the students, and as the students sat down, he went forward, turned around, and saw 46 eyes in close proximity staring at him. Thus, with no professional training, his college teaching career began. Michelle, on the other hand, benefited from the opportunity to teach as a part of a teaching practicum, with a community of others at her same level of competence and an experienced teaching supervisor. Of course, this helped to decrease Michelle's anxiety related to teaching when it was a new endeavor for her and build community with peers at the same developmental phase.

Usually, the acute anxiety occurs when the novice is trekking on a mountain path that is too narrow and the situation is novel (i.e., doing a specific professional task for the first time). Perhaps there is a strong evaluation climate. The situation often becomes arduous because the anxiety of self-consciousness and focusing on oneself makes it more difficult to attend to the complex work tasks. A moderate level of anxiety can improve performance, but high levels of anxiety reduce performance by directing the individual's attention to both reducing the external, visible effects (e.g., trembling and wet hands, unsteady voice) and lowering the internal anxiety level so that one can think effectively.

Opposed to pervasive performance anxiety, hovering like a menacing rain cloud, are fears about specific things. The list can be endless, although there are some specific favorites, for example, being speechless with no idea what to say to one's client, losing control of a classroom of active students, or using a health procedure that causes unpredicted pain. Together, anxiety and fear can seriously heighten the stress level for the novice.

THE FRAGILE AND INCOMPLETE PRACTITIONER SELF

At the beginning of any new human role – walking a bridge along the mountain path from the known and secure competence of the past to the unknown and the insecurity of the future – we usually feel unsure. Examples abound: the first time with a new date, landing at the airport of a city on a foreign continent, the first day at a new job, or the early days of parenting. The novice is trying on new clothes and new ways of being in the world to create a *practitioner self*. We are using this term, related to one used by Ellwein, Grace, and Comfort (1990), to describe the vigorous interior construction work of the novice in creating a practitioner identity. Trying on clothes takes many forms over many days, weeks, and months. With the awkwardness of a new adolescent play-acting in the adult world, the novice is trying to act like an advanced practitioner. All of us as novices, like all of us as adolescents, go through it. A classic method used here is what we call "imitation of experts" (Skovholt & Rønnestad, 1992b).

Like an adolescent, the fragile and incomplete practitioner self shifts through a series of moods: elation, fear, relief, frustration, delight, despair, pride, and shame. This raw mixture of emotions is a predictable outcome when the novice practitioner self steps into the practitioner world. Although this world produces valuable food for the slow development of practitioner expertise, it is also the context for the "series of humiliations" experienced by the rookie in the practice world. The novice self is fragile and, therefore, highly reactive to negative feedback. There is not much muscle, and the immunology system is stressed. Age and experience in allied jobs tend to mute the various novice effects. For example, the 40-year-old counseling student who has worked as a hospital aide tends to have a less intense reaction to this elevated stressor than does the inexperienced 23-year-old counseling student.

The following accounts from new student teachers, taken from student diaries by Galluzzo and Kacer (1991), show the emotional reactivity we are discussing here:

The students began asking me questions over my head. Questions that I found no material on. I handled it wrongly. . . . I was embarrassed and getting worked up. The students laughed at me and that really hurt.

(p. 15)

It was the dullest, driest lesson that was ever recited . . . the students were bored out of their minds . . . I felt like crying. The lesson was over in about a half hour. I thought that it would last two days. Worst of all the students were saying I was boring. That was the worst insult of all. They didn't like me.

(p. 16)

I felt very disgusted and almost indignant toward the kids because they could not grasp the things I was trying to explain.

(p. 21)

These preoccupations, both with self by the novice and the sense that the practitioner self is on stage, are analogous of the adolescent sense of being exposed and illuminated while on stage. There is then, of necessity, a self-focus for the novice because of a need to protect and nourish the fragileness. The difficulty is that this occurs at the same time that one is preparing for a career where the needs of the Other – the client, student, or patient – are the central focus of the work. A supportive senior practitioner as mentor can mute the self-protective, defensive focus and help keep the novice open to learning and growing while focusing on the needs of the Other. This clash between a self-focus and another-focus while creating a practitioner self produces another elevated stressor for the novice.

SUMMARY

Two phrases, "talking about the elephant in the corner" and "finding a voice," describe the value of articulating the unarticulated. This powerful curative result within groups has been called the "universality of experience effect" (Yalom, 1985). The aim of this chapter is to produce this universality of experience effect by describing a landscape peopled by each of us when a novice. More specifically, the intention is to provide a positive trinity of validity, clarity, and hope for current novices, their teachers, and their supervisors. The goal is a recognition reflex to terrain, as we encounter the valleys and hills, the rocks and soil, and the watering holes. Hopefully, the map of terrain descriptors will help in navigating the journey that all of us, as novices, must take.

Although this chapter has focused on novice stressors, often the novice journey is also filled with excitement, joy, hope, and positive promise. Our hope for you: less stress and more joy during the novice days!

SELF-REFLECTION EXERCISES

As you read this material, you may be a beginning practitioner in counseling, therapy, teaching, or health care. Perhaps you are a student in a training program at the graduate or undergraduate level, or you may now be more experienced; however, like everyone, you were once a rookie.

1.   Regardless of your experience level, how do you react to the description of the elevated stressors experienced by the novice? Do they ring true or not so true for you?

_____

_____

_____

_____

_____

_____

_____

_____

2.   Perhaps of more importance, what could be some long-term implications of your novice experience on your capacity to be a resilient practitioner?

_____

_____

_____

_____

_____

_____

_____

_____

NOTE

* *Tarasoff* is a case in which the client threatened to kill someone and the practitioner did not warn that person. After the person was murdered, the court said that the practitioner was wrong not to warn.

5

HAZARDS OF PRACTICE

When I am affected by a woman's story or someone tells me something about a domestic violence situation, I can't stop thinking about it. I feel for that person. I think about them all day every day, and I can feel their pain. I know it's not the pain they feel but in some sense I feel pain for them. I'm frustrated and irritated, and I want to fix it . . . I've taken on someone else's trauma, and not only am I doing my job but someone else's job too, and I start to realize that this is not healthy.

> – D. Boyland (cited in van Dernoot Lipsky
> and Burk, 2009, p. 124)

I am interviewing my new outpatient, Lisa, a fidgety young woman with darting eyes that avoid contact with my own. [She says] . . .

"I sat on my bed in the dark with a loaded gun to my head, completely numb, just getting the courage to pull the trigger. And then, out of nowhere, my cat jumped on my lap! I dropped the gun and just started crying. And then I called my boyfriend. I couldn't even talk, but he just knew it was me. He came right over and drove me to the hospital."

When I suggest that her cat could have just as easily startled her into pulling the trigger, Lisa's leg motions cease and, for the first time, she meets my gaze head-on.

"That would have been OK, too."

My adrenaline gives a mild surge, but my eyes meet hers unflinchingly. We have our work cut out for us, I think. "So what do you imagine would have to change in your life for you to feel differently about that?" I say out loud, alert to every nuance, verbal and nonverbal. She meets this question with a long, thoughtful pause . . .

A clock silently logs the minutes on my desk, its glowing red numbers managing the procession of patients in and out of my office in this busy HMO health center, where a multitude of lives in turmoil intersect with my own. My time is a semiprecious commodity to the insurance company that pays for it. My patient's time? She clearly puts no value to it at all.

– G. Garfunkel (1995, pp. 148–149)

DIFFICULT ELEMENTS OF OUR GRATIFYING WORK IN THE HELPING PROFESSIONS

Working in the helping professions means making highly skilled professional attachments, involvements, and separations over and over again with one person after another. To really matter to the Other, these must be I–Thou relationships, not I–It relationships, to use Martin Buber's (1970) terms. This means these relationships are full of respect for the Other, understanding of the Other, and energy for the Other. As Skovholt and D'Rozario (2000) found in studying students' best teachers, these are caring relationships.

What makes this work so difficult? It often has to do with the reality of these interpersonal encounters. Establishing and maintaining these relationships takes hard work. This means they take enormous energy from the practitioner. This is demonstrated in the 2009 Academy Award nominated French movie *Class*. The movie is about a teacher and the students in one classroom in France, a classroom packed with 13- and 14-year-old students, many from immigrant families. The movie vividly portrays the students' yearnings, confusion, and needs. The movie is based on the teaching experience of Francois Begaudeau, who plays himself. He works really hard to engage the students and respond to their multiple needs, ways, and wants.

The difficulty of the work relates to our hope to make a difference, with our inability to tolerate so much ambiguity, with the distress we vicariously feel from those we attempt to assist. Here are some specific hazards that make work difficult with clients, students, and patients. You may have your own list of hazards, especially if you are an experienced practitioner.

Hazard 1: The Other wants a quick solution; we disappoint with an offer of slow success

Good therapy, like good cooking, takes time.

– M. Piper (2003, p. xxiii)

Our research-supported, ethical offer to each client/student/patient/mentee is that their lives can get better; there can be less distress and more joy and competence. However – and there is a big *however* – it takes time. Such disappointment for the client/student/mentee/patient! And for us too, to see the other person so disappointed. To be in a helping profession and not be able to offer quick help – now, that is hell.

Of course, sometimes quick help works. For example, in "One Hour of Career Counseling and 30 Years of Influence," Cynthia McRae (2010) describes how one hour changed her life forever. However, difficult problems, such as a child suddenly losing both parents, require time – lots of time – before a new identity can emerge.

This is the gulf – between wish and reality – where a stages-of-change theory (Prochaska & Norcross, 2001) has helped practitioners understand this reality. The six stage model of change (discussed more in the next pages) helps the practitioner try not to speed up the process more than is possible. Going very, very fast down a hill on a bike can seem like a good idea until it isn't. So, too, with the human change process.

Often people do not want to hear that substantial human growth and development takes time. There are examples everywhere: needing physical therapy for an injury, learning a language, developing a large 401k account, learning how to parent . . . and finishing the third edition of this book. Can it be NOW? No, it can't be now.

Yet, we must say that into this gasp of disappointment for the Other there are many offers of quick help. Tom has heard plenty of them over his decades in the field. Seduction is a powerful word; it usually means things seem so hopeful at the front end of the seduction funnel and then later terrible at the back end of the seduction funnel, when the person comes out in even worse shape. Methods promoting quick change are often seductions. Tom's first teaching job was teaching speed reading. The promise at the time was that speed reading methods would help a person read a book in an hour; unfortunately, comprehension did not go along with speed. That method dropped away. Most too-fast-to-work methods do eventually drop away in human growth and development.

After a first counseling interview, when the client has described the difficulties in her or his life and has a painful amount of one or more of the distress emotions – anxiety, depression, anger – and wants the pain to go away *now*, Tom has learned, after hundreds of hours of counseling experience, to sometimes address the disappointment by saying: "I wish I could give you an injection right now and have all the pain be transformed to joy!" Tom tells them that therapy work is about three times as powerful as teaching: ". . . and I have done decades of both . . . but I do not have the ability to do an injection-type transformation!" He tells them, "Maybe somebody else can promise that, but when I read the best research on therapy and counseling outcome (Lambert, Garfield, & Bergin, 2004), I do not see validated quick change."

Hazard 2: Sometimes we cannot help because we are not the right person at the time

The Other may be searching for someone to help them . . . and they may be looking for someone different from us. We may not be the right practitioner for them. The demographic variables may be wrong. As Tom gets older, he gets more right for some clients, more wrong for others. He is the wrong gender for some women clients who are seeking a female therapist and the right gender for some women clients who seek a male therapist. We may not have the right experiential background or the specific competence needed. For Michelle, sometimes her perceived age, gender, and style fit, and sometimes they don't.

The Other comes to us with a whole history, hundreds and hundreds of hours, of people encounters. We may consciously or unconsciously remind the Other of a person who cared deeply for them . . . or one who betrayed them deeply.

Often the right helping person is some years older – not too few or too many, the same gender and ethnicity, seen as a competent example of success, is personally warm and energetically present. It's hard to be this right person for every student, client, patient, mentee.

An interesting example of this hazard occurred with our original master therapist research. Since interviews by doctoral students Len Jennings, Mary Mullenbach, and Michael Sullivan were the data collection method for these studies and we had no research funds, it was necessary to make nominations of therapists in the 3-million-person population base of the Twin Cities metro area. Using three criteria for selection as a master therapist, 103 therapists were nominated at least once. Those with four nominations or more served as the interview group. This group had a total of 77 nominations and the final qualitative portrait was not of one person but a composite of the 10 (Skovholt, Jennings, & Mullenbach, 2004). This is how nominations can be a valid selection method. When Tom asked Len, Mary, and Mike to rank the 10 as master therapists, after each had interviewed all ten, they had some consistency but some variability, too. This is striking example of this hazard: Sometimes we are not the right person.

To this same point, these master therapists communicated a sense of humility. They accepted the idea that they would not be the right helper for everyone. One said it was important to go on vacation long enough to realize that the world would go on just fine without you: ". . . the trick is to be gone long enough . . . so you recognize you're entirely replaceable. That you are absolutely replaceable" (Mullenbach, 2000, p. 100).

For the novice, this sense of being the wrong helper can be especially difficult to accept. Maslow's famous quote, "If the only tool you have is a hammer, [you tend] to treat everything as if it were a nail" (as cited in Goldfried, 1980, p. 994), symbolizes the effect of limited competence. In time, practitioners experience a "series of humiliations" when their wrong demographics, life experience, or competence level do not meet the needs of the client, student, or patient. This is difficult for the practitioner because of a basic occupational need to feel that one is making a positive difference in human life.

Hazard 3: The readiness dance; there is often a readiness gap between them and us

Here we are discussing the serenity prayer's message of controlling the things you can control, letting go of those you cannot, and understanding the difference.

The newly trained firefighter rushes out of the station, with the siren blasting and lights flashing looking for the fire wherever it is, ready and eager. The novice – not veteran – firefighter may be ready before the fire is a fire! Over-ready is the mindset of the newly minted novice.

The helping professions offer a developmental process. This means that the goal of the practitioner is to facilitate improvement in the person's functioning. The goal is movement on a continuum. How would you have done as a new, first-year college student at age 15? Would 25 be a much better age to begin college because of academic readiness? Ten years can make a big difference. Some 30-year-old new parents would have been overwhelmed at 16, and some 16-year-old parents would be great at 30.

Readiness can also be a matter of first experiencing the "school of hard knocks." As examples: A friend's daughter was more receptive to his ideas after she had been out on her own and *knew more* than when she was home and *knew less*. Helping others as a career counselor may work better – the client may be more receptive – when the client's own career search process has first failed.

In the helping professions, we often worry about our undercommitment, disinterest, and burnout, but overcommitment is also an issue. Readiness is about matching our commitment and readiness to work at change with the Other's commitment and readiness. This "readiness dance," which in its best form closely matches the two people, is especially difficult for the novice who is trying to judge "dose" and "timing" without much practice.

A classic problem in the helping professions is the offering of programs to people who are not ready. Prochaska and Norcross (2001) summarize research findings on a transtheoretical model of behavior change. The six-stage model of change has the following stages: precontemplation (no plans to change), contemplation (awareness of the problem but no decision to change), preparation (awareness of the problem and some attempts to be different), action (actively engaged in change processes), maintenance (work to maintain changes made), and termination (ended the change process, no longer have to work to avoid relapse). Prochaska and Norcross's review of research studies on stages of change indicated that pairing knowledge about the client's stage of change with type of intervention can positively impact the treatment. Prochaska, DiClemente, and Norcross (1992) described a health maintenance organization (HMO) in which 70% of the eligible smokers said that they wanted help with smoking cessation. A program was developed and offered, but only 4% of the smokers signed up. Like firefighters ready to fight a fire, novice helping practitioners often misread smoke for fire. One of the reasons that being highly skilled at matching with the client on readiness is so important is because it is easy to trip the client's ambivalence regarding change, and hence resistance is increased. Master practitioners are talented at increasing motivation and decreasing resistance in part by not rushing in prematurely to help.

See Table 5.1 for a chart of the Readiness Gap.

Like those health professionals who prepared materials for smoking cessation but were disappointed when few people showed up for help, the helping impulse is thwarted for us, too. Training programs select practitioners who yearn to help and share a deep desire to care for others. We can easily be more ready than the Other. This is a natural occupational hazard.

Finding the right blend of professional attachment with the Other can be difficult. One can be uninvolved in the attachment, and this, of course, is not good. One can be overinvolved, and this, too, is not optimal.

Tom remembers being an academic advisor for high-risk college freshmen. At the time, he was teaching career development theory and practice to graduate students and a career planning class to freshmen. He was an experienced academic advisor and career counselor, and had written articles on career counseling in professional journals. In fact, he was overprepared for the academic advisor task compared with other faculty member advisors who excelled in their academic specialties in fields like English, physics, and mathematics.

Tom was really ready to help these high-risk college freshmen advisees, but the task "went South," as former Minnesota Twins' baseball manager Tom Kelly said when things go wrong.

Table 5.1 The Readiness Gap

Stages of Change	Client, Student, and Patient	Counselor, Therapist, Teacher, or Healer
Precontemplation		
Contemplation		
Preparation	The Readiness Gap	
Action		
Maintenance		
Termination		

Sources: "In Search of How People Change: Applications to Addictive Behavior," by J. O. Prochaska, C. C. DiClemente, and J. C. Norcross, 1992, *American Psychologist, 47*(9), pp. 1102–1114; "Stages of Change," by J. O. Prochaska and J. C. Norcross, 2001, *Psychotherapy, 38*(4), pp. 443–448.

Tom would give these advisees his time, talent, and energy in looking at the big picture of their educational and career futures. After all, we want practitioners to assist disadvantaged individuals to find their way through the American reward maze. But in time, Tom changed his behavior when his efforts were consistently met by advisees with only, "Would you sign the paper for the classes?" They did not come for a deluxe version of educational and vocational guidance. They came because bureaucratic regulations forced them to get his signature. The Readiness Gap! Tom came to see that his own excessive helping impulse produced the gap.

Here is another example. Earlier in Tom's career at the University of Florida, he joined other new faculty members from many parts of the country to start a Department of Behavioral Studies. They were to offer innovative, cross-disciplinary courses to honors undergraduates. The new faculty had spent years in graduate school preparing for the task. At fall orientation, the new assistant professors sat at tables to meet the new students – some of the best graduates of Florida's high schools. With great animation, the faculty members described the content of new cross-disciplinary courses, such as Power and Violence. The new students responded by asking, "What courses do you have before lunch?" Again, the Readiness Gap. Michelle notices this again and again in her therapy work with graduate and undergraduate students. Excited to engage and jump in, Michelle is aware of the importance of listening, noticing and getting a sense of where the client is in their readiness for change in order to form a strong alliance and move towards change in the therapy process.

Readiness is also a matter of the natural human maturity process – when the client, student, or patient can understand in a broader, deeper, less egocentric way. Sometimes we have little power to affect it. After all, "you can lead the horse to water, but you can't make it drink," and "the teacher will appear when the student is ready." Until then, you, the helper, are *invisible, unrecognizable,* and *inaudible:* "I can't hear a word you are saying, only the echo of my mind."

We cannot all be lucky enough to have the attention and commitment of the airplane passenger listening to instructions on the use of oxygen in the midst of intense turbulence and cabin depressurization. This is why the work can be difficult. Those in the helping professions want to believe that they make a difference in human life, but sometimes they do not. At times, we feel ineffective, and the feelings are accurate – we *are* ineffective! The key is that, in time, the counselor, therapist, teacher, or healer, like the veteran athlete, learns when to expend energy and when to preserve energy, when effort matters and when it does not. As stated earlier, the practitioner also learns the lesson that too much practitioner eagerness can bring on, in a subtle way, client, student, or patient resistance. And this creating of resistance is something that skilled practitioners learn not to do because it can really derail success. When the client, student, or patient is fighting the professional person, failure in the helping process may be around the corner. Success is hard when the stars are aligned and much more difficult when they are not.

When people are not ready, what can you do? Sometimes we just have to wait. Miller and Rollick (2002) propose Motivational Interviewing as a way to increase readiness. Within the context of this counseling style, a therapist employs empathetic listening to gain an understanding of the client's problem and to minimize resistance. After rapport is developed, the therapist works to explore how a person's goals and values might interact with their desire to change. Motivational Interviewing helps the client face her ambivalence about change in her life. Tom has found it valuable to help the client address all the losses, as well as gains, that can come with life changes. This can help the Other take a deep breath and start the slow change process.

Hazard 4: Often people ask for help because they have a seemingly unsolvable problem that must be solved

Some of the most difficult and stressful situations people face involve making choices when all options involve significant loss. "Can't live with him, can't live without him" is just a poetic saying, until it becomes more personal and real. At that point, the person is on a desperate search for a solution that does not involve great loss. For example, just imagine that you cannot continue to live in an intimate relationship with a partner or spouse because of one or more things that make the situation intolerable. Conversely, losing the other person to the greater world and not having all the wonderful and ordinary aspect of the relationship is also intolerable. Now you approach a helping professional for a happy solution . . .

In life, sometimes neither approach or avoidance works. These are the ingredients of hopelessness and demoralization that Frank and Frank (1991) suggest are central when individuals seek help. When we are stuck in life and unable to find a solution, the result is often a feeling of low self-efficacy and high despair. In this situation, it is usually difficult for helpers to have a strong, quick impact. If it were easy, the person would have solved it already. And, if the person could have avoided it, it would have been avoided. We all do both of these: solve or avoid problems. When neither is possible, we ask for professional help.

And the professional helper can help. Our experience as therapists and counselors is that answers can come but they usually take time and a certain amount of agony for the client along the way. Often these situations mean a choice between two bittersweet options, both involving doors opening and doors closing in one's life. The person's life can move forward, but the process of getting there is not like life on a cruise ship.

Examples here include the counselor's work with a parent of a very rebellious teenager. The parent will not abandon the teenager but is unable to reach the teen to stop the angry, rebellious activity. A counselor can be effective here but not in the sense of finding an immediate, positive solution. Another example: A teacher of children with learning disabilities struggles to help them get up to grade level, a difficult task given the children's abilities. The physical therapist works to increase the mobility of a patient with osteoporosis who needs to get past a hip fracture. The possibility for improvement is limited. All of these practitioners are operating within the common arena of "a seemingly unsolvable problem that must be solved."

We want to state here that although the "unsolvable problem that must be solved" situation does not scream out for quick solution, it can be very rewarding work for the practitioner. The solution is a good working alliance between the practitioner and the Other and a process that they follow where they carefully consider options and go through the necessary grieving. Then the world often opens up and the client-student-patient moves on to an authentic choice for her or his future. This can be gratifying work for the practitioner.

Hazard 5: Sometimes it means working with individuals who are not "honors students"

Honors students can get better, improve, and learn anywhere. Harvard professors may do little for the students who come in brimming with resources and skills. If the professors do not harm them, the students will be successful, and the professors can later bask in their success. In the past, Schoefield's (1974) term *YAVIS* (the acronym for young, attractive, verbal, intelligent, and socially skilled) was a way to describe desirable psychotherapy clients – that is, those who could improve rapidly. As a practitioner, if one does not get in the way, one can feel successful. There is a natural tendency for practitioners in the helping fields to gravitate towards clients, students, or patients who have resources (e.g., motivation, ability, limited problems) that will fuel the success of the practitioner's helping effort. This way, there is improvement, and the practitioner, feeling competent, can bask in the positive change. For example, one of the ironies of the modern university is that there is more status attached to teaching honors courses or advanced doctoral seminars, in which the students have so many skills, than in teaching basic, developmental courses in which the students are less able and the instructor's work can be more difficult.

Hazard 6: Those we try to help may have motivational conflicts

Motivational conflicts in the helping professions have historically been discussed under the concept of "secondary gains." In some government programs, when one gets better, he or she may lose benefits. For example, we have a social work colleague who said, looking back at a job she had in the past, the work was too frustrating because her VA hospital patients lost disability pay if their depression decreased in severity. Imagine the possible motivational conflicts for a person who gets money while disabled but loses funding when able to work again. Imagine being a helper there and trying to make an impact.

In the past, Tom had a counseling client in this kind of situation, someone who received monthly disability payments because of a mental health diagnosis. Losing the diagnosis meant losing the payments and becoming vulnerable to the legal demands for funds from a former business partner. As a younger practitioner, Tom did not understand the profound impact this situation had on his ability to help the client change. He would have charged ahead, being naive about how much the client had to lose to change.

Tom remembers the grieving of an economically disadvantaged African American woman who was finally getting her BA degree. Grieving when a great success was at hand? It was confusing because success meant triumph over long odds in an oppressive environment. Success, however, also meant losing her former peer group, a rich source of friendship. Suddenly, she was not so accepted by the rest of the group.

In one research study, Hagstrom, Skovholt, and Rivers (1997) interviewed advanced undergraduates who were unable to decide on a college major. They were often frozen in the decision-making process, not by simple issues such as lack of information or decision-making skills, but by a highly complex set of conflicts that were difficult to resolve.

Motivational conflicts also refer to being sent by others, such as parents or the court system (e.g., for remedial classes in math, an anger management workshop, stop smoking information). The motivation is outside oneself: outplacement – *sent by others;* driving while intoxicated and chemical abuse classes – *sent by others;* academic probation and mandated work with an academic advisor – *sent by others;* dragged to marriage counseling by one's spouse – *sent by others.* One of the classic red flags predicting limited success in human services is external, not internal, motivation for seeking help. And this, as we discuss in Hazard 3, is why Motivational Interviewing has become popular (Miller & Rollick, 2002).

In Tom's counseling work, he has seen many male clients sent by their female partners/spouses. It has often been like pushing the rock up the hill vs. rolling the rock down the hill. Combining (1) the female nature of counseling, right down to pastel wall colors, low lighting, Kleenex in full display, soft chairs, a focus on vulnerable feelings; (2) male role demands of toughness and invulnerability, to be like an oak tree; and (3) being sent by others can be a tough combination. All over the world, teenage and young adult males are harvested for war for their specific community/ethnic group/country. For this, young males are hardened as they grow up. A willingness to harm others does not fit with empathy for others. Tom calls this the 180-degree male role conflict – trained for war, expected to later nurture. This means that males often have conflicts with the client role in which they are expected to reveal their vulnerabilities and fears. Sometimes males can overcome these fears and start to see that getting help can be very positive for them. Others never get there. Motivational conflicts again stir the pot!

Hazard 7: Sometimes they project negative feelings onto us

> At the best of times, people project on their pastor their fears of judgment, their anger at God, and many other feelings. In moments of severe stress, the tendency to misperceive the pastor is even stronger.
>
> – Mitchell & Anderson (1983, p. 118)

Veteran teachers call this *excess baggage,* a term meaning that the student brings extra, painful feelings from interactions with teachers in the past. Here are other examples: In school, did teachers treat you as if you were your older brother or sister? Did they call you by his or her name, assume you had his or her characteristics? Communication can get worse with new lovers as relationships get more serious because projections from each person's past – especially betrayal or abandonment types of narratives – can enter the conversation and make understanding and trust much more difficult. The euphoria of early relationship chemistry gets replaced by ghosts (or sometimes angels) from the past.

These are examples of the dynamic of projection and transference. Our clients, students, and patients can bring intense transference reactions to us with their past pain, hurt, anger, and fear related to helpers and authority figures. We get their unrecognized stubbornness, resentment, anger, and lack of cooperation.

The projections of early feelings and internal schemas can be especially strong when the consequences of the helping relationship are very important for the one being helped; that person does not feel much power in the relationship and the rules of engagement are fuzzy. This is not the fault of anyone; this is just very human. An unexamined example is the relationship between doctoral advisors and doctoral students in PhD programs. This is a very important part of higher education and in modern society, where intellectual property is central for economic prosperity. Yet, professors as advisors, across so many fields (e.g., history, physics, literature, mathematics, sociology), get no training in the art of the doctoral relationship. A negative transference reaction from a student to the professor or the professor to the student can harm the work just as a very positive transference can energize their work together. Many professors are naturally skilled at this relationship work; some are not. None get any direct training in it.

High school teachers often experience angry, disappointed, distressed parents and personalize the parental reaction. It can be difficult to understand the transference element and not be personally hurt. The mark of an expert at attachment and connection may be the ability to do this well even when the client, student, or patient brings hurtful past interpersonal experiences that create very understandable fear (Harmon et al., 2005).

Tom was unaware of his innocence when first teaching disadvantaged, historically unsuccessful college students. He thought that they would welcome him as "Tom," the good guy ready to help them. He did not know that he represented all the teachers from the past who had flunked, humiliated, and shamed them in school, the mandatory prison they attended for years. To them, he was often just another oppressive adult.

Hazard 8: *They have needs greater than the social service, educational, or health system can meet*

All practitioners have examples of how success would be enhanced with more resources. For example, every day high school students plead for tutoring help at schools where there are few tutors. In physical and mental health, practitioners are constantly trying to squeeze out resources for patients and clients within the arid world of limited insurance coverage for services. Difficult clients can be those who fail, not because they are personally difficult, but because the system does not provide enough resources for success.

These kinds of limited resources were evident during the years 2012–2015 in the VA system in the United States. Military veterans kept coming home from war zones with intense physical, emotional, and spiritual needs to only be put on waiting lists, or not even put on the lists. The VA was swamped with infinite human need; the system provided only finite resources. So many Veterans with legitimate human suffering didn't get their needs addressed.

In contrast, some clients, students, and patients do not overwhelm the system. They may quickly succeed at the task. They have the motivation, skills, and resources to get better, and we, as practitioners, can bask in their success and are nourished by successfully helping another human being. Even now, let us imagine a world of clients, students, and patients who are easy to assist. Let us dream; bring them on. But of course, the world is not that way.

Hazard 9: *Our inability to say no – the treadmill effect*

> She [the special education teacher] . . . felt her enthusiasm ebb in the face of overwhelming problems presented by dozens of students.
> **– M. J. Smetanka (1992, p. 1B)**

> The general experience of Australian doctors is stressful and demanding . . . with the need to balance work and personal responsibilities, too much to do at work, responsibility at work, long work hours, and fear of making mistakes.
> **– The National Mental Health Survey of Doctors and Medical Students in Australia (2013, p.4)**

> When we stop caring about what people think, we lose our capacity for connection. When we become defined by what people think, we lose our willingness to be vulnerable.
> **– B. Brown (2012, p. 169)**

As a strategy to meet the needs and constant demands of clients, students, or patients, the practitioner often reacts by running faster and faster. Soon the pace is dizzying, and the surroundings blur. The practitioner gets numb and can't think or process experience or feedback. And when we cannot process our professional experiences, we cannot learn and improve. Yet, that seems secondary while on the treadmill where the pace just seems to increase.

This major professional stressor concerns our desire to help, our difficulty in saying no, and the resulting overload. In "The Heroic Syndrome," Stone (1988) described his "good intentions and heroic strivings" as ultimately an Achilles' heel that needed to be changed for long-term professional vitality. His prescription: "The word 'no' belongs in the helping vocabulary." Here is his description of his work while a psychologist at the University of Iowa Counseling Center:

> I received a call from a resident assistant (RA) at about 1:00 a.m. on a Saturday night after a football game. He stated that "a young man was in his room, dripping blood from cuts in his arms and acting very strange." He pleaded, "Couldn't you come down?" I was still somewhere in the twilight zone as I heard this description, yet responded, "Sure." I went to get my John Wayne uniform and wake up the trusty steed. As I was motoring to the rescue, I became aware of how little I knew of the situation. Such things as the name of RA, specific residence hall, security issues, medical needs, and so on drew a blank. I finally woke up and lowered my Superman cape, and went to the security office to gather some information.
>
> Although the situation was resolved in a positive manner, the potential for harm was also present, regardless of my heroic although misguided intentions. The incident crystallized for me the importance of becoming informed before blindly attempting to save the world. My good intentions and heroic strivings are no substitute for informed and competent practice. There are limits!
>
> My personal incident also sensitized me to the potential for the heroic phenomenon within the counseling profession and higher education. I have witnessed the heroic drive among counseling center leaders and practitioners as I listen to them describe their responses to their unique campus situations – 24-hour on-call duty, treating long-term clients with limited resources, serving as the hero on campus by becoming all things to various campus constituencies. For example, a counseling center may find it difficult to say "no" to a part of the campus community needing long-term treatment, although the center does not have the necessary resources – 24-hour on-call service, sufficient staff, and easy access to inpatient facilities. Given the limited resources, long wait lists, and a brief therapy orientation to student developmental tasks, many counseling centers may not be an appropriate treatment facility; that is, use of such a center may be counter-therapeutic for long-term clients. Of course,

the long-term treatment question for counseling centers is more complex (e.g., a question of availability of appropriate referral sources), but to the degree that heroic intentions of counseling centers are not matched by adequate resources and competent practice, they become prone to the heroic syndrome.

I am not troubled by heroism, but I have relearned that the heroic drive needs to be tempered by realizing the necessity of limits. The word no belongs in the helping vocabulary.

My discussion has to end here because I just received an emergency call. I've got to roll. The struggle continues.

(p. 108)

Stone's dilemma is the dilemma of all of us in human services, education, and health care. It concerns the tension between two elements: good intentions/heroic strivings and the "no" of turning one's back on human need. These two pulls on the heart and mind of the practitioner are extremely difficult to reconcile, especially for the novice counselor, therapist, teacher, or health professional who is often confused about how hard to try in the helping role. Practicum, clerkship, practice teaching, and internship sites often receive excessive services from students in training whose strong intentions and heroic striving naturally lead to overextension. This process occurs year after year, like the swallows returning to San Juan Capistrano, with each new wave of students in training. It happened with us, Tom and Michelle, and our own classmates; did it with you and your classmates? Learning boundaries and saying no seem to come later.

There was the public health nurse in Chicago (L. Smith, personal communication, 1982) who had a 550-person caseload, and the school counselor in New York (R. Severson, personal communication, 1987) who tried to be fully available for 400 students and to please all the relevant groups – the school administrators, his counseling colleagues, the students, and the parents. Often, the ability to set limits and say no only occurs with exhaustion and the realization that the individual cannot physically or emotionally maintain the pace over the long haul of 30 to 40 years or even a shorter haul of months or weeks. For Hill (1988), it came only after she had become totally overwhelmed as *the* college counselor for hundreds of students. She wrote:

Nine years ago I accepted the position of college counselor at a private liberal arts college of 800 students. I entered with 4 years of community counseling experience but was new to the needs and expectations of a college system. Seventy percent of the position was designated for directing and providing personal counseling and programs, and 30% was designated for teaching one psychology course each semester and serving on departmental committees. In addition to the college counselor, there was one career counselor.

My first year was chaos. Ongoing, and at times simultaneous, situations occurred that required immediate attention be given to students, staff, and faculty. For example, class lecture preparations and test design and evaluations were left to the late evenings because of the high demand of 35 to 40 hours of psychotherapy per week. (There were times when 3 or 4 students were simultaneously needing immediate counseling.) I was called out for approximately two middle-of-the-night emergency calls per weekend because a poorly trained housing staff was unable to identify, respond to, and refer students with problems in their early stages of development.

Needless to say, I felt exhausted, angry, hurt, and numb. I wanted the college system to reward me for my hard work and to rescue me from the overload. Neither occurred. I went to an extreme, working lunches, evenings, and weekends before I was willing to say to myself; [sic] "I have done all I can do and it's not enough." At the end of the first year I faced a cathartic moment, which became a turning point in my life. I realized that I had the choice of quitting or rescuing myself and the position. I chose the latter.

(p. 105)

How does one learn to say no yet avoid indifference and apathy? For many, as Hill said here, the proper point of tension often occurs after the practitioner becomes overextended and exhausted. Noting this professional exhaustion inspired the first writing on burnout (Freudenberger, 1974). In the years after Freudenberger first used the term *burnout*, many books have addressed this topic, including Baker (2003), Larson (1993), van Dernoot Lipsky & Burk (2009), Mathieu (2012), Norcross and Guy (2007), Rothschild (2006), and Wicks (2008). We now have many other warning words, such as *emotional depletion, secondary trauma, compassion fatigue, vicarious traumatization,* and *trauma exposure response.*

Hazard 10: Living in an ocean of stress emotions

The capacity for compassion and empathy seems to be at the core of our ability to be wounded by the work.

– B. H. Stamm (1995, p. ix)

The incidence of stress-related problems for teachers has been dramatic in studies that have investigated this phenomenon. Surveys have demonstrated that up to 90% of all teachers may suffer from job-related stress and 50% of all teachers indicate that stress is a serious problem for them.

– M. T. Schelske and J. L. Romano (1994, p. 21)

In the helping professions problems may be a physical, academic, or emotional. Often a component is the Other's emotional distress. Confusion, frustration, discouragement, anxiety, and anger are common. Unable to solve their own problems, the Other often experiences a strong dose of what we name *demoralized hopelessness*. Frank and Frank (1991) state that it is the job of the professional helper to work with demoralization. Hopelessness is a strong predictive sign of suicidal ideation. We use the term *demoralized hopelessness* to communicate the level of human distress that we are often asked to address.

One reason it is important to describe the intensity of client, student, and patient distress is that "forewarned is forearmed" helps us prepare to practice self-care over the long haul. When we understand that the task is stressful, we can prepare for it. The job of the practitioner in the helping professions often involves attaching and being wired emotionally to the Other. That is the essence of empathy, being wired as if one's battery is connected to the other's battery to jumpstart it. The wiring often involves the negative emotions, meaning the stress emotions, resulting in the practitioner living in an "ocean of stress emotions." In time, practitioners learn how to be both wired to these distress emotions and separate from them. Learning this skill is intricate and takes time.

Being wired to these stress emotions can be professionally toxic and a threat to the helper's emotional and physical health. Support for this idea comes from research on the physical health of individuals experiencing chronic stress, such as caregivers of Alzheimer's patients (Vitaliano, Zhang, & Scanlan, 2003).

While working as a practitioner, which of these client, student, or patient stress emotions are most difficult for you to experience internally, as you connect in an empathetic way with the Other?

Fear
Confusion
Rage
Helplessness
Cynicism
Sorrow
Isolation
Loneliness
Estrangement
Anomie
Lack of motivation
Hopelessness
Anger
Desperation
Bitterness

To understand the strength of these negative emotions on you as a practitioner, imagine each of these as a toxic agent attempting to enter your body. Which are most powerful and compelling? What is difficult or debilitating about these emotions for you?

Because working in this ocean of stress emotions is taxing, practitioners sometimes wish to remove themselves. For example, Tom once thought of opening a Joy Clinic, a place for only happy emotions. People would come when everything was going well. Unfortunately, he realized that business might be kind of slow. Later, he thought of a flower shop, an ice cream store, a candy shop, or a plaque and awards store. At these kinds of places, everybody seems happy. There are many positive emotions.

The intensity and scope of human distress that comes to practitioners should not be underemphasized. Human beings are an extremely intelligent, able, and creative species and have the capacity to solve many complex problems. All of us are very skilled at problem solving. As we stated earlier in this chapter, people often seek out helpers *only* when they can't solve their problems by themselves, that is, when they have seemingly *unsolvable* problems that must be *solved*. It is the combination of unsolvable and must-be-solved that leads people to experience demoralized hopelessness.

In the working alliance between the practitioner and the Other – in the intensity and vividness of the counseling session, the educational classroom, or the hospital room – what is too much involvement and what is too little involvement in the negative emotions of the other person? We know that lack of empathetic involvement in the emotions of the Other is often considered poor practice in the helping professions. An uninvolved, callous, disengaged, "burned out" helper is what every counselor, therapist, teacher, and health professional hopes to avoid becoming. Yet, the other extreme, over-involvement in these stress emotions, may be more precarious and dangerous for the helping process and our own well-being. How then does one regulate emotional involvement in the flow of human data, the life stories, of our clients, students, and patients? What is too much involvement; what is too little in this ocean of negative emotions? Decades ago Norman Cousins (1979) made a compelling case for the impact of positive emotions and laughter on the health of the individual. In contrast, does the intensity of negative emotions change the helper's emotional immunological system? Are there analogies here to the effect of passive smoke on the nonsmoker or asbestos fibers on the person in the room?

Hazard 11: The covert nature of the work

The previous hazard suggests that ambiguity and lack of closure can make success feel elusive. This next hazard introduces another element that interferes with work satisfaction. Practitioners in the helping professions often cannot talk about their work. For example, the psychotherapist may have achieved an incredible breakthrough with a client that is life changing. However, the practitioner must enter her or his personal life after work with details of the day's relationship-intense work and identifying information about the Other sealed in a vault in one's mind. Maintaining confidentiality is essential in our work.

How may euphoria, about the day's success in helping others, be expressed? It is muted and sketchy. Imagine that! You want to tell friends and family about your day – doesn't everybody want to do that? – but you cannot because of confidentiality provisions that protect the privacy of the client, student, or patient.

Confidentiality is an important and valuable aspect of these professions and is a catalyst for the work to occur, such as in psychotherapy in which the client reveals very personal information. The privacy and confidentiality provide an environment that promotes client trust and willingness to open up the self for exploration. Although this is a very positive aspect of the work overall, it binds practitioners to put a wall between the work self and the personal self. Therefore, the practitioner must have an internal mind vault to store the 3-D movie of the relationship-intense work of that day, week, month, year, decade.

Practitioners in the helping fields and government spies share a common bond, a secret life they cannot reveal. The negative side of this is that a practitioner in these fields is unable to share the successes, failures, frustrations, and confusion of the work outside of the professional context; therefore, the value of social support from others, connection to others, and understanding by others as ways to reduce work stress gets greatly compromised in the helping fields.

Let us note that professional consultation and clinical supervision, conducted within the ethical guidelines of the field, are very helpful activities in mitigating the professional and personal isolation that can occur for practitioners because of confidentiality provisions. We know of one group of highly respected female practitioners who have conducted peer consultation on a regular basis for 30 years. Bravo!

Hazard 12: Constant empathy, interpersonal sensitivity, and one-way caring

> As we reached the edge of the cliff, my first thought was "This is unbelievably beautiful."
>
> My second thought was, "I wonder how many people have killed themselves by jumping off these cliffs?"
>
> **– van Dernoot Lipsky and Burk (2009, p. 1)**

> Empathy is a double-edged sword; it is simultaneously your greatest asset and a point of real vulnerability.
>
> **– D. G. Larson (1993, p. 30)**

The very act of being compassionate and empathic extracts a cost under most circumstances.

– C. Figley (2002, p. 1434)

Reading these three quotes brings home the message that, yes of course emotional depletion is always nearby for the practitioner in the helping professions. Practitioners are successful because they can do "high touch" – relate to others by way of expert people skills. Yet, this work takes effort. The practitioner must concentrate, be involved, and work at it until depletion – not total depletion but relative depletion – sets in. Interpersonal sensitivity demands that the practitioner understand the complexity of human relationships, including concepts such as projection and transference, which mean the feelings that the Other projects, like in a movie, onto the practitioner. For example, if you have followed an older sibling in school and teachers seemed to keep treating you like your sibling rather than yourself, then you have experienced projection or transference.

The psychoanalytic–psychodynamic tradition has been most useful in illuminating transference–countertransference concepts (Corsini & Wedding, 2010). Maintaining a clear awareness of transference–countertransference issues is not always easy for counselors, therapists, teachers, and health professionals trying to establish positive human relationships with individuals that they attempt to assist. Working in a high-touch professional relationship amid the transference–countertransference flotsam is very difficult but of critical importance in achieving excellent human relationships. And, of course, being able to establish excellent human relationships is a marker that sets apart those in the helping professions. But it is swimming upstream and hard work. Working free of our own distortions is a difficult goal because it means that we must take off the layperson's perceptual lens.

As mentioned in Hazard 7, Mitchell and Anderson (1983) describe the stress of the transference reaction in the professional lives of those in an allied helping field, the clergy. They write, "At the best of times, people project on their pastor their fears of judgment, their anger at God, and many other feelings. In moments of severe stress, the tendency to misperceive the pastor is even stronger" (p. 118). Members of the clergy, wanting like other helpers to be perceived positively, can often be confused and distressed when those that they seek to help react to them with strong negative emotions.

With countertransference, which is our own distorted reactions to the Other (Sexton & Whiston, 1994), we must work to understand the wide array of perceptual filters that we bring to the helping relationship: our personal history; our major demographic variables, such as age, ethnicity, religion, sex, and socioeconomic status (SES); our family of origin genogram and its biases; our trauma and pain; and our cultural encapsulation within geographic and national boundaries. Understanding all of these perceptual filters, and their impact on our reaction to the Other, is hard, hard work.

Thus, although transference and countertransference provide rich data for the helper of others, making use of this data means swimming against the current. The temptation is always to turn around and go with the current, with the lay reaction of just being human. Fighting this temptation is both a primary stressor and hard work. Excellent helping practitioners, however, maintain the interpersonal sensitivity within the one-way caring relationship.

Hazard 13: Regulation oversight and control by external, often unknown, others

A medical doctor told Tom of being scolded by an administrative clerk the day after admitting an adolescent to the hospital. The evening before, he had seen the adolescent while he was on emergency room duty. He made a medical decision, based on 20 years of practice, that inpatient care was warranted. The next morning, the administrative clerk, an anonymous person in another state, told him that the admission was unwarranted.

This new layer of administration between the practitioner and the one in need in human services, education, and health care has a positive goal – to reduce excessive costs and increase quality of care. From the practitioner's point of view, however, the main result is often increased stress. The ingredients for the increased stress are less control but increased responsibility by the practitioner, more detailed paperwork without pay for the additional work, and contradictory messages to increase and decrease services at the same time. There are many difficulties. For example, should the mental health practitioner highlight the client's problem areas when asking for authorization of more treatment? A yes might increase the stigma of emotional illness; a no might decrease the chance for authorization.

Hazard 14: Elusive measures of success

Sometimes in this world the best you can do is plant the seed, attend patiently and reverently to a reality you cannot change quickly or even in your lifetime, yet be present to suffering you cannot banish.
— K. Tippett (2007, p. 58)

In the helping professions, it is difficult to gauge success. If the professional impulse is to counsel, teach, or heal, then success must relate to the amount of counseling, teaching, or healing. Or does it relate more to the amount of improvement by the client, student, or patient? Or is it some combination of these qualities – effort by the practitioner plus improvement by the Other? Is it the quantity of the practitioner's effort or the quality? Is it gain scores – how much the client, for example, has improved compared with earlier or compared with the general population? If the person in need is significantly impaired, do we expect less? If he or she is highly functional, do we expect more? For example, should a physician who routinely sees terminally ill cancer patients judge success or failure by whether these patients stay alive? If not this criteria, what?

Professional stress in the helping professions is closely tied to the complexity of the human condition, the elusiveness of concrete results, and the difficulty in measuring success. In the ambiguous and murky world of counseling, therapy, teaching, and healing, who is responsible for improvement? About this, a graduate student in the helping professions wrote:

> Related to feelings of success and failure in the helping professions is the issue of responsibility . . . Not only was the overresponsibility sometimes unproductive, or even counterproductive, with the clients, it was horribly frustrating to me to often feel like a "failure" with my clients. I too frequently imposed my view of success, then beat myself up when they couldn't achieve it.
>
> (Thorson, 1994, p. 3)

Maybe we are doing a good job if our supervisor says we are, but then *maybe* the supervisor is in error. *Maybe* we are doing a good job if our clients, students, or patients like us. *Maybe* liking us is irrelevant for their growth. Haven't we all, with time, come to appreciate and gain from practitioners, such as a demanding teacher in high school, whom we disliked at the time because they were pushing us hard? For example, Tom had an extremely demanding football coach in the past but has come, in time, to appreciate having that coach.

Perhaps success is related not to results but rather to skilled effort. In other words, the counselor of acting out, angry adolescents can measure success by how much an adolescent client becomes more cooperative, social, and achieving, or the counselor can measure success by how much he or she practices professional skills to a maximum level. Do we focus on outcome (the client's changes) or process (our own professional effort), or is it a combination of these two? Should one reduce expectations regarding outcome if the level of need, dysfunction, disease, or dis-ease is greater? When do reduced expectations help to fuel a cycle of failure, rather than interrupt it, so that the practitioner colludes in the failure rather than attempting to stop it?

Even if we decide that realism rather than idealism should be a goal, how do we move in that direction? This question often emerges for practitioners from the older dilemma of realizing that one's professional efforts (one's power, influence, commitment, energy, and competence) are not enough. This realization usually occurs through a "series of professional humiliations," which occur when one's best efforts produce only failure.

Even when avoiding perfectionistic expectations, the practitioner faces a new dilemma of how to transform expectations. How is the practitioner to distinguish between being realistic and giving up? Giving up is a process in which the counseling, teaching, or healing practitioner colludes in a cycle of failure and somehow the Other was at fault; the inadequate client, student, or patient failed. This is when helping becomes toxic, the victim becomes revictimized, and blaming the victim becomes a powerful, destructive enterprise. The liberators have become prison guards who continue on because they like the salary and retirement benefits, the security, and the status, but they no longer care enough to really be powerful helpers of the Other. And being a powerful, plugged-in helper of the Other really matters.

According to Angus et al. (2010, p. 359), accumulative research evidence shows that patient reports of a strong, collaborative alliance early in therapy are consistently correlated with overall positive therapeutic outcome, across diagnostic subgroups and therapeutic approaches. A practitioner who has given up is no longer attached, and without the attachment, the collaborative alliance, so well documented in the above citation as an instrument of human change and transformation, is unplugged. Powerlessness results. How can this destructive process be distinguished from the very different process of becoming realistic; that is, gaining a more elaborate, textured understanding of the difficulty of human change and moving to less grand expectations of oneself as a practitioner? Sorting out realistic and possible vs. idealistic and unreachable is a Hazard of Practice to be sure!

Hazard 15: Normative failure

A common experience of teachers is to feel the pain of opportunities missed, potential unrealized, students untouched.
— W. Ayers (1993, p. 7)

[Sometimes] the classroom is so lifeless or painful or confused – and I am so powerless to do anything about it – that my claim to be a teacher seems a transparent sham. Then the enemy is everywhere: in those students from some alien planet, in that subject I thought I knew, and in the personal pathology that keeps me earning my living this way. What a fool I was to imagine that I had mastered this occult art – harder to divine than tea leaves and impossible for mortals to do even passably well!
— P. J. Palmer (1998, p. 1)

One of the most distressing parts of being a practitioner in the helping professions is the often desperate search for concrete standards of success versus failure. The personal threat is often severe, and one's career search and occupational identity are at stake. There is often a sense of ambiguous but pervasive anxiety related to this question of "Am I any good at this work?" One element of this dis-ease is the need to differentiate normative failure from excessive failure. Resolving this question is very important for the novice practitioner. Increased professional experience often brings more clarity to this distinction. This, in turn, tends to greatly reduce pervasive professional anxiety as one moves from novice to advanced practitioner (Rønnestad & Skovholt, 2013, and Chapter 11 of this book). After learning to define normative failure versus excessive failure, the novice must begin to clarify whether he or she is on the normative failure rate or high failure rate. Being able to place oneself on the normative side also reduces one's free-floating worries about professional skill.

Central to this focus on professional performance is the term *normative failure*. It is a startling term. People most often enter the helping professions with an intense desire to make a significant impact in the lives of others – to heal, educate, reduce hurt, stop pain, increase competence, provide insights. Accompanying this desire, there is often an only partially understood sense of using a powerful method of change, a feeling of one's own potency in helping others make positive changes. Related to this, there can also be an urgent attempt to rescue the Other from some version of significant pain-stress-hurt-loss. Thus, the concept of normative failure can be a startling jolt.

Those in the helping and caring professions can be extremely distressed when they feel that they have failed in helping. Linville (1988) describes such an experience:

> I was in my first position as a school counselor and soon found that I was expected to do much more than talk with students who had problems. I learned that I was also the director of the school district's home-bound program. I tried to be conscientious, but my world seemed to be a jumble of interviews with students, parents, and teachers; of trying to deal with classroom and playground emergencies; and of jumping from one thing to another. I was not quite sure who or what I was supposed to be.
>
> One morning I found a note on my desk. A boy in the upper grades who had leukemia now required home-bound instruction. He was only a name and an added responsibility for me, part of my duties. I shook my head. I had begun fitting students into categories, "Problems" and "Duties," and I slipped Tim, the boy with leukemia, neatly into the "Duties" category.
>
> I made my telephone calls. I called the teacher who worked with home-bound students and asked when she and I could visit the boy. I called Tim's mother, and we set up a time for the visit.
>
> The teacher and I visited the home. I didn't know what to expect, but Tim was dressed and he was up and around, a little pale perhaps, wearing a brown sweater to keep warm, but happy to see the teacher.
>
> "I'll be back on Friday," the teacher said. "Maybe you can have all of your assignment done by then."
>
> Tim came up to me. "When will you be back?" he asked.
>
> "I'll come back a month from today," I said cheerfully. "That will be Tuesday, the 28th. I'll see how everything's working out."

"What time will you be here?" Tim's mother asked.

"About one o'clock," I said.

"Come back," Tim said.

He stood just inside the door, holding one of his books.

Arrangements had been properly made. Another of my assignments had been completed. When I was back in the office, I made a note in my appointment book about the visit on the 28th.

I was soon involved with Parents' Night, with some boys who were leaving school at recess, and with two teachers on a teaching team who had stopped speaking to one another. The month went fast. The day I was to visit Tim came, but the school superintendent came by to talk to me, and I forgot to check the appointment book. Then the superintendent asked me to go to lunch, and when I got back to the office it was two o'clock.

"Tim seemed all right," I said to myself. "I'll stop by another day when I'm in the neighborhood." . . .

A month passed, and I stopped at a grocery store on my way home from school. It was an evening in early winter, and I was glad to walk down the brightly lit aisles of the store after walking through the evening darkness outside. I stopped by the produce counter and picked up a head of lettuce.

I looked up and there was Tim's mother, pushing a grocery cart. She pushed it slowly, and her lips moved as if she were trying to remember something. There was a large orange box of cereal in her basket with a picture of a baseball player hitting a home run on the side.

I said cheerfully, "Hello. Do you remember me?"

"Yes," she answered.

"How's Tim doing?"

This time she didn't answer. She only looked at me.

"I hope . . ." I started talking because everything seemed so quiet.

Suddenly she spoke. "He died," she said in a harsh voice.

I gathered up the usual words of sympathy and smoothed them out. She kept looking at me, and I shifted the head of lettuce in my hands. I stepped back a little. I thought she was looking at me as if she hated me.

"He thought you were coming," she said. "He waited for you. He had his work ready to show you."

I still remember every sharp detail of the scene – her face with the tight lines of grief by her mouth, the stacks of produce, the bright lights of the store. Her hands were gripping the round handle on the grocery cart. She looked at me and said softly, "You hurt him."

She pushed the cart hard and walked away. I stood there. I put down the lettuce and walked out of the store. It was dark outside, no touch of evening left. The lights fell across the parking lot in pale and wavering lines. I waited a while before I opened the door of my car. I felt as if I had turned my back on another human being.

Since then I have kept duplicate appointment books, but, far more than that, I began to think about what I was really doing. I realized that I had a responsibility to others, that I could not keep people waiting through long afternoons, that being busy (often idle busyness) was no excuse. My essential function was to be there and not leave people all alone, waiting for a word from me. I saw that failure in my work could go far beyond not meeting job specifications. I realized that children were not Problems and Duties, that human contact was more than making proper arrangements, that beyond the performance of assignments were human needs reaching toward me – and I had not been there. A little boy in a brown sweater had been waiting, and the afternoon was long.

(p. 101)

Malcolm Linville wrote this piece, which he titled "The Long Afternoon," years after the incident happened, yet it was traumatically stitched into his memory, as we can sense with his words: "I still remember every sharp detail of the scene." Failing the vulnerable people we serve can leave us so distressed. The great majority of people in the helping professions are very conscientious, with high internal standards for their work, like those expressed by Malcolm Linville. Yet, our performance can also be overwhelmed with demands and difficult problems. Linville describes that, too.

We may know at one level that the patients of expert doctors sometimes die, but this profound understanding of the reality of professional success and failure doesn't penetrate our own professional self-concept. Somehow, we believe that we will succeed in our own healing of others, and our clients, students, patients will change and get better. With further experience and a clearer reality, practitioners realize that they are like doctors whose patients die. All our will, all our work, all our competence will sometimes not be enough. This means that, in time, the practitioner must develop the capacity to accept lack of success – normative failure – as a component of the work. Being able to come to this realization, accept it, and incorporate it into one's professional self-concept is important for long-term, high-quality professional functioning. In our research, experienced practitioners often were, in effect, talking about acceptance of normative failure when they described their own shift in expectations as they moved toward being "realistic" (see Chapter 11 of this book).

Hazard 16: Cognitive deprivation and boredom

The novice, at sea in heavy waters, tries hard to maintain the craft and avoid sinking. It is often an anxiety-filled voyage, composed of quick changes, new challenges, occasional calm, and a veneer depth of professional confidence. Like a powerful, churning sea, the novice is never sure of the professional challenge to be faced in the upcoming minutes, hours, and days. It is often intense, involving, engrossing, and sometimes very exciting in a positive vein. It is *not* boring.

For the senior practitioner in the high-touch fields, the challenge can be 180 degrees from that facing the novice. For the veteran with years of experience, the sea is calm, the route predictable, and the work tasks, now mastered, can be the same as before and before and before. This situation is especially true for a practitioner working in a very prescribed arena in terms of the scope of the work and the job environment. Sure, the payoff is reduced anxiety and increased professional confidence. That counts for a lot. The problem is that the intellectual stimulation is lessened, the routine has become boring, and task repetition grates like an old wound. The stimulation of novelty, with its sugar high of energy, is gone. The obnoxious, unpleasant, unwanted, and routine tasks, which do not seem too bad for the novice who is simply trying to stay afloat, can be felt as deadening by the veteran practitioner.

Tom remembers thinking that work activities can be divided: 20% is loved, 60% is okay, and 20% is disliked. When beginning in a helping profession, the person eagerly starts up the career mountain and pushes through the disliked tasks. Many decades later, the percentages can remain similar, but the person can react differently to them. The 20% disliked can become Really Disliked, as in the hazard of cognitive deprivation and boredom.

Whether the practitioner is a novice or seasoned practitioner, the client, student, or patient is, of course, fully invested in his or her personal needs, as should be the case, and wants very much to have a practitioner who is fully invested too. The unwritten, unspoken contract desired by the one in need is that the practitioner be strongly engaged in the Cycle of Caring of empathetic attachment, active involvement, felt separation, and re-creation. For example, remember in Chapter 3 the research that found that, most of all, people want a caring teacher. They want to feel they matter to the practitioner.

With boredom, there is a lack of novelty to stimulate the practitioner. One kind of novelty relates to the practitioner as a cultural anthropologist. One vocational choice inventory asks if the person is more interested in people or things. For counselors, therapists, teachers, and health care workers, it is people. People – their lives, choices, thoughts, feelings, and ways in the world – enchant the practitioner. It can be exciting, like a big tip for a taxi driver. Being with people, therefore, is very rewarding because the practitioner keeps learning about other people and from other people. When one knows enough about one aspect of human life and the curiosity factor is satiated, then the cultural anthropologist reward disappears. Tom remembers working at the University of Florida Counseling Center as a psychological counselor for 18-year-old college freshmen. He found it interesting to try to understand all the permutations and combinations of these students' lives. Yet, after four years of it, Tom felt that he knew more than enough about being 18. He was getting bored with the same thinking, struggles, worries, and developmental vistas. He wanted out and was lucky to expand his client load to include a bigger variety of people.

Aside from learning about people through involvement with them, practitioners are stimulated in their search for more professional competence. Good practitioners always want to find ways to work effectively with those that they serve. Using one's own mind to search for ways to improve can be immensely stimulating intellectually.

For example, imagine that there is a seventh-grade boy in front of you. He is in school but not doing well. You, the teacher, are charged with engaging him. What route will you take? Or imagine that you are a physical therapist with a patient who fails to do critical exercises at home. What will you do? Or you are a school counselor leading a group of children from divorcing families. These children have never been together before to discuss this difficult topic. How will you lead the group so that the children will benefit?

These challenges stimulate the practitioner; however, at some point, especially with a narrow population or problem, the practitioner has seen and done it all before, and *boredom sets in.* The counselor has heard the story many times before; the teacher has taught the subject over and over; the physician has repeatedly performed the medical procedure. The rub is that the client, student, or patient needs an energized practitioner, but the practitioner is bored. The practitioner can be engaged by new work but may be trapped by "golden handcuffs," the financial benefits given to those who stay in a position for many years. In short, this problem of cognitive deprivation and boredom is a significant hazard in the counseling, therapy, teaching, and health fields.

Hazard 17: Cynical, critical, negative colleagues and managers

It is not unusual to see faculty in midcareer don the armor of cynicism against students, education, and any sign of hope. It is the cynicism that comes when the high hopes one once had for teaching have been dashed by experience – or by the failure to interpret one's experience accurately.
– **P. J. Palmer (1998, p. 48)**

The work can be hard – so hard that van Dernoot Lipsky and Burk (2009) proclaim that we have to develop "trauma stewardship." In the same vain, we have, since our first edition in 2001, called for all of us in the helping professions to become "resilient practitioners." With a supportive work group and a good boss, the job can be positive and fulfilling. When colleagues are negative or the boss is incompetent, reality is more burdensome. Cynical colleagues spread a highly infectious disease. This disease of negativity is easy to catch. It is also a seductive disease because, when one first gets it, he or she feels better. Some venting can be very helpful, yet when the negativity faucet is fully open, hope fades. Cynicism, in the air, is especially dangerous in the relationship-intense helping fields. Clergy, professors, physicians, counselors, and others in the relationship-intense fields, members of the people occupations, need the stress-buffering effect of positive colleagues, which is a long distance on a continuum from the nonbuffering effect of negative colleagues.

A second factor relates to the needs of those we serve. The caring desired by the Other, whether client, student, or patient, is most empowering when it contains the active ingredient of hopefulness. In fact, Frank and Frank (1991) argue that helpers are sought out when a person feels demoralized, with the chief curative agent being hopefulness. But how can one offer hope within a critical, cynical work environment?

Administrators get paid more because they help create the important work environment. We are reminded of the work of Carkhuff (1969), whose research suggests that the client cannot function psychologically at a higher level than the helper. In a parallel fashion, it is hard for a worker to function at a higher level than the boss. With a great boss, everyone can sail; with a poor boss, the environment leads to no sailing or poor sailing by all on board. In the helping professions, bosses are incompetent if they are very critical or unfair. They also are poor performers if they do not support ideal conditions that enable counselors, therapists, teachers, or health workers to fully implement the Cycle of Caring with those that they serve. And please remember a basic premise of this book – only energized helpers can continually care for the Other in need and do it over and over again for person after person. *Cynical, critical, negative colleagues and managers are a danger!*

Hazard 18: Legal and ethical fears

We used to be on our toes of concern for the kids, now we are on our heels of worry about ethical and legal threats.
– **25-year veteran teacher and counselor participant in other-care and self-care workshop (1996)**

It is important to start by noting that legal and ethical complaints have been nurtured by illegal and unethical behavior of practitioners in the helping and caring professions. Misuse of power to meet one's own needs, general incompetence, and other unethical behaviors are not to be tolerated. But here we are talking about the wider arena of potential legal and ethical complaints and instances where the practitioner is wrongly accused. At times practitioners feel pulled away from the important work of attending to the client by fears and concerns of ethical and legal issues, as the quote above illustrates.

Hazard 19: Practitioner emotional trauma

After many years of hearing stories of abuse, death, tragic accidents, and unhappiness . . . my exposure to other people's trauma had changed me on a fundamental level . . . Rather than stay in touch with the heart that was breaking, again and again . . . I had started building up walls.

– van Dernoot Lipsky & Burk, 2009, pp. 2–3

Last week on one day I had eight appointments, all with people who had been terminated from their jobs. After that day I wanted to crawl in a hole [to escape the painful feelings].

– Matt Johnson, counselor of newly "downsized" employees (personal communication, August 1996)

We have described the practitioner dilemma of needing to connect with the Other by using one's "soft side of the turtle" rather than the hard shell. Yet, unfortunately, doing this produces a side effect – practitioner emotional trauma – as surely as strong medicines produce side effects. Terms we have cited at various places in this book used to describe the impact on the practitioner are *burnout, emotional depletion, vicarious traumatization, countertransference, compassion fatigue, secondary trauma, trauma exposure response,* and *ambiguous professional loss.*

This construct overlaps the earlier described ocean of distress emotions, but it goes beyond that to experiencing the reality of difficult events in the lives of our clients, students, and patients. These include vicariously experiencing and understanding sexual assault, chronic physical pain, unexpected failure in school, betrayal in friendship, student neglect by parents, severe financial loss, a child's death, physical attack, sudden job loss, deceit within marriage, a fatal car accident, onset of a serious illness, and severe existential anguish. Over the years of a practitioner's career, many of these events and others are described by clients. Often, for history taking and diagnostic purposes, the counselor, therapist, teacher, nurse or other helping professional must hear the details of the experience. Later, in counseling or therapy, for example, the desensitization protocol may entail countless times of recalling the experience to help the client reduce the traumatic elements of it. The therapeutic process for the client can, over time, produce a vicarious traumatization or secondary trauma experience for the practitioner. Therapist Sussman (1995) describes it this way:

> Prone to overidentifying with clients, I tend to experience much of their emotional pain and internal struggles as if they were my own. The permeability of my ego boundaries may facilitate empathic contact, but it also leaves me vulnerable to emotional overload. Especially when working with more disturbed individuals, hearing and digesting their stories of past and present abuse can be highly disturbing.
>
> (p. 21)

A parallel process can happen for health professionals who repeatedly hear of the vulnerability of the human body to disease and injury. The human body in front of them that has been attacked by disease or injury is not unlike the body that they themselves possess. Educators also experience versions of this vicarious stress when they interact with struggling students unable to learn and with little family support. For all of these conscientious, caring practitioner the following words are not too far away: "there but for the grace of God go I."

Another kind of practitioner emotional trauma involves "taking in" the hostility of the client, student, or patient toward the practitioner. For example, there is the angry reaction of a parent to a teacher at a parent–teacher conference, the intense affect liability of a teenage client to a youth counselor, or the hostile behavior of a patient to a nurse. This negative reaction from those that we try to help can be quite stressful because it can hit the "soft side of the turtle" part of us with which we attach and it can negate our primary occupational need of being helpful. Learning how to have emotional boundaries, but not emotional walls, helps a person become a resilient practitioner. More on that in later chapters!

Hazard 20: Practitioner physical trauma

Sometimes things go beyond severe overload, the ocean of negative emotions, ambiguous professional loss, and normative failure, so that the "underside of the turtle," the soft defenseless part, the area that attaches the helping or caring professional to the Other gets physically hurt.

The most frightening form of practitioner physical trauma is direct attack by clients. In the *Boston Globe* on August 21, 1999, a headline stated, "Social Worker Slain Outside Client's Home." The first paragraph reads, "A social worker whom colleagues described as dedicated to his job counseling troubled youths and trained to deal with violent situations was shot dead yesterday, allegedly by a member of a family he had gone to visit" (Milbouer, 1999, p. B1). A nightmare came true for a 30-year-old practitioner, married with children, just trying to do his job.

In research on this topic, Guy, Brown, and Poelstra (1990, 1992) discovered that 40% of their sample group of 750 predominantly full-time psychological practitioners had been physically attacked by clients during their careers, and 49% had received serious verbal threats against their health and safety. These kinds of traumatic events led to many different concerns about safety. For example, 28% often or sometimes were concerned about the verbal threats toward their physical safety, 17% were often or sometimes concerned about physical attacks on their loved ones, and 7% were often or sometimes concerned about being murdered. This in turn led to a variety of protective measures against client threats. For example, this sample group frequently refused to treat certain clients (50%), discussed safety issues with loved ones (30%), installed a home security alarm system (13%), or kept a weapon at home to protect themselves against present or former clients (5%). This study provides sobering data regarding this issue of practitioner primary trauma.

Both Kinnetz (1988) and Zeh (1988) describe highly traumatic experiences while they served as counselors. Both were physically attacked by their clients and traumatized by these events. For Kinnetz, it occurred while she worked in a maximum-security psychiatric unit; for Zeh, it was in a shelter for runaway adolescents. Kinnetz describes her experience:

At the beginning of my counseling career, I was employed as an art therapist in an adult male, forensic, maximum security psychiatric unit. The job was difficult because I had never before worked with an all-male population, let alone one that was explosively violent. Angry patient outbursts were common. For example, in one scuffle a patient cracked the jawbone of a hospital aide, and, on another occasion, a patient knocked his doctor nearly unconscious in an unprovoked attack. Nearly paralyzed with fear during the first few days, I stayed in the protective nursing station away from the patients, leaving only to come and go from work. My fear of being harmed lessened considerably, however, when I realized that the hospital staff was very tightly knit and could be counted on to work as a team, especially in emergencies. So, despite the limitations imposed by the strict safety requirements, I began to feel challenged to stay on the ward and to establish an art therapy program.

My discomfort did not completely disappear, however, as I sensed tension in the patients as well. Although I never actually observed a blatant example of staff abuse, I became aware that some of the staff's behavior was less than professional. It seemed to me that, at times, their methods of patient restraint were too strong and bordered on abuse. Certainly, the patients were both verbally and physically abusive to staff as well [as] to each other, and any staff intervention was aimed at rapidly defusing a potential fight and reestablishing compliance with hospital routine. A client-centered approach would have been ludicrous in this situation, because immediate control had to be externally imposed to protect other patients. It was obvious that very strong measures were needed. But how strong, and what kind?

My dilemma was this: Do I report my suspicions in an effort to stop overly aggressive restraints, and risk being told that the force was really necessary? Or do I continue to observe the strong-arm control and be ensured of the protection of the staff? I could depend on the staff to promptly come to my aid should a fight threaten to break out, and was afraid that if I reported my suspicions, I might upset some of them and lose their protection. My fear won out; I did not report anyone until I left the unit for another position.

One of the factors that helped me to decide to leave was when a patient attempted to rape me. I had been escorting him to another part of the hospital when he suddenly grabbed me around the neck and twisted my arm behind my back. He held a contraband razor to my throat and dragged me into an empty room. Fortunately, I was able to free myself and run back to the unit for help. But I continue to wonder whether help would have come so quickly if the staff knew that I was considering reporting them for excessive force.

Years later, I still have not come to terms with the issue of whether I should have reported the possible abuse earlier. This incident has sparked many internal dialogues on the general issue of how I can best take care of myself without sacrificing my client's care. I have found that it sometimes becomes necessary for me to pull back momentarily from the continually intense and demanding emotional needs of a client. This is essential to preserve my own emotional reserves and to prevent eventual burnout. These client needs are less life threatening than the attempted rape, but my time-out response to them is no less important over the course of therapy. Certainly, if I withdraw every time the client becomes emotionally demanding, it would be a major therapeutic error, and my effectiveness would be severely compromised.

The ability to be fully engaged with the client in his or her struggles is a powerful curative factor. But if I allow myself to become emotionally overwhelmed and burned out, the long-term result is a compromised effectiveness. Not only is one client affected, but all my clients and even family and friends suffer. Although the strong-arm measures on the unit were extreme, perhaps (but perhaps not) they were justified to preserve the unit's functioning and ultimately to benefit the patients. Similarly, without taking care of myself emotionally, I cannot help clients learn to take care of themselves.

The unresolved nature of this question continues to keep me searching for balance. Too much therapist emotional withdrawal is not in the client's best interests, but continual emotional availability to the client is draining and dangerous, particularly in the absence of sufficient external therapist support. It is imperative that I monitor my own internal state as well as attend to my clients' emotional well-being. I judge my immediate internal state as a balance of present emotional and physical reserve, counterbalanced with the amount of support and replenishment that I can count on in the near future to replace the outgoing supply. This self-monitoring can be considered an extension of caring for my client. Although self-monitoring is not sufficient in itself to prevent therapist burnout, it goes a long way in helping me remain effective in both the short-term and long-term. Nonetheless, it is an ongoing, elusive dilemma – where is the balance between my needs and the needs of those I serve?

(p. 87)

This is a gripping story by counselor Kinnetz. Both her experience and that of Zeh, mentioned earlier, are examples of practitioner physical trauma. These are acute wounds to the "underside of the turtle" part of the practitioner self. Fortunately, physical harm is a relatively rare occurrence; unfortunately, when it does occur it can be a hazard of great trauma for the practitioner.

HAZARDS SUMMARY

Work in the helping professions can be engrossing, exciting, and deeply satisfying! It is important to emphasize this point to you, the reader, because we have just described 20 hazards of practice. It is also important to note that the sting of the hazards can be lessened if we face them directly, if we become mindful of them. The popular historic saying, "Forearmed is forewarned," is our intention with this chapter.

For veteran practitioners, there often are difficult incidents over the years of practice that lead to a loss of innocence. The most traumatic incidents, such as the suicide of a client, are stressful and, at the time, bring on daydreams of other, hopefully more positive, occupational choices. What are the lessons from these incidents? For one, practice can wound the practitioner. Often one's vulnerability is unknown. The person may not have known before that a field that can do so much good can also wound its practitioners. Innocence is not knowing how the "soft side of the turtle" can produce practitioner vulnerability.

Reading this chapter of hazards may lead a person to question the wisdom of entering any of the helping or caring professions. Bodily experiences when reading this chapter can include feeling a pit in one's stomach, an increase in anxiety, or the beginnings of a headache. It can be hard to read about hazards of practice. We have also tried to communicate the positive feelings in Chapter 2, "Joys, Rewards, and Gifts of Practice."

The overall goal of this whole book is to portray first the wonderful qualities of the work and, in contrast, the stressful qualities of the work and, consequently, the need for professional resilience and self-care on an ongoing basis.

SELF-REFLECTION EXERCISES

In this chapter, we discussed many difficulties that can affect the work of the practitioner. We suggest that you review the chapter and then pick five from the list of hazards. As a next step, fill out the following:

1. Hazard number _____ Name: _____

    Why has this been a significant practice hazard for you?

    _____

    _____

    _____

_____

_____

_____

_____

_____

_____

_____

_____

What methods have you tried to alleviate its impact? How successful have you been?

_____

_____

_____

_____

_____

_____

_____

_____

_____

2. Hazard number _____ Name: _____

Why has this been a significant practice hazard for you?

_____

_____

_____

_____

_____

_____

_____

_____

_____

_____

What methods have you tried to alleviate its impact? How successful
have you been?

_____

_____

_____

_____

_____

_____

_____

_____

_____

_____

3. Hazard number _____ Name: _____

Why has this been a significant practice hazard for you?

_____

_____

_____

_____

_____

_____

_____

_____

_____

_____

_____

What methods have you tried to alleviate its impact? How successful
have you been?

_____

_____

_____

_____

_____

_____

_____

_____

_____

_____

_____

_____

4. Hazard number _____ Name: _____

Why has this been a significant practice hazard for you?

_____

_____

_____

_____

_____

_____

_____

_____

_____

_____

_____

What methods have you tried to alleviate its impact? How successful
have you been?

_____

_____

_____

_____

_____

_____

_____

_____

_____

_____

5. Hazard number _____ Name: _____

Why has this been a significant practice hazard for you?

_____

_____

_____

_____

_____

_____

_____

_____

_____

_____

What methods have you tried to alleviate its impact? How successful
have you been?

_____

_____

_____

_____

_____

_____

_____

_____

_____

_____

6

HEMORRHAGING OF THE CARING SELF: BURNOUT, COMPASSION FATIGUE, VICARIOUS TRAUMA, AMBIGUOUS ENDINGS, AND PROFESSIONAL UNCERTAINTY

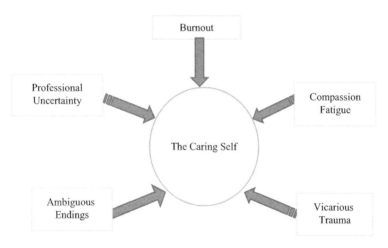

Figure 6.1 Spears that hemorrhage the caring self

The words "hemorrhaging of the Caring Self" can bring on fear and trembling! These are words used by the existentialist writer Søren Kierkegaard in: *Fear and Trembling* (Kierkegaard, Hong, & Hong, 1983).

Although the five spears (illustrated in Figure 6.1) can stab at the helping professional's Caring Self, please keep in mind, as you read this chapter, the title of Chapter 2: "Joys, Rewards, and Gifts of Practice." Also, note that we will give resiliency tips in future chapters. For now, we are digging deeper into professional stressors . . . so keep your seatbelt on as we go for this ride together.

These five concepts all provide windows into stressful realities for the helping practitioner. Naming a problem gives the person a chance to address it and limit its negative consequences. A good example of this is the famous naming of "the problem that has no name," which was the way Betty Friedan described the limits faced by educated adult women in mid-20th-century America. Her naming of the problem energized and reenergized the women's movement. Here we are naming burnout, compassion fatigue, vicarious trauma, ambiguous endings, and professional uncertainty as contributing factors to the hemorrhaging of the Caring Self. These five concepts describe both separate ideas and overlapping ideas. Here, we are less interested in concept purity and more interested in offering topics of value to practitioners. We will devote the largest share of space to burnout, since it is the oldest and most researched term.

BURNOUT

> After working in community mental health for five years, I was burned out, or burned up, by a sense of hopelessness after overextending myself to help people and no one seemingly appreciated my efforts.
>
> – M. E. Young (1997, p. 45)

You may wonder where the term *burnout* came from. In the early 1970s, Herbert Freudenberger was a practitioner in New York City at a community agency focusing on drug abuse. At the time, drug abusers were often called "burnouts." Being called a burnout meant that the person no longer cared about anything except drugs. As a consequence of a slow erosion of motivation and competence, the person was not capable of much or interested in anything except getting high on substances. Hence, one became a burnout.

In 1974, Freudenberger published an article titled "Staff Burnout" in a psychology journal. Freudenberger attempted to describe a loss of will among the practitioners who worked with these addicted clients. He used the word *burnout* in this way for the first time, and the term was born. This first article on burnout began:

> Some years ago, a few of us who had been working intensively in the free clinic movement began to talk of a concept which we referred to

as "burn-out." Having experienced this feeling state of burn-out myself, I began to ask myself a number of questions about it. First of all, what is burn-out?

(p. 159)

In the 1980s, the term *burnout* hit a chord. It quickly became a popular way to consider exhaustion and disquiet at work. It had what measurement people call face validity, meaning that it captured something that practitioners could identify as real. Soon, a number of authors wrote books on burnout in various occupations, such as human services (Cherniss, 1980), teaching (Cedoline, 1982), nursing (McConnell, 1982), and medicine (Wessells et al., 1989). From 1980 to 1985, there was an outpouring of 300 academic articles on burnout (Roberts, 1986). Schaufeli, Leiter, and Maslach (2009) estimate that over 6,000 journal articles, books, chapters, and dissertations have been published on the topic of burnout in the 42 years since the term was identified.

Searching the literature 20 years after the term was first used, Söderfeldt, Söderfeldt, and Warg (1995) found many descriptions of the term. Although the descriptions were different, key words reveal commonalities. These key words are fatigue, frustration, disengagement, stress, depletion, helplessness, hopelessness, emotional drain, emotional exhaustion, and cynicism. These words point to a profound weariness and hemorrhaging of the self as key components of burnout. This profound weariness and hemorrhaging of the self makes the concept of burnout one that is understood by counselors, therapists, teachers, health professionals, and clergy, too.

LACK OF CLARITY: WHAT REALLY IS BURNOUT?

Paradoxically, although the concept of burnout seems understood by all, it does not seem to really be one specific thing. One could ask, what does it really mean, and what is the research summary at this point many years later? The answers are murky. It has been hard to find strong, consistent statistical relationships regarding burnout. Söderfeldt et al. (1995) wrote, "Overall, there are weak indications of any pattern in the associations, except that they generally seemed job related" (p. 642), and concluded that "burnout should be considered a multidimensional syndrome" (p. 644). In their review of burnout in research and practice, Schaufeli et al. (2009) reported that the concept of burnout has different meanings across international contexts. For example, in Sweden and the Netherlands, burnout is a medical diagnosis. A wide variety of variables have been found, in at least one study or another, to be associated with burnout.

Sölderfelt, Sölderfelt, and Warg (1995) wrote about factors that contribute to burnout in social workers. Citing relevant research studies, they divided the contributors to burnout into three areas of Work Related, Client Related, and Worker Related. Together, they wrote, this trilogy of factors led to social worker, and more generally, in our view, to practitioner deterioration in the relationship-intense professions. Work Related Factors include low work autonomy, lack of challenge on the job, low degree of support and role ambiguity. Client Related Factors include negative impression of clients and empathy. Worker Related Factors included chronic low-level stressors.

WORK OF MASLACH

Christine Maslach, a psychology professor in California, is considered one of the leading burnout researchers. (This is opposed to being a burned-out researcher. Tom heard her speak at a professional conference and she was quite energetic.) The Maslach Burnout Inventory, a popular research instrument (Maslach & Jackson, 1981), and her books, *The Truth About Burnout* (Maslach & Leiter, 1997), *Burnout: The Cost of Caring* (Maslach, 2003), and *Banishing Burnout: Six Strategies for Improving Your Relationship With Work* (Leiter & Maslach, 2005), have been well received.

Maslach and Leiter (1997) give their definition of burnout: "Burnout is the index of the dislocation between what people are and what they have to do. It represents an erosion in values, dignity, spirit, and will – an erosion of the human soul" (p. 17). They go on to describe three key work dimensions in which a person could be fully engaged or burned out (p. 24) in Table 6.1.

Regarding the causes of burnout, Maslach and Leiter (1997) take a strong work-climate view. Instead of focusing on the individual practitioner, they say "burnout is not a problem of the people themselves but of the social environment in which people work" (p. 18). They cite six specific work environment sources of burnout: work overload, lack of control, insufficient reward, unfairness, breakdown of community, and value conflict. As an example of their view of burnout, we are using a long citation from

Table 6.1 Three dimensions of engagement/burnout

Fully Engaged	Burned Out
Energy	Exhaustion
Involvement	Cynicism
Efficacy	Ineffectiveness

Maslach and Leiter (1997, p. 34) – their description of the case of Julie, a public school teacher:

> Julie taught history and literature to eighth graders in a public school and had a reputation as an outstanding teacher. Students loved her, parents called to get their child enrolled in her class, and the principal rated her as one of the best. Young and successful, Julie was expected to have a long and distinguished teaching career. But this year, Julie decided to quit. Her decision came as a shock to everyone; some of her colleagues cried when they heard the news.
>
> At one time Julie was completely dedicated to the job because it allowed her to do things she valued highly – to make a difference in the world, to have a positive impact on other people's lives. But today she doesn't feel the job is worth it. At one time she brought enormous energy and commitment to her work, putting in long hours and agreeing to do all sorts of "extras" above and beyond the call of duty. Now she is exhausted just going through the motions and doing the bare minimum. At one time she was deeply involved with her students, attentive to their progress and achievement in learning, sensitive to their individual needs. Now she is more negative and cynical about their motivation and skills. At one time she was confident that her efforts would pay off, that the kids would get a better education and a better start on life because of what she and other teachers were able to accomplish. Now she questions whether the students are really getting what they need; she even worries that children are getting damaged by overworked teachers like herself. To Julie, trying to do good came at too high a price.
>
> What is noteworthy about Julie's case, and many others like it, is that the negative slide to burnout started from a position of strength and success rather than from one of weakness . . . In terms of skills and motivation, she was at the top of her class – one could hardly ask for more. As one of her colleagues said, "Julie was 'on fire' from the beginning, not like some of those teachers who never even 'light up' in the first place. She had a passion for teaching, and it is so depressing to see that disappear." Indeed, losing the best and the brightest – people like Julie – is the most devastating cost of burnout.

SEVEN SOURCES OF BURNOUT

What led to the erosion of Julie's engagement with teaching? A close look at her case reveals the presence of the mismatches between job and person that we described in Chapter 1. Maslach and Leiter (2008) identify seven domains of the workplace environment: workload, control, reward, community, fairness, values, and job–person incongruity.

Work overload was a major factor from the beginning. Julie spent intense 8-hour days in the classroom and extra hours – after school, in the evening, and on weekends – to prepare for class, grade homework, and attend meetings. Although she had a great deal of control over how she taught her class ("When I close that door, the class is all mine – just me and the kids"), she had a *lack of control* over the district policies that led to increased class sizes and decreased teaching resources. Like other teachers, she received a low salary that was clearly *insufficient reward*; she didn't mind so much when she was young and single and just starting out in the profession, but later it posed a severe financial burden. Furthermore, low salaries are the most visible symbol of the lack of respect for teaching. Julie's wages fueled her sense that there was an inherent *unfairness* in the system ("Why am I working so hard, doing so much, and yet getting so little in return?"). The bickering, political infighting, and competitiveness between the teachers in her school made her feel alienated from them, and thus there was a *breakdown of community*. There was a growing *value conflict* between what Julie was trying to achieve in the classroom and the "extras" she was being asked to do by the school. As she put it, "The last straw was when they wanted me to spend a lot of time pulling together all this material to prepare an application for a 'good school' award – there was far more concern about getting the award than actually doing the things that would make us a good school!" (Maslach & Leiter, 1997, pp. 25–26). Finally, Julie experienced *job–person incongruity* as she determined that trying to do good in this setting cost too much in terms of personal sacrifice and lack of unambiguous rewards. In other words, the organizational environment no longer fit for Julie.

Maslach and Leiter's (2008, pp. 500–501) correlates of burnout and engagement address each of the seven problem areas described in the case of Julie. We have put the alternatives in Table 6.2 and labeled them burnout creation and burnout prevention.

There is strong research support for the Maslach and Leiter (1997) belief that the cause of burnout is often in the organization, not the individual. Their interventions, therefore, are to change organizations. We think that this

Table 6.2 Seven areas of burnout creation/prevention

Burnout Creation		Burnout Prevention
Work overload	vs.	Sustainable workload
Lack of control	vs.	Feelings of choice and control
Insufficient reward	vs.	Recognition and reward
Breakdown of community	vs.	A sense of community
Unfairness	vs.	Fairness, respect, and justice
Significant value conflicts	vs.	Meaningful, valued work
Lack of fit (incongruence) between the person and job	vs.	High job–person fit

approach has merit, but it is also myopic and dangerous for practitioners. Actually, Maslach and Leiter (1997) support this caution in their description of the contemporary work environment:

> The workplace today is a cold, hostile, demanding environment, both economically and psychologically. People are emotionally, physically and spiritually exhausted. . . . The idea of the workplace as an efficient machine is returning to undermine the ideal of the workplace as a safe and healthy setting in which people may fulfill their potential through intrinsically rewarding work for which they are given fair compensation.
>
> (pp. 1–2)

What if one's work environment is not a place that constantly addresses the psychosocial stress of the staff? It reminds us of the play *Waiting for Godot* (Beckett, 1997), in which two individuals waited and waited for a man named Godot to show up so that they could go on with their lives. He never did, and the play ended. The moral of the play for practitioners: Be careful about waiting for others to care for you.

Consider the two work settings described by Molassiotis and Haberman (1996) in their research on bone-marrow-transplant nurses. This is a caring profession group at high risk for stress and burnout. They have the grief work that accompanies engaging in the Cycle of Caring with dying patients and their families. In one setting, there was a supportive environment that addressed staff psychosocial needs. This was not present in a second setting, and the stress and burnout level was higher there. Hopefully, in the second setting, some of the nurses took charge of their own self-care and did not "wait for Godot."

We are reminded of many settings in which we have worked. Some were burnout creators and some burnout preventers. In the bad settings, no one rescued us. It was up to us to create an environment that worked. In the absence of psychosocial support, counselors, therapists, teachers, or health professionals must create it for themselves and "create a professional greenhouse at work," a concept identified in the chapter on sustaining the professional self.

There are some exceptions to this rule. One successful, systemic, organizational intervention is that of Gysbers and Henderson (2005). Instead of waiting for others to create a positive work environment, they have taught school guidance counselors how to do it for themselves.

MEANING AND CARING BURNOUT

The term *burnout* has helped us lift a shade and see more clearly through a window to the realities of the practitioner's world. The symbolism involved with the word burnout relates to the extinguished flame, which is the motivational force in the caring professions.

It is helpful to distinguish between two styles of burnout; one is meaning burnout, the other caring burnout (Skovholt, 2008). Meaning burnout occurs when the calling of caring for others and giving to others in an area such as emotional development, intellectual growth, or physical wellness no longer gives sufficient meaning and purpose in one's life. Individuals in the caring professions derive much "psychic income" from helping others. In religious terms, such occupations are often labeled a calling, a calling to something of great value. When the meaning of the work disappears, an existential crisis can develop, and meaning burnout can result. Meaning burnout occurs when the meaning of the work has been lost and the existential purpose for the work is gone.

This may occur for any number of reasons. It may be that the activity – such as counseling adolescents, teaching children to read, or nursing the frail elderly – becomes routine, boring, and seemingly insignificant for the practitioner. It may be that the practitioner entered the occupation in part to satisfy his or her own personal needs. This in itself is not a negative factor in job choice. Yet, when it is a predominant factor and the need is filled, then the meaning of the work can decrease. Here are some examples: There is the "wounded healer" who feels healed after counselor training and work in the field. A teacher may have entered education to prove that he wasn't dumb, after feeling that way in high school. Now, years later, he feels intellectually competent and no longer has to prove himself. How about the wellness nurse who was attracted to the field because of her own body image distress earlier in life? Now, she has better feelings about herself. Each of these individuals has lost some of the original meaning and purpose in their occupational choice. However, new meaning in the work can emerge. If it does not, meaning burnout can grow.

Another kind of meaning burnout occurs when the practitioner no longer feels that the work is helpful to the client, student, or patient. This can be a "crisis in meaning" time because if the work is not useful, and the point is to be useful, then why continue? Examples here are a job in (a) an agency where too many cases and too much paperwork make good work impossible, (b) a school that seems to promote a "revolving door" of failure rather than student success, and (c) a health setting where the finances do not permit the practitioners to operate in a competent manner. One colleague working with substance abuse talks of the relapse problem bringing on meaning burnout for him. He wondered how the work could be meaningful when relapse seemed to be more of a reality than recovery.

The second type, caring burnout, is the most popular way of describing burnout. This type focuses very strongly on the professional attachment–involvement–separation–re-creation process that all practitioners engage in over and over again with their clients, students, and patients. As described in an earlier chapter, the quality of the attachment to the person in need is of central importance for client, student, or patient gains. (For example, think of your favorite teacher. Was his or her interest in you *as a person* a central element of what you treasured about this teacher?) This idea corresponds with research in the helping professions described in Chapter 3. "Indeed, of the multitude of factors that account for success in psychotherapy, clinicians of different orientations converge on this point: The therapeutic relationship is the cornerstone" (Norcross, 2010, p. 114).

If the inevitable separation with the client, student, or patient does not too severely deplete the practitioner, then he or she can attach again. But if the process drains the person, perhaps each time just a little – just as the plaque in arteries builds up little by little – then the life force, the blood flow for the counselor, therapist, teacher, or health professional, is gradually choked off. This is the caring burnout process. One could also use the analogy of a battery. The battery keeps getting energized or drained. When drained enough, there is no spark, no life.

Professional attachments and separations that deplete the practitioner, such as too many ambiguous professional endings and losses, can lead to a subsequent inability to attach. The three subscales of the Maslach Burnout Inventory (Maslach & Jackson, 1981) seem to capture this process – emotional exhaustion, depersonalization, and lack of personal accomplishment. Okun and Kantrowitz (2008) provide a description that fits with this description of burnout:

You may be suffering from burnout when you feel exhausted and are unable to pay attention to what someone is saying; you find yourself reacting more impatiently and intolerantly than you have in the past; your sleeping and eating habits change or you experience a new physical symptom; or you find yourself dreading the beginning of the workday and lacking enthusiasm, motivation, and interest.

(p. 302)

An older reference shows that burnout has been a problem for a long time (Corey & Corey, 1989):

Continuous contact with clients who are unappreciative, upset and depressed often leads helpers to view all recipients in helping relationships in negative terms. Practitioners may care less, begin to make derogatory comments about their clients, ignore them and want to move away from them. Dehumanized responses are a core ingredient of burnout.

(p. 167)

The most important point that we are making here is that the presence of losses and the absence of gains in the Cycle of Caring of empathetic attachment → active involvement → felt separation → re-creation contribute to burnout. This definition of caring burnout, as opposed to meaning burnout, is focused specifically on the most important work task in the high-touch occupations. Caring burnout is the result of a decreased ability to professionally attach with the next client, student, or patient because of the cumulative depletion and negative energy generated over many previous episodes of work between the practitioner and the client, student, or patient. We define caring burnout as disengagement of the self from the empathetic attachment → active involvement → felt separation → re-creation. Hopefully, there are bountiful joys, rewards, and gifts of practice. It is best when the work itself, active engagement with the Other, produces energy rather than depletion. When depletion occurs more than a positive effect, energy is drained from the battery. Without a spark, burnout occurs.

Both meaning burnout and caring burnout are destructive realities because the end of active engagement by the practitioner means the end of competent practice in counseling, therapy, teaching, or health work. Mediocre work can occur, but expertise in these fields needs the active engagement of the self. You ask, what is one to do about burnout? Our attempt to answer that question can be found throughout this book where we offer both answers and strategies to manage burnout.

COMPASSION FATIGUE

In the helping profession, practitioners may experience difficulties from continual exposure to hearing clients discuss suffering and trauma in their lives. A term parallel to burnout in some ways, yet distinct, Figley identified the concept of *compassion fatigue*: "the natural consequent behaviors and emotions resulting from knowing about a traumatizing event experienced by a significant other – the stress resulting from helping or wanting to help a traumatized or suffering person" (Figley, 1995, p. 7). In his later work, Figley expands his initial definition to include "a state of tension and preoccupation with the traumatized patients by re-experiencing the traumatic events, avoidance/numbing of bearing witness to the suffering of others" (Figley, 2002, p. 1435). Figley asserts that compassion fatigue results in higher levels of helplessness and a feeling of being isolated from a support network. Compassion fatigue represents a difficulty for the practitioner in regenerating and renewing after engagement with clients/students/patients and an inability to engage successfully in the re-creation phase of the Cycle of Caring. Without re-creation, moving through the work of the Cycle of Caring becomes problematic.

Compassion fatigue results from exposure to hearing about or supporting a client who has suffered from a traumatic event or events. Some researchers (Jenkins & Baird, 2002) use the terms *secondary traumatic stress* and *compassion fatigue* interchangeably, referring to the same concept, as defined above. They go on to draw similarities between the terms: "Secondary trauma, vicarious trauma and burnout are similar in resulting from exposure to emotionally engaging clients via interpersonally demanding jobs, and represent debilitation that can obstruct providers' services" (p. 425). The concept of vicarious trauma will be explored below. It is important to note that some authors indicate that compassion fatigue can occur without exposure to traumatic material; it can result through chronic exposure to the Other's suffering. Newell and MacNeil (2010) indicate that "the experience of compassion fatigue tends to occur cumulatively over time; whereas vicarious trauma and secondary traumatic stress have more immediate onset" (p. 61). In the literature, there is some disagreement about the definitions and uses of the terms we are exploring in this chapter; however, precise definitions that separate these terms are of more importance to researchers. We are focused on helping helpers manage the cost of caring.

Individuals in the relationship-intense professions are exposed to the stories of the Other. We stand by and create a container to hear and hold the stories of our clients/students/patients. Sometimes these stories are heart wrenching and difficult to hear. Compassion fatigue comes when one hears the telling of the Other's story as traumatic or when the chronicity and severity of client/student/patient suffering over time is great.

Sometimes there are factors that predispose us to feeling particularly impacted by a story – for example, if there is some parallel with our personal lives or the stories of those we hold dear. For example, as a mother of a young child, it is difficult for one social worker we know to hear of traumatic events happening to children, even if the events are far off in a client's history. An instinct to protect, along with the awareness of how vulnerable children are and how the results of treatment in childhood are often alive in people far beyond childhood, is particularly poignant at this stage in this practitioner's life. When the practitioner's life stage/story intersects with the chronic hearing of a traumatic event, this has the potential to create compassion fatigue. Additionally, other variables, such as a practitioner's own trauma history or being in the early career stage paired with a high degree of trauma work and insufficient self-care, can predispose the practitioner to compassion fatigue and vicarious traumatization (discussed below).

Other times it is not about the intersection of bearing witness to traumatic events and personal variables within a practitioner's life. Sometimes it is just so painful to take in the suffering of the Other.

VICARIOUS TRAUMA

Repeatedly being exposed to stories of trauma can begin to alter the worldview of the helper. Distinguishing itself from other related terms that we discuss in this chapter, *vicarious trauma* tends to shift the helper's inner cognitions about the world. A comprehensive and clear definition comes from Hernández, Engstrom, and Gangsei (2010), who state: "*Vicarious trauma* refers to the cumulative effect of working with traumatized clients: interference with the therapist's feelings, cognitive schemas, memories, self-esteem, and/or sense of safety" (pg. 69). Vicarious trauma typically comes on quickly and can overwhelm the practitioner. McCann and Pearlman (1990) indicate the "profound psychological effects, effects that can be disruptive and painful for the helper and can persist for months or years after work with traumatized person" (p. 133). As you can see from the quotes above, the impact of vicarious trauma can be pervasive for the practitioner.

The practitioner is tasked in the empathetic attachment and active involvement phases of the Cycle of Caring with engaging empathetically with the Other and trying to understand the subjective experience of the client/student/patient. In attempting to understand the subjective experience of the Other, especially in cases where trauma is present, the practitioner is a witness to the painful emotions and at times horrific experiences of the Other. In a practice made up of work with clients who have experienced significant trauma, the possibility of vicarious trauma grows. Here, from Jordan (2010) is a poignant example of the vicarious trauma experienced by therapists working with combat veterans.

> VT is the repeated exposure of the therapist to the combat veteran's traumatic experiences (e.g. having seen dead bodies or remains, fear for their own and others' safety and lives, fear of being attacked or ambushed, having seen dead or injured Americans . . . injured women/children and being unable to help . . .
>
> (p. 226)

Other examples include the counselor working with the refugee population and hearing stories over and over again of the loss of family, country, and home. Many practitioners bear witness to pain of a family whose loved one has died through senseless acts of violence, such as mass shootings that come with no cause or warning. Trauma such as this is hard for anyone to hold and even harder to hear over and over. How do practitioners walk the line of protecting themselves from ongoing heartbreak for the Other while continuing to do the work of the Cycle of Caring over and over again with each client/student/patient and maintain empathetic engagement each time the practitioner hears another's story? True compassion involves a certain vulnerability, really caring for the Other while being able to maintain a sense of self and separateness. This is a hard line to walk, especially when work exposes the practitioner to stories of trauma across many clients/students/patients.

AMBIGUOUS ENDINGS

> I would like to beg of you, dear friend . . . to have patience toward everything that remains unsolved in your heart. Try to love the *questions themselves,* like locked rooms or like books that are written in a foreign

language. Do not now look for the answers . . . at present you need to live the *questions*.

– Rilke, 2000, p. 35

Two famous poets, Rilke (2000) and Alice Walker (cited by White, 2004) have written about embracing the questions rather than desperately searching for the answers. In their spirit, we can say to practitioners who hit the ambiguity of the work – dwell with the questions, be patient while engulfed in questions. Being in the questions is a way for practitioners to reduce the stress of the ambiguity.

Wise words from Rilke and Walker, but how can the helping professional live without answers? Like a house painter who is blind and has no feedback about his painting! This plight can invade the vitality of helping professionals who start the I-Thou helping relationships with the client-patient-student only to have it end . . . without an ending.

When Tom was conducting a practitioner resiliency workshop in Norway in 2014, one of the participants, a nurse on a hospital unit, said it was hard to have a connection with a patient, return to the hospital the next day and see that the patient's name was no longer on her hospital door. The patient was discharged during the night, never to be seen again. If the job requires few human emotions of connection, then "people come and people go, some say yes and some say no." However, the resilient practitioner uses the human connection to make an emotional, caring bond with the Other. And when humans have emotional bonds, sudden, unexpected, or unresolved endings can be distressing and zap one's vitality for other bonds. The cost of a broken connection for the helper usually shows up later in the vitality level of the helper in establishing a relationship with a new Thou in the I-Thou relationship.

To describe these 'ending without endings' we are using the term *ambiguous endings*. This is one of the five spears that stab at the Caring Self. (In the first and second editions of *The Resilient Practitioner*, we described this wounding of the helping professional as *ambiguous professional loss – ending before the ending*. Now, in this third edition, we use the more descriptive term of *ambiguous endings*.)

As we have said so often in this book, the laser focus of the helping professional is on improving the life of the Other – the client for counselors; the patient for nurses, MDs, and other health professionals; the student for teachers, lecturers and professors; the parishioner for the clergy; the employee for those in human relations. Ethical violations occur when the laser focus is not on the welfare of the Other. One important ethical principle used to protect the Other is confidentiality and privacy. In the counseling relationship, for example, the client controls his or her coming or going into or out of the counseling relationship. A person may come to appointments and then suddenly stop coming. Consider this situation within the Cycle of Caring, discussed in Chapter 3. The counselor and client go through Phase 1: Empathetic Attachment and begin, and then enter Phase 2: Active Involvement. But Phase 3: Felt Separation never occurs. The good-bye is unclear, indefinite, absent. How then does the counselor do the Re-Creation Phase? Re-Creation is very important for the counselor to have vitality for the next Cycle of Caring with the next person as the work of the Cycle goes on. When Felt Separation does not occur, there is no good-bye. The result is an ambiguous ending. For example, with a client who does not come for a second appointment, the career counselor may say to herself: "Did the client get better? learn anything? feel less distress? think I was a poor counselor? wish to tell me something?"

Into this morass of broken professional relationships comes clarifying language from the work of Pauline Boss. To describe the agony people feel when their loss is ambiguous, she used the term *ambiguous loss* for the first time in Boss & Greenberg (1984). The American MIA soldiers in Vietnam were one of the first examples she described, as in: "Is Dad gone forever . . . or is he coming home sometime?" A spouse with dementia is another: present and absent at the same time. In the book, *Loss, Trauma, and Resilience: Therapeutic Work With Ambiguous Loss,* Boss (2006) describes these two kinds of ambiguous loss: (1) A person is physically absent and psychologically present (e.g., absent parent) and (2) a person is physically present but psychologically absent (e.g., addicted spouse). Both of these types of ambiguous loss can produce extreme stress. Why? Lack of closure. Pauline Boss is describing a way that the natural grieving process gets intensified, or frozen, or both.

Over lifetimes, people experience so many attachments and so many losses of these attachments (attachments can be to so many things – one's high school, one's first home, an important early romantic relationship, beliefs that are no longer believed, one's parents, babies that become adults, a first language no longer used, and the list goes on and on). As a friend once said, "With every hello there is a goodbye." Such an utterly simple statement, but so profound.

From the Boss term of *ambiguous loss* to our term of *ambiguous endings*, the commonality is the lack of concrete results and closure for those in the counseling, therapy, teaching, and health professions. Both Tom and Michelle have experienced this many times as practitioners. From other practitioners, we have heard many stories of ambiguous endings. These are actual accounts told to us from people in the caring professions.

• A counselor at a residential treatment center worked very hard with a teenage female runaway, and he and his wife became very committed to this

young, troubled teen. They got attached. Then one day, the teenager suddenly left the center, and they never heard from her again.
- A counselor in training told her supervisor that she wanted to have a different supervisor, but the counselor would not say why. The supervisor had to deal with this rejection – this attachment and then separation – without knowing why.
- A teacher spent the year with an at-risk fourth-grade boy, trying amid a room full of 31 children to give him enough attention to improve his poor academic performance. She was very invested in his progress. Just as he started to finally make major strides in April of the school year, after months of effort by the teacher, he was suddenly removed from his home and put in a foster home in another town. She never saw him again.
- A few years ago, a counselor saw one of her clients at a social event. The client seemed uncomfortable and later did not come back for counseling. Why? Did the social situation make a difference? The counselor never knew.

An elementary teacher told this story of a stressful ambiguous ending:

> I spent much time working one-on-one with Christina, documented daily her behaviors. She was difficult to work with and I was exhausted at the end of each day but in time she appeared to be happy, healthy, and clean. She did better in academic and social areas. I was excited and happy for her! . . . One day her parents called to say they were leaving the state and she wouldn't be returning to school.
>
> I remember feeling very uncomfortable, sad, and angry. I had "lost" Christina when we were just making progress. While she had been a challenging student to work with, her sudden disappearance truly bothered me. I had no opportunity to say good-bye or to wish her well. I felt like I wasn't "finished with her"; we still had more things to do . . . I still occasionally think about her and wonder how she is doing. I believe I am also realistic in knowing that there will be similar incidents regarding lack of closure during my teaching career.
>
> (Smith, personal communication, 1996)

Reflecting on the ambiguous nature of the work, S. Hage (personal communication, February 1994), a counselor in campus ministry, said:

> Perhaps here lies one of the most difficult personal challenges of being a counselor. We most likely will never know the fruits of our work. We are very often the people who sow the seeds or water the soil of the harvest we will never see.

The constant demand for helping professionals to attach, be involved, and separate over and over means that this process must be done in a way that is energizing to the individual practitioner. Ambiguous endings produce the opposite result; they drain the practitioner. This is one of the five spears that stab at the Caring Self.

PROFESSIONAL UNCERTAINTY

The unexplained – especially the fearful unexplained – cannot be tolerated for long . . . Giving a name to chaotic, unruly forces provides us with a sense of mastery or control.

– Yalom, 1995, p. 84

. . . in medicine . . . The steps are often uncertain. The knowledge to be mastered is both vast and incomplete. Yet we are expected to act with swiftness and consistency.

– Gawande, 2007, p. 4

There are different sources of professional uncertainty that flow like rivers into the Swamp of Ambiguity for those in the helping professions (Skovholt & Starkey, 2012). Professional uncertainty acts as one of the five central spears that Hemorrhage the Caring Self. When we, as humans, feel this uncertainty, we are drawn to clear, simple answers. Many years ago, Tom wrote a short piece for adolescents titled "Total Package Belief Systems," which was an attempt to describe the power and attraction of simple, clear answers for adolescents who were sensing the confusion, paradoxes, and jarring disconnections within the adult world. With a focus on the political world, Eric Hoffer captured the urge for certainty in his book *The True Believer* (1951). Hoffer was quite a character, a longshoreman at the wharf in San Francisco by day and a phi-losopher by night.

For counselors and others in the helping professions, uncertainty shows up when faced with the unique life of the client. Common questions in ses-sion can be: What do I do? What is right? How to proceed? What theories/ techniques/strategies to use? And the questions go on and on . . . while the client/patient/student sits in anticipation and hope, waiting for help. This can be stressful, *especially* for the novice helper. Imagine, then, the magnet-type power of books that are called treatment planners. They give a list of things for the helper to pay attention to – read the list and you are good to go. It is like painting by numbers or cooking something with six steps to follow. Such structure is important and positive for beginners, but great poets, wonderful teachers, and master therapists have long shed such simplicity. Let us note here Rønnestad's (1985) advice, when writing about the early struggles of the novice, that structure and tips on how to proceed are valuable but premature closure is to be avoided.

Here now are three sources of professional uncertainty that flow into the Swamp of Ambiguity.

The first source of professional uncertainty: Human complexity

Human beings are the most complex of all species . . . and you, the reader, have chosen to work to competently help this most complex species! Why not spend your career energy really knowing everything about something intricate enough – grass or snails or wood or swans? Did you realize the implications for choosing the most complicated living, and that means changing, species? The biggest headache is that we will never know, as in really know: What is central when helping the Other? Is the source of the difficulty part of nature? Is it part of nurture? Is it a mix and of what percentages?

To really describe the intricacy, Tom has sometimes used the term complex ambiguity, but that seems like overkill. It is hard to put the complexity into words. However, *complex ambiguity* as a term can seem accurate for the novice practitioner who, for example, faces a new suffering client who talks and talks, giving out copious information yet leaving the novice swimming in data and unsure how to proceed.

Irv Yalom, a Stanford University Medical School Professor, says it this way:

the capacity to tolerate uncertainty is prerequisite for the profession. Though the public may believe that therapists guide patients systematically and sure-handedly through predictable stages of therapy to a fore-known goal, such is rarely the case: instead . . . therapists frequently wobble, improvise, and grope for direction.

(Yalom, 1989, p. 13)

The second source of professional uncertainty: Competing ways of knowing

Is it gerontology, geography, genetics, or geology that most reveals clear human truths? Maybe it is not a *field of study* but a *way of knowing*. How about the scientific method? One's own dreams? The sacred scripture in the Bible? The written or spoken word of other great religions? In these days of the 21st century, perhaps the most remote human tribes hold truths varnished away by the digital age. Here is one small example of how we can understand using different methods: Do we know most about human emotions by (1) blood pressure readings? (2) listening to early Elvis or Bach? (3) viewing the magnificence of a Norwegian fjord or the Grand Canyon?

Regarding ways of knowing, in the helping professions, we think of five different ways of knowing: (1) the empirical scientific research method;

(2) qualitative methods, especially interview methods in which the data is analyzed for themes; (3) the power of professional experience with hundreds of clients/patients/students who are often described by practitioners as their greatest teachers; (4) wise elders – mentors, teachers, clinical supervisors – who guide us with tips on what is important and what is not; and (5) our own personal lives, which serve as a powerful laboratory that gives us internal cognitive schemas for human psychology.

The third source of professional uncertainty: So many micro sources of data for the helping professional

There is some overlap between this way of knowing and the last one. In our research interviews with novices in the counseling and therapy professions, we found that they had six different sources of influence in their search for professional competence (Skovholt & Rønnestad, 1992a).

The beginning helper has so many questions and just wants clear answers. Instead, the answers and near answers come as if they are from the proverbial fire hydrant as a source of water for a thirsty soul. The water gushes out, the answers gush out. So many answers from so many places. Here are the sources of influence:

Theories
Research
Clients
Professors
Supervisors
Mentors
One's own therapists
One's own personal life
One's peers
One's colleagues
The social/cultural environment

Regarding just this last category, the social/cultural environment, clear directions are relative truths embedded in culture, tradition, and time. For example, Kottler and Carlson (2014) tell of encountering an esteemed helper in rural Zambia who had a whole different way of healing.

In reaction to all of this, one of our novice counselor research participants said: "Something grabs you and you run with it for a while" (p. 24). Then some other source of influence pulls the beginner in another direction. Quickly understood and comprehensive theories are embraced by the novice who is experiencing the Swamp of Ambiguity. If these theories could speak, they would say: "Focus on one major piece of the elaborate human story you are hearing while you try to understand the bigger picture." The novice's reaction to this life jacket: "Great. I'll do it." Here are different examples of something to focus on:

cognitions are central
ask about family of origin and attachment patterns
ask open-ended questions
listen to affect
the working alliance is key
try an eye movement technique
be multiculturally sensitive
the last minutes of the interview are most important
the first minutes of the interview are most important
everything has meaning
relax – counseling takes time and the client will come back to the crucial part
target the core conflicts

. . . and the list goes on and changes as new ideas arise – or, as senior practitioners say, as "old ideas are wrapped in new paper."

SUMMARY

Professional uncertainty jolts the practitioner forward . . . searching, searching, and searching for certainty and solid ground as the Swamp of Ambiguity looms ahead. The heart quickens as the practitioner seeks answers that are firm, sure, accurate, true.

The search for a simple, encompassing answer is often doomed. Yet the search goes on. Yes, there are many answers in a relative sense . . . and some answers are better than others. Yet, in the helping professions, the caring professions, the relationship-intense professions, the complexity of human nature overwhelms the thirst for complete certainty.

The topic of human complexity does not attract a lot of interest among practitioners in the relationship-intense professions, especially novices. They really love the methods that shrink the complexity to manageable dimensions via an easy-to-understand method. We, Tom and Michelle, did the same when we began.

One of the great paradoxes of professional training in the helping professions is that the novice enters the field assuming that she will know the answers at graduation. She will know the right way to precede, the right methods to use, the precise answers to ethical situations – as well as the wrong answers. It doesn't work that way! As the saying goes, as the circle of knowing grows, the circle of not-knowing also grows. Professional uncertainty acts as a central spear to Hemorrhage the Caring Self. The resilient practitioner must learn how to ride the wave of uncertainty while homing in on relative truths and effective ways of helping. These are keys to satisfying work.

SELF-REFLECTION EXERCISES

First, consider all of the different meanings of burnout discussed in this chapter.

1. Of all the different meanings of burnout, which definition speaks most directly to you?

_____

_____

_____

_____

_____

_____

_____

_____

_____

2. Using your understanding of burnout, how much does this definition define you at this time? Circle the number.

1	2	3	4	5
Not at all	A little	Some	A lot	Totally

Describe the key factors in your rating.

_____

_____

_____

_____

_____

_____

_____

_____

Part II

Part II

7
WHAT IS HUMAN RESILIENCE?

THE DRAMATIC INCREASE IN PSYCHOLOGY IN THE USE OF THE TERMS *RESILIENCE* AND *RESILIENCY*

The increasing use of the term *resilience*, as seen in Figure 7.1, is symbolic of the shift of psychology from a focus on "what is wrong" to a focus on "what is right" in human development. Here is an example of that shift: Fifty years ago at our university, the University of Minnesota, all students took the MMPI Inventory. It is an instrument to measure "what is wrong" with scales

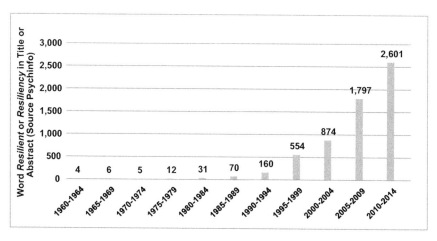

Figure 7.1 Growth in popularity of psychological term *resilient* or *resiliency*

to measure different versions of psychopathology. The original MMPI clinical scales indicate either problems or the absence of problems. Now, college students often take instruments that measure positive attributes. They get results that point out their greatest strengths . . . all positive options, no dysfunction terms. The shift has been from psychopathology to positive psychology (Lopez & Edwards, 2008).

WERNER AND GARMAZEY, GRANDPARENTS OF RESILIENCE RESEARCH . . . AND A NOD TO MAAS

In the study of resilience the same shift has occurred. This is most evident as we look at two pioneer researchers, Emmy Werner and Norman Garmazey, whom we could call the grandmother and grandfather of resilience research because of their extensive focus on this topic.

But first, a nod to the first citations using these terms. Early use of the terms resilient and resiliency (one of four we found between 1960 and 1964) was in 1963 by Henry Maas, Professor of Social Work at the University of British Columbia. He studied adults who had been separated from their parents during World War II. Here is a quote from his abstract:

> Twenty young adults, who as preschool age children were separated from their parents during World War II and placed in group care nurseries were interviewed and given . . . [psychological tests]. It is concluded that human personality is sufficiently plastic and resilient to resist long-term effects resulting from early childhood separation.
>
> (Maas, 1963, p. 34)

Back to the resilience grandparents, Werner in Hawaii and Garmazey in Minnesota. Initially, both were psychopathology oriented – as in, how do poverty, racism, family instability, and similar factors create major psychological problems for children? Both were surprised to find that some children in these environments actually thrived. Eventually they used a term that was originally used by Tredgold in 1818 to describe timber that would bend but not break (cited by McAslan, 2010). That term was *resilient*.

Werner and her colleagues started their research in Hawaii in 1954 (Werner et al., 1971). They had 698 children and their families in one research cohort. They assumed the children would exhibit vulnerability because of their unstable, stressful lives, and at age 10 not be doing well. They found that some of these children were actually doing well! Here is the word *resiliency* for the first time in their research: "The remainder of the children who underwent severe perinatal stress survived the first decade of their lives with amazing resiliency and flourished in homes with adequate educational stimulation and emotional support" (Werner et al., 1971, p. 74).

They continued their study for many years. Of 201 high-risk research participants, at age 32 they assessed 72 of the 201 as doing well (Werner & Smith, 1992). Resilient! Here is an inspiring quote from Werner, which also shows the power and importance of the helping professions.

The life stories of the children of Kauai now grown into adulthood teach us that competence, confidence, and caring can flourish, even under adverse circumstances, if children encounter persons who provide them with secure basis for the development of trust, autonomy, and initiative. From odds successfully overcome, springs hope . . .

(Werner, 1992, p. 267)

Norman Garmazey was another pioneer, the grandfather of resilience. Working at the University of Minnesota, he began a project to research the children of emotionally disturbed parents. Garmazey began by describing his research as the Risk Research Project, examining what makes children vulnerable to psychiatric conditions. Gradually his thinking changed so that he looked for the markers of invulnerability.

In a 1971 article titled "Vulnerability Research and the Issue of Primary Prevention," he explored the topics of psychological vulnerability and invulnerability. He discussed research by Heston and Denny in 1968 that found that some individuals who grew up in difficult situations had, as adults, adaptive personality traits. Later in the article, he wrote: "these 'invulnerable' children remain the 'keepers of the dream.' Were we to study the forces that move such children to survival and to adaption, the long-range benefits to our society might be for more significance" (Garmazey, 1971, p. 114).

So he gradually did. The Risk Research Project changed to Project Competence with one report titled "Project Competence: The Minnesota Studies of Children Vulnerable to Psychopathology" (Garmazey and Devine, 1984). Fast forward to 2015 with the Garmazey tradition. Ann Masten, once one of his graduate students and now an eminent resilience researcher, has captured the history and current status of resilience in her 2014 book, *Ordinary Magic: Resilience in Development.*

RESILIENCE: THE ABILITY TO BOUNCE BACK

Here is an answer to our chapter title's question: What is human resilience? It is, simply said, *the ability to bounce back.* The word comes from the Latin word *resilire,* "to leap back." As Masten writes, "the concept of resilience continues to refer generally to positive adaption in the context of risk or adversity" (p. 9). Rutter (1985), the British psychiatrist, is considered one of the most important scholars in the study of resilience. In their excellent review in the journal *European Psychologist,* Fletcher & Sarkar (2013) state that most definitions have two core two parts: (a) adversity and (b) positive adaption. Together, (a) and (b) fit perfectly with *The Resilient Practitioner.* People in the helping professions face client adversity as part of their everyday work (e.g., the client who presents with sudden relationship loss, career indecision, addiction relapse, parenting stress, overwhelming elder care, bankruptcy, sexual abuse, school failure). Fletcher and Sarkar (2013) say that resilience is not a static trait but a process that can be developed: "resiliency is a capacity that develops over time in the context of person–environment interactions" (p. 15). In keeping with our approach in *The Resilient Practitioner,* they also state that "individuals operating in a demanding performance environment on a daily basis would be deemed to exhibit resilience if they evaluate stressors as an opportunity for development and consequently received peer recognition for their work" (p. 16). The Fletcher and Sarkar (2013) list of how to build resilience includes the following: reduce negative thinking and beliefs, manage energy (we call it *vitality*), learn good problem solving skills, cultivate gratitude, and have strong relationships.

We expand on our own list of ingredients for resilience in the following pages of this chapter.

BALANCING CARING FOR OTHERS AND CARING FOR SELF

In life, it is important to first take good care of yourself. If you don't, you can't take care of others!

— Tom's mother, Elvera Meyer Skovholt
(August 1994; at age 85)

Still true!

— Tom's mother, Elvera Meyer Skovholt
(September 2002; at age 93)

If I am not for myself, who will be for me, if I am only for myself, what am I, and if not now, when?

— Hillel (as cited in Neusner, 1984, p. 32)

Overall, we recommend that therapists do for themselves the self-nurturing, self-building things they would have their clients do. Increasing our awareness of our needs and remaining connected with our bodies, our feelings, and other people will strengthen us as individuals and allow us to choose to continue to do this important work.

– L. A. Pearlman (1995, p. 62)

LOSING ONE'S INNOCENCE ABOUT THE ASSERTIVE NEED FOR SELF-CARE

The following describes the work of mental health practitioners in the military:

Many of the patients who fill the day are bereft, angry, broken. Their experiences are gruesome, their distress lasting and the process of recovery exhausting. The repeated stories of battle and loss can leave the most professional therapist numb and angry.

(Carey, Cave, and Alvarez, 2009, p. 1)

This statement about the work of military therapists helps us see the importance of assertive self-care. Remember the goal is to thrive as a practitioner while offering the deeply meaningful and valuable work of the helping, healing, teaching, and spiritual/religious professions.

Earlier chapters of this book were intended to alarm you, the reader, with these chapter titles: "The Elevated Stresses of the Novice Practitioner," "Hazards of Practice," and "Hemorrhaging of the Caring Self." Did we, Tom and Michelle, cause an alarm go off inside of you? Hopefully we did; we need to lose our innocence about the need for assertive self-care. With foresight, we can be forewarned. Too often in the helping fields, we focus on the immediate tasks at hand and the intense human needs before us, rather than thinking of how we must take care of ourselves if our self, the healing agent, is to thrive for the decades of our work.

In addition to realizing that the work is difficult, and – we keep stating! – often very rewarding, let us all keep the thought in our minds and hearts that helping practitioners, teachers, healers are people too, with their own lives that often contain the normal stress and strain of life during these early decades of the 21st century. That often means time and money pressure, multiple-role demands, and high workplace expectations to perform. The result is often a series of stress-related problems. This can be understood by examining the results of a study (Table 7.1; Mahoney, 1997, p. 15) in which helping practitioners were asked about a variety of personal problems.

Table 7.1 lists a variety of stress-related conditions, some job related, some personal-life based. When one combines the hazards of practice in Chapter 5 with personal-life stress, it is clear why there is an assertive need for practitioner self-care.

Table 7.1 Mental health professionals' previous year personal problems endorsed by 20% or more of the sample (*N* = 86)

Problem	Percent
Concerns about the size or severity of their caseload	48.2%
Episodes of irritability or emotional exhaustion	46.5%
Problems in their intimate relationships	41.2%
Doubts about their own therapeutic effectiveness	40.7%
Insufficient or unsatisfactory sleep	39.5%
Chronic fatigue	37.2%
Feelings of loneliness or isolation	33.7%
Episodes of anxiety	31.8%
Feelings of disillusionment about their work	27.1%
Episodes of depression	25.3%
Frequent headaches	20.9%

Ingredients of balancing include:

1 *An attitude of altruistic egotism* – Selye (1974), the pioneer researcher in body–mind medicine, described the helper of others as needing to also be concerned with the welfare of the self. He called for a stance of altruistic egotism. Given Selye's credibility as a pioneer of the concept of stress and its toxic effects, his ideas warrant attention. Veteran psychology practitioners J. Buchanan (personal communication, 1995) and E. Nightengale (personal communication, 1995) coined similar concepts – holy selfishness and self-attentiveness. By holy selfishness, Buchanan means that the individual must hold his or her own welfare as a holy or sacred obligation. For Nightengale, self-attentiveness means having a focus on one's needs and concern for others. Here, we are talking about an obligation in attitude that involves a constant allegiance to one's own well-being as necessary for competent other-care.

2 *Continual behavioral monitoring of one's other-care–self-care balance* – Buchanan's holy obligation to oneself is more than attitudinal. It also involves an obligation to monitor oneself and constantly be nurturing of self. Robinson (1992) describes "brownouts," episodes of forgetfulness and inattention, among helping professionals as early warning signs of insufficient self-care. Veteran helping professionals often develop personal signs indicating that they are approaching a point of danger. When the practitioner works in a highly stressful environment, this means monitoring and nourishing oneself, just as diabetics monitor their insulin levels. This describes actual behavior engaged by the practitioner to check for signs – physical, emotional, social, spiritual, and intellectual – that one's self is seriously depleted. For example, Stevanovic and Rupert (2004) studied behaviors that psychologists employ to sustain

their careers and found that the second highest career-sustaining behavior was maintaining balance between professional and personal lives.

Hage (2010) describes the importance of balancing self-care and care for clients in her work:

> I learned how important it was to provide a consistently caring presence with Peter to let him know I would be present with him unconditionally, no matter what pain or hurt he shared with me. I also learned, as time progressed, that I needed to keep a certain level of emotional distance, to maintain a separate space for reflection and self-care, to be effective in my work as a counselor.
>
> . . . The "lesson" and the challenge of my experience with Peter is one that I continue to deal with almost daily in my work as a teacher, mentor, researcher, and clinical supervisor. How do I truly and fully care for my students, mentees, supervisees, and their clients, while setting appropriate limits, to ensure that the work is truly empowering instead of disabling and also doesn't leave me depleted? It seems that as professional helpers we need to learn to live with the tension of this paradox – caring and simultaneously letting go. A danger is that, to avoid the tension and ambiguity of this paradox, we may turn to self-protection and project a "hard shell" with our clients and students.

(p. 183)

THE NEED FOR MORE SELF-CARE AT TIMES OF PERSONAL CRISIS OR EXCESSIVE STRESS

Self-care is always important. At times of personal crisis or excessive stress, when ability to function well may be severely compromised, it is even more important. There are, as we all know, bountiful examples of either personal crisis or excessive stress (e.g., the serious injury of one's child, a sudden loss of family income, a major geographic move, the death of one's parent, the emergence of a chronic disease for oneself, the loss of one's intimate partner, destruction of one's property because of the force of nature). The research on self-care strategies can be helpful at these times, as described, for example, by Turner et al. (2005). Following are two examples of a serious family illness that had an impact on the practitioner. First, Schorr (1997) discusses how the personal crisis affected his ability to listen to his counseling clients:

> In my sessions with clients, there would be frequent reminders of our black cloud [my wife's diagnosis of leukemia]. One man complained about a woman he knew – she was weird but that was because she had cancer. Another client had a son who killed himself after he was diagnosed with

leukemia. Another came in numb with grief over the recent cancer death of a housemate. When clients would tell stories in which the mention of disease was a minor note, I had to restrain myself from asking questions merely to satisfy my own insecurity. Or to let my mind drift off into worrisome tangents.

(p. 57)

Pollack (1988) describes her own experience as a person in the caring professions who experienced extreme stress:

The timing was right when I entered graduate school. The youngest of my three children had reached age 10, my husband's career was stable, and I was 37 and ready for a new challenge. I was going to explore my long-time goal of working with adults, with an emphasis on older adults. Two years later, during my spring break, I found myself facing the severest challenge of my life. At first we thought it was the altitude of the Colorado ski resort that was making my husband . . . ill. When the doctor said it was colon cancer we were totally shocked. . . .

Immediate surgery provided temporary relief. Although we were far away from family and friends, the hospital had become like a cocoon, with its kind and caring staff. I felt a sense of terror when we left. Back at home in Maryland, I felt nearly unbearable anxiety while waiting for the results of further surgery. I will never forget my feeling of devastation when the surgeon told us the cancer had metastasized and the prognosis was poor.

The next 11 months were an emotional roller coaster. Why him? Why me? I felt shock, sadness, and disbelief. I was angry at the doctors who took away our hope, joyful during experimental treatments that shrank the tumor, distressed at the appearance of another malignancy, happy with his recovery from the second surgery, depressed as it became clear that it was only temporary, encouraged by the good days, cheered by the jokes we shared about the situation, and distraught at my impending loss. . . .

As his condition worsened, I tried to prepare the children, urging them to read books about death and to talk with us. . . . My grieving started long before his death. Never before did I realize the strength I had. Indeed, I had never before been put to the test.

. . . As I look back and reexamine my experience in facing his death, I am keenly aware of what helped me to integrate it, of what may similarly help my clients to come through devastating transitions successfully. According to the Transition Model (Schlossberg, 1984), there are three components in how one copes with any transition: the situation, the environment, and oneself. All of these contributed to my understanding of what I was going through and my eventual adaptation. In terms of the situation, I knew what it meant to be an "off-time" or early widow. There were no rules or role models, no one to guide me, and no one who would understand my feelings at a gut level. Consequently, I learned to become more self-reliant, independent, and capable of making decisions.

Not only was the transition off-time, but it was unanticipated and outside my control, so there was a high degree of stress. This was balanced by an environment of tremendous social support from family, friends, and my department at the university. I could not have survived without the constant telephone calls, concern, and continuous offers of help. I was surprised at my initiative in creating a support group of single women to share common concerns.

In terms of myself, I discovered that I used many coping strategies. Giving in to my sad feelings helped me get through them. I jogged every day, which helped me reduce the stress. I talked to myself, reassuring myself that things would get better and that I could handle the situation. I also talked to trusted others and learned it was more helpful to be listened to than rescued. The emotional pain made the world look gray and bleak, but I felt that the pain lifted, and with it, my spirit, when I was able to have a sense of humor. Although not changing anything, it did provide temporary relief. The process took time; there were many setbacks. I discovered that there is no "best" coping strategy that works in all situations, but no matter how difficult the situation, I will eventually find a way to cope with it.

By working through my own loss I feel better able to help others, particularly the elderly population, for whom loss is a common theme. Facing death has enabled me to grieve, to learn, to grow, and to be a better counselor.

(p. 117)

This was such a life-changing, critical incident for Pollack! All of us have bursts of stress coming from life events. For short periods of time, one just tries to hold on and get through it. For example, an intern was trying to hold on for three more months before she could leave her internship in a distant city and return home. At the time, though, she was coping with the stress of a major geographical move, the sudden death of her brother in a traffic accident, and an inadequate internship stipend, as well as the demands to perform at a high level to meet the expectations of internship supervisors.

The balancing equation can be especially precarious in times of extreme stress. How do we do adequate self-care during these disequilibrium periods, these times of exhaustion, pain, despair, and disquiet? A short answer to a difficult question is that we must continue self-care but do so at an accelerated pace. Van Dernoot Lipsky and Burk (2009) address this dilemma throughout their book, *Trauma Stewardship: An Everyday Guide to Caring for Self While Caring for Others*.

CODEPENDENCY AND SELF-CARE

When considering how a practitioner might balance self-care and other-care, the term *codependency* is helpful for those of us in the relationship-intense professions in pointing out factors in excessive self-sacrifice. It is also a concept that should be used sparingly because much of the self-sacrifice and giving in the caring professions is central to the work, helpful to others, and meaningful to the giver.

Helping professionals at risk for excessive codependency-type behaviors would do well to address the short-term seduction and long-term destruction of an excessive other-care orientation. A core aspect of the term *codependency* is an abandonment of self, and this ultimately has severe implications. Abandonment of self, however, like all strong seductions, can have great appeal. The appeal is often in avoidance of the self and its own growth. There may be unresolved grief, strong ambivalence, or great risks that are avoided through abandonment of the self. It can draw one in like a strong magnet.

Severe codependency, as abandonment of self, is a behavior that should be a warning to high-touch practitioners. Years ago, Tom worked with a client. After her husband was killed, she totally invested herself in her children. After a long period, she stopped running, faced the reality of her grief, and started the healing and moving-on process. Yet, for us helpers, running from ourselves and our needs can be a temptation because denial of reality can solve short-term problems. Helldorfer (as cited in Robinson, 1992) describes the clergy, a helping profession, as composed of many individuals engaged in such "addictive caring."

Women writing about women's lives often describe female socialization as focused on an "ethic of care" and nurturing human life, with concern for others as a strong value. This is a major theme of Gilligan's *In a Different Voice* (1982), Ruddick's *Maternal Thinking* (1989), and Chodorow in *The Reproduction of Mothering* (1978). Montagu (1974) expressed a similar sentiment in *The Natural Superiority of Women*. This ethic of care may be a very positive trait. After all, how can helping professionals not endorse it? But it may also produce extra risk for a high other-care, low self-care focus among those who are oriented this way by the three elements of personality, gender, and membership in a helping profession (e.g., females who are elementary or secondary teachers, social workers, nurses, rehabilitation counselors, psychotherapists, or physical therapists).

The opposite option – too little other-care and too much self-care – also tips the balance. Although understandable, self-absorption carried to an excessive level is also out of balance. To abandon clients, to meet only our needs, to do excessive self-protection, to listen to their struggles and solutions and apply them to us and to our own problems, or to use the "hard side of the turtle" to avoid involvement, is excessive self-care. We can listen to client, student, or patient concerns – their struggles and strategies – and use them excessively to bring us back to our own lives. For example, a client loses a job and reacts to it with disbelief and inaction. We say to ourselves that we would handle the situation better if it happened to us. We use the client's behavior to focus on our own well-being. Without knowing it, we are focusing on ourselves.

The ability to naturally turn one's focus onto the Other is, we must remember, a wonderful attribute for those we serve. The opposite focus for practitioners – self-care at the expense of other-care – is potentially unethical and destructive to the well-being of the often vulnerable individuals who we help. Unethical, exploitive helping professionals are often focused on the needs of the self. One example comes from the encounter groups of previous decades in which charismatic, self-focused leaders often produced deterioration in group members (Lieberman, Yalom, & Miles, 1973). A second example comes from the unethical, exploitive therapists who violate professional boundaries to satisfy personal needs (Pope & Vasquez, 1991).

PSYCHOLOGICAL WELLNESS AS AN ETHICAL IMPERATIVE

Barnett, Baker, Elman, and Schoener (2007) describe ongoing self-care to promote psychological wellness as an ethical imperative for psychologists. They emphasize that self-care is important both for our personal lives and as an essential ingredient for our work as practitioners. When the practitioner is not mindful of the consistent need for self-care, other-care may suffer. Barnett, Johnston, and Hillard (2006) assert, "Self-care is not an indulgence. It is an essential component of prevention of distress, burnout, and impairment. It should not be considered as something 'extra' or 'nice to do if you have the time' but as an essential part of our professional identities" (p. 263).

SELF-REFLECTION EXERCISES

One of the themes of this chapter and, in fact, the whole book is the need both to lose one's innocence about the grinding nature of the work and to actively practice resiliency development. We use the term *innocence* to describe the belief by practitioners that they can escape either insidious or overt burnout effects without active prevention efforts. Let us ask you: How is your practitioner innocence quotient, your PIQ? How do you react to this idea that actively practicing resiliency development is important?

_____

_____

_____

_____

_____

_____

_____

_____

_____

_____

_____

_____

_____

8
SUSTAINING THE PROFESSIONAL SELF

I am grateful to have the opportunity to hear my clients' stories and learn from them. I look forward to having more clients to smile about, squirm about, and wonder about.

– S. Chambers (2009, personal communication)

METHODS OF SUSTAINING THE PROFESSIONAL SELF

1) Meaningful work
2) Maximizing the experience of professional success
3) Avoiding the grandiosity impulse and relishing small "I made a difference" victories
4) Thinking long-term
5) Creating and sustaining an active, individually designed development method
6) Professional self-understanding
7) Creating a professional greenhouse at work
   a. Learning environment where practitioner growth is encouraged
   b. Leadership that promotes balance between caring for others and self
   c. Professional social support from peers
   d. Receiving support from mentors, supervisors, or bosses
   e. Being nurtured from your work as mentors, supervisors, or managers
   f. Learning how to be professional and playful

8) Using professional venting and expressive writing to release distress emotions
9) Being a "good enough" practitioner
10) Understanding the reality of pervasive early professional anxiety
11) Increasing cognitive excitement and decreasing boredom by reinventing oneself
12) Minimizing ambiguous endings
13) Learning to set boundaries, create limits, and say no to unreasonable requests

SUSTAINED BY MEANINGFUL WORK

Occupation is essential.

– V. Woolf (1990, p. 503)

The only ones among you who will be really happy are those who have sought and found how to serve.

– A. Schweitzer (1975, p. 87)

Do all the good you can,
By all the means you can,
In all the ways you can,
In all the places you can,
At all the times you can,
To all the people you can,
As long as ever you can.

– Although attributed to John Wesley, the author is unknown (according to John Wesley expert R. Thompson, Director, Wesley Center, personal communication July 21, 2015)

Practitioners often choose their work because they perceive it to be of great value. The work to benefit other members of the species *Homo sapiens* can provide enormous meaning and purpose. You may remember the George Bernard Shaw quotation earlier in this book: "This is the true joy in life, the being used for a purpose recognized by yourself as a mighty one; . . . the being a force of Nature instead of a feverish selfish little clod of ailments and grievances" (as cited in Larson, 1993, p. 2).

Tom knows a remarkable public school teacher whose work is infused with meaning. Coming from a home with a shaky foundation, she received needed transfusions from teachers during the difficult hinge days between childhood and adolescence. Now, with great energy, enthusiasm, and competence, she helps young people. Her work, of great help to them, is rich in purpose and meaning for her. This inoculates her from burnout. All win.

The sense of purpose and meaning is most at risk when, for example, a caseworker senses that her work accomplishes little good and that her clients are caught in destructive, bureaucratic systems. It is when the counseling, therapy, teaching, or healing seems to have little effect that we reach despair because our *raison d'etre* for choosing this work – to make a difference in human life – is threatened. We call this meaning burnout.

The problem is not the choice of the work itself, like it is with some other jobs. We could all name career fields that do little to further the development of our species and others that are very destructive to human life. That is not true of our work; at least, it is not true of our intentions. We are trying to make the world a better place, each in our own small way (e.g., to ease the physical pain of a post-surgery patient, to provide safety to mothers and children in a shelter, to reduce the anxiety of a college freshman away from home for the first time, to assist in reducing the shock of sudden joblessness). This means that the search for meaning and purpose in life, such a major life crisis for so many individuals at this time in history, can be less of a crisis for us because our work intrinsically gives us meaning.

For some practitioners, formal religion offers a rich structure of beliefs that provide meaning and purpose and help them confront mortality with answers and assurance. For many others, formal religion seems not to offer assurance or answers for the larger life dilemmas. In either case, we are suggesting that our work can provide meaning because we have often sought this work to make a difference. Victor Frankl, in *Man's Search for Meaning* (1946/1959), addresses this concern, as do many powerful existential writers, such as Rollo May, Paul Tillich, Søren Kierkegaard, Irving Yalom, Albert Camus, and Jean-Paul Sartre.

Ernest Becker has produced one of the most impactful books of the last half-century in its focus on the meaning and meaninglessness in modern life. In *The Denial of Death,* Becker (1973) suggests that we, as a species, spend an enormous amount of time and energy in denial of our own mortality. For many practitioners, the work of generativity (promoting the lives of those younger than us) gives meaning and helps manage the internal fears related to 'leaving the human dance while it is still going on.'

Many of us know stories of individuals who, in later life, radically changed their life's work to engage either professionally or as a volunteer in work that nurtures human life. The search here is often for more meaning or purpose and is an attempt to tie oneself more directly to the species and its survival. It is a kind of immortality, an identification with our species' history or future, and it is analogous to the way that grandparents partake in the future through the lives of their grandchildren.

As practitioners, our crisis of meaning burnout concerns the sense that we are not being very effective. If we can feel effective, we can obtain the kind of meaning that can offer great sustenance to the self. For the sustenance of the self, therefore, we must find a way in our work to feel that we are succeeding, even if it is in very small ways.

MAXIMIZING THE EXPERIENCE OF PROFESSIONAL SUCCESS

One generation plants the tree, another gets the shade.
— C. Warner (1992, p. 301)

Having an impact . . . is crucial to [practitioner] career satisfaction. Jobs that allow active, skillful involvement that produce tangible results are inherently sustaining and rewarding . . . Constant giving in a one-way relationship, without feedback or perceived success, is hard on anybody . . . Unrealistic expectations may be especially manifested in terms of expectations of client growth. The same urge to help and to be seen as helpful that propels many into the therapeutic professions often fosters grandiose notions of completely turning people's lives around.
— W. N. Grosch and D. C. Olsen (1994, pp. 8, 15, 16)

What is success in the helping professions? How can we judge our success? Consider the four quadrants of practitioner success in Figure 8.1. The amount of practitioner control of each dimension varies greatly.

We tend to focus on the top left dimension in Figure 8.1: whether the person we are helping gets better (e.g., learns more, walks better, is less shy). Our validation of professional competence and self-worth seems to come mostly from this dimension. Because our whole reason for professional functioning is to be helpful, the usefulness of our efforts naturally seems most valid. It is the recipient of our help – the client, the student, the patient – to whom we relate most closely and who also can judge our work. Does not the patient of the physical therapist have the most contact and an investment in judging the professional's efforts? Yet, this is the dimension over which we have the least control. This is an important point. For example, one semester Tom taught a PhD seminar and a college freshman remedial course. The two class cultures were two different worlds. The first group loved learning, had high student self-efficacy, and had a history of positive connections with teachers. They gave Tom high student evaluations. The second group was

Client / Student / Patient Change	External Recognition by
or Appreciation	Supervisors and Peers
Practitioner has Limited Control	*Practitioner has Limited Control*

Four Dimensions of

Practitioner Success

Expert Content	Practitioner's Mastery
Knowledge	of the Working Alliance
Practitioner has High Control	*Practitioner has High Control*

Figure 8.1 Four dimensions of practitioner success

the opposite; they didn't intrinsically love learning, thought of themselves as dumb, and had long histories of conflicts with teachers. Teaching the second group was harder and more exhausting, and they were more critical in their student evaluations. No wonder teachers, counselors, health care providers often gravitate during their work life to those most capable of being active in the I-Thou relationship.

Both with teachers and counselors, there is a focus now in 2015 to tie student achievement and client remission of symptoms to practitioner effort. This can be valuable work, but practitioners can 'game the system.' Teachers can teach to the test and counselors can focus on reduction of negative affect, leaving unaddressed bigger human development issues.

Students in graduate programs in the helping professions are admitted because they have been very hard-working and very successful in their own efforts. The formula is: Success comes from my efforts to push me to succeed. Now, however, in practice, success is tied to another person and their efforts. This person is the client, student, patient, or parishioner. We do not control the life of another person. How frightening if the practitioner could do this. So to judge our success by this dimension of client outcome alone is potentially damaging to long-term sustenance of the professional self. In addition, success is so hard to judge. The client, student, or patient may take in the practitioner's help, but like the inside of a dry sponge on water, the absorbed help may go undetected, unexpressed, or unappreciated.

Regarding the upper right part of the figure, we also have limited control. We choose our supervisors with as much freedom as we chose our parents. Sometimes we are lucky, sometimes not so lucky. Peers, too, are a mixed bag. They can be friends who give much, but they can also be fierce competition in an arena where jealousy is exchanged more often than support. Excessively tying one's own sense of professional success to any of these external sources – client, supervisor, peer – can make us feel out of control, which can produce high levels of job stress.

In contrast, we can control two other dimensions: our professional expertise and the quality of our involvement in the relationship process with our clients/students/patients. Professional expertise means knowing about our field and keeping up to date on theories, techniques, methods, research, and strategies. All practitioner fields continue to explode in knowledge. Through hard work, we can excel in acquiring professional knowledge.

Of equal importance is the relationship, the working alliance that we create with those that we serve. It is important for us to be fully present with the Other in the counseling, therapy, teaching, and healing process (Castonguay et al., 2006; Strauss et al., 2006). Do we understand the process of involvement in these kinds of relationships, and are we able to be fully involved? This is an extremely important dimension of professional functioning.

For two of the four dimensions (expertise and the helping relationship), our efforts dictate our success. We can, therefore, have some control over our work and derive some satisfaction from it. For example, when teaching a college psychology course to prison inmates, Tom worked on the subject matter, his teaching style, and his relationship skills with the students. It would have been a setup for professional discouragement if he had expected the inmates as students to write excellent papers, do very well on the tests, or praise Tom as a teacher. Tom looked for small gains for them and expected little positive feedback. However, he did work to be prepared and teach well. Using this approach, the course went well, and he remains excited and pleased about this teaching experience.

The student may fail; the patient may die; the client may continue with substance abuse. We may be distressed by these results, but we must continually reflect about the other two dimensions, relationship and expert knowledge: Did I do the relationship work well? Was I professionally attached and involved? Was my knowledge base sufficient?

Sometimes we get external recognition. Savoring it at the moment can be important for long-term professional vitality. We usually use the term *savor* when discussing food. It means to linger over the food – to enjoy the taste, the smell, the texture – before it is gone. The savoring process gets missed in the mad rush of fast eating. So, too, we practitioners sometimes go madly from one occupational responsibility to another, rushing from one thing to the next without savoring the success.

Michelle and Tom have learned, over time, how transitory the moments of satisfaction with our work can be, in part because, at its heart, it often involves the professional attachment – active involvement – separation – re-creation process that has few concrete and permanent results (e.g., the 12th-grade English class goes very well but then ends and that same group of student and teacher will never be together again; the cardiac rehabilitation patient completes the program and returns home; the displaced worker no longer needs job assistance and emotional support after finding a new job).

Like all other practitioners in the caring professions, Tom remembers struggling for a long time while trying to become an adequate practitioner. Just in terms of his teaching role, there were many stress-filled hours. He described this in an article, "Learning to Teach":

I was driving down the freeway from Missouri to Florida, with spouse and baby girl next to me in the Ryder rental truck. Soon I would begin working as an assistant professor at the University of Florida with a split faculty/psychologist position. One thought kept recurring: "How will I be able to teach? I've received no formal training in the art and science of teaching." . . . [W]here was the training to be a professor? I thought of my sister, an elementary teacher in Minnesota, who had received extensive training before beginning to teach. My mind wandered off to other occupations – hairstylist, airplane pilot, bricklayer, surgeon. Did any of these professions let loose their new graduates without any practical training? How was it, then, that I had received no systematic, organized instruction in teaching?

After days of daydreams and driving, I reached Gainesville, and the academic year began. I spent the first year on a do-it-yourself training program. . . . My self-training was deficient. . . . There was no systematic, organized sequence of learning experiences and no feedback from experienced master teachers. . . . In those first years of teaching, traumas and disillusionment coexisted with a few victories.

(Skovholt, 1986, p. 8)

There are many factors that impinge on the recipient's reaction to our practitioner attempts. Once, Tom took a time management course. It was difficult for him to really appreciate the instructor's efforts because he was frustrated by all the time demands in life. He felt very strongly that he didn't need time management; he needed more time, less to do, or a culture in which human life was not defined by time-obsessed schedules. None of these were possible. Only time management was an option, and the instructor did his job. But Tom's evaluation of the course and instructor expressed his frustration with the bigger picture of the rat race and, in that sense, was unfair to the instructor. If he judged his success by Tom's reaction, he would be disappointed. As another example, one time in a mediation situation, one of our colleagues was pleased by the work of the mediator but was too exhausted by the conflict and loss that was mediated to be appreciative. If the mediator depended on our colleague's reaction for validation, she would be disappointed and depleted. Do patients in the recovery room, coming out of anesthesia after surgery, ever really express their appreciation for the gentle, expert care that they receive? Probably not. They are confronting their own disorientation and discomfort and are concerned with little else. If the recovery room nurse judges her success by the appreciation of her patients, will she not soon be discouraged by her professional efforts? If she attempts to receive most of her personal self-esteem validation this way, will these relationships sustain her? And what if the high school teacher relies heavily on student reactions for her self-esteem?

It is important to say again, as we have earlier in this section, that results do matter in the age of accountability, outcome standards, and managed care. But they have always mattered. Here, we are addressing the intensity of this dimension for practitioner long-term vitality. In the dimension of our efforts related to client, student, or patient outcome, it is important to match our expectations to the possibility of positive change.

AVOID THE GRANDIOSITY IMPULSE AND RELISH SMALL "I MADE A DIFFERENCE" VICTORIES

When considering results, watching one's expectations can be useful. Sometimes if we expect less in terms of client, student, or patient gains, we can be more satisfied. We do not mean becoming lazy or accepting mediocrity. It can be a paradoxical task. Helping professionals often want so much to help that they get caught up in wanting to make a big difference for many people. Sometimes pushing for big changes actually empowers the client's ambivalence and resistance about change and makes improvement less possible. Reducing expectations and focusing on small changes can be more empowering for both people in the helping relationship.

THINK LONG TERM

Professional development is a long-term process (see Chapter 11). From the expertise literature of Chi, Glaser, and Farr (1988), Ericsson et al. (2006), and Ericsson, Prietula, and Cokely (2007), we know that it takes thousands of hours to develop high-level skill in a complex human craft such as counseling and therapy, high school teaching, or nursing. Breaking down big educational and career steps into small steps is a well-used method and motivational strategy. Considering the long haul is also important. In the wilderness of northern Minnesota, some canoeists start paddling hard in the first hour of the first day. How about the next five hours? The next day of another six hours of paddling? The day after that? The day after that? Practitioners work 30 to 40 years. Thinking long-term and building professional and personal self-care into this decades-long adventure can change one's perspective and approach. Think of the toddler learning to walk; it is a process, an adventure of attempts, feedback, and more attempts. In time, with experience, the toddler walks and then runs. So does the resilient practitioner.

CREATING AND SUSTAINING AN ACTIVE, INDIVIDUALLY DESIGNED DEVELOPMENT METHOD

To stay alive, one must eat. To stay alive and grow professionally, one must eat voraciously and then digest the new professional food. Refusing or "throwing up" the food – that is, denying it or distorting work-related feedback – can lead to stagnation and pseudodevelopment (Rønnestad & Skovholt, 2003, 2013). We discuss this topic here and in Chapter 11.

In contrast to college and university training in which we are told how to develop through class requirements, as practitioners after school we are now in charge of our own development. The use of continuing education credits in many fields is an attempt to ensure development, but the requirement of going to classes reflects an earlier, less developed approach. Highly functioning senior practitioners keep the learning process going over the long run but vary in their development methods (Rønnestad & Skovholt, 2003, 2013).

One key element is openness to new information and to feedback about one's performance. This entails a nondefensive stance, as in Rogers's (1961) description of the fully functioning person and Maslow's (1968) self-actualized personality structure. In both descriptions, openness and perceptual accuracy are key. When the individual must distort information or shuts off new information, then development is stifled. This is a reason why experience alone does not seem to increase expertise. We have all met experienced veterans in our field who are seemingly less skilled than newer practitioners. One reason is that the veteran is not growing from the increased experience.

Aside from openness, one must continually feed oneself with data from practice and from the bigger world of ideas and theories. From the interviews during our N=100 research project (Skovholt & Rønnestad, 1992a) we were told that one highly functioning practitioner in our community reads five books at once; another works collaboratively with four other practitioners on different projects to keep developing. Both of these senior practitioners are voraciously feeding themselves professionally with new content, new ideas, and new alternatives that they add, modify, and shed with their ongoing professional working method. Highly respected by their professional peers, each has a finely tuned, individually designed development process.

Last, professional reflection as a catalyst for one's development is important. Reflection has recently received much attention as a key developmental process in the professional growth of counselors, therapists, teachers, and health practitioners. Swanson (2010) discusses the use of reflective practice with teachers, while Dubé and Ducharme (2015) discuss its use in the nursing field, and Mann, Gordon, and MacLeod (2009) review the literature related to reflective practice in health professional education. Neufeldt and colleagues (1996) identify key elements of the process as starting with an initial problem or point where the individual is puzzled and unsure. The individual's personal and cognitive flexibility, plus a supportive work environment, furthers the reflection process, which is guided by a search for understanding. They write:

> The intent to understand what has occurred, active inquiry, openness to that understanding and vulnerability and risk-taking rather than defensive self-protection, characterize the stance. . . . To contribute to further development, reflections are profound rather than superficial, and are meaningful.
>
> (p. 8)

The end point, using one's experience to form detailed internal cognitive schemas results in professional improvement as a practitioner. Benner and Wrubel (1982) describe elements of this process when they say:

> Experience is necessary for moving from one level of expertise to another, but experience is not the equivalent of longevity, seniority, or the simple passage of time. Experience means living through actual situations in such a way that it informs the practitioner's perception and understanding of all subsequent situations.
>
> (p. 28)

These viewpoints are similar to our own three-part view of this essential process for professional development: professional and personal experience; an open, supportive work environment; and a reflective stance. Receiving uncensored performance feedback and ideas from other sources, being open to it, and taking time for it are essential elements of reflection as a developmental process. The closing off or distorting of feedback, with little time given to it, along with an absence of reflection, provides elements for professional stagnation as described, for example, in Chapter 11.

It may be that the spacious campuses of American colleges and universities – the benches and the grass – serve the serious, intellectual reflective function. After class, these environments encourage students to ponder, wonder about, consider, discuss, and contemplate the content of the past class. This is important because the opposite – experience without reflection – does not produce the same amount of professional growth. The requirement that professional psychology doctoral interns spend at least 25% of their time on direct clinical work, rather than 50% or 75%, represents this stance; professional development entails more than just direct experience (Kaslow, Keilin, & Hsu, 2010).

The reflective process is stunted in work environments in human services, education, and health where productivity is measured by volume, and practitioners are kept continually busy and, by necessity, practice in a hectic, repetitive style. The problem is that repetitive practice alone tends to produce the same behaviors, cognitions, and affective reactions, rather than creative professional growth and improved work by the practitioner. There is little evidence that experience alone produces expertise.

PROFESSIONAL SELF-UNDERSTANDING

As important as methods may be, the most practical thing we can achieve in any kind of work is insight into what is happening inside us as we do it. The more familiar we are with our inner terrain, the more sure footed our [work] – and living – becomes.

– P. J. Palmer (1998, p. 5)

Finding healthy ways of maintaining a strong sense of self is a prerequisite for effective functioning as a professional helper.

– W. N. Grosch & D.C. Olsen (1994, p. 31)

Self-awareness is a strongly emphasized value in a variety of the career fields we are focusing on with this book. We have used so many terms to describe the rainbow of these fields: high-touch, helping, relationship-intense, caring, resilient. The psychotherapy professions have especially endorsed one's own therapy as a method to develop self-awareness and increase personal maturity as a way to make one's professional work more effective. Other helping professions often include training experiences in self-development as part of the education of helping professionals. Grosch and Olsen (1994) provide a valuable discussion on the personal background of helping professionals. For example, they make a surprising declaration when they say:

The great paradox revealed by professional burnout is that, although helping others can and should be a way to transcend ourselves, many of us embark on helping careers not out of a genuine concern for others but rather out of a need to be appreciated by them.

(p. 170)

Using the work of self psychologist Kohut and family theorist Bowen, Grosch and Olsen (1994) suggest that family of origin roles are instrumental in the excessive needs that some helpers bring as adults into their professional work:

In dysfunctional families, boundaries may be absent or violated; in fact, parent–child roles are often reversed. Rather than receiving the mirroring [validation] they desperately need for the formation of healthy and cohesive selves, children wind up needing to provide mirroring for their parents.

(p. 93)

Grosch and Olsen (1994) point out that many individuals attracted to the helping professions received validation and admiration for their helping attempts early in life. They suggest that these attempts may have occurred in families in which the helper, as a young person, took on the role of an adult, perhaps in a highly stressed family, and received this validation rather than in the normal mirroring and admiration of healthy child and adolescent development described in self psychology theory (Kohut). If the person then, as an adult, enters one of the helping professions, the style may continue.

The person enters an occupation in which caring for others is a primary role. The individual already knows how to care for others – listening, putting the Other's needs first, nurturing the Other. These skills are sometimes hard for others who are not socialized this way, but the helper cannot be sustained over the long run just by validation from recipients. If the individual centers his or her life on caring for others and does not develop other, more balanced interpersonal relationships – that is, relationships in which the individual is not the giver but also the receiver – then the benefits from the helping role are the only source of the individual's sustenance. This source of sustenance, however, is limited because the client, student, or patient does not have a primary obligation to care for the helper and meet his or her needs. Ethical violations, in fact, occur when the helper's needs become primary in the relationship. In addition, the recipient is often not in a place to help the Other because he or she is too distressed to focus on the Other.

The essential point here is this: When the child does not receive developmentally appropriate validation from significant adults, the self develops in a different way, seeking self-worth through pleasing, supporting, and understanding others. This need for admiration is then sought in adult work by working extra hard to help others. This deep longing for appreciation is so often thwarted, of course, because the client, student, or patient role is not designed to meet the basic self-esteem needs of the professional helper. For those who need admiration, approval, and validation from clients, students, or patients, the situation is quite precarious. Consequently, "when we do not understand and deal with our craving for admiration and need to be seen in given ways, we tend to get angry and resentful" (Grosch & Olsen, 1994, p. 119). These authors suggest that Bowen's concept of differentiation is useful in suggesting how we need to learn to separate our own sense of self and its basic needs from the professional attachments we make with those we serve. Understanding this family of origin dynamic can be important for understanding unrealistic work expectations and preventing emotional depletion.

Berry (1988) uses the terms *messiah* and the *messiah trap* to describe the extreme helping of others as a defensive interpersonal type. Although this messiah idea may be simplistic, Berry does touch on some important ideas, such as family-of-origin roots and expressions of this style in pleasing, rescuing, counseling, and teaching. She described her own awakening as: "I thought I was doing the 'right' thing by helping people. But by helping others, I avoided being intimate with them. We [other helpers and I] were much more comfortable helping than we were asking for help" (p. x). (See Figure 8.2.)

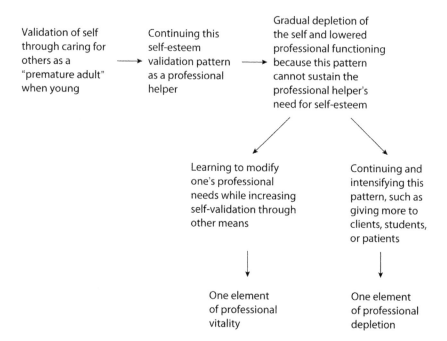

Figure 8.2 Possible outcomes from an excessive focus on helping others

A related area in which professional self-understanding is important concerns attachment. Within developmental psychology, attachment theory is now widely used to understand, explain, and predict interpersonal relationships, such as success at intimacy. One of the premises of this work, which is now being extended to other relationships such as work collaboration, is that past relationship patterns have an impact on present relationships. For example, Bachelor and Horvath (1999) summarize the therapist attachment research to suggest that "therapists tend to re-create earlier interpersonal patterns in the therapy relationship and treat clients accordingly" (p. 158).

This research is very important for the caring professions because the important common factor in the helping fields is the cycle of empathetic attachment → active involvement → felt separation → re-creation. If the practitioner has a poor personal history of attachments, the chance of doing good work is at risk. This is another reason for professional self-understanding.

CREATING A PROFESSIONAL GREENHOUSE AT WORK

No man is an island.

— J. Donne (1975, p. 87)

Speech pathologist Carole Sellars who works with children who have disabilities said:

It's absolutely the most wonderful place to work. It's spiritually rewarding and mentally rewarding. I bet I laugh more on my job than anyone I know. The children and families with whom I work have literally stolen my heart out of my chest. I'll never have a vacancy in my department. Once you're here, you're here.

(Majeski, 1996, p. 5A, reprinted with permission of Pioneer Press)

The work can be hard. We are constantly asked to increase human competence in areas such as social skills, learning, and health. A stressful work environment can make it even harder. As we discussed in Chapter 6, Maslach and Leiter (1997) make a strong case for organizational factors as the key to burnout. We agree; however, we also urge you as a practitioner not to wait for the organization to serve your needs. We urge you to actively create your own greenhouse at work. A greenhouse, as you know, is an environment where many factors – temperature, soil, and water – are ideal for growth. Here are elements that seem to create a greenhouse effect at work:

A learning environment where practitioner growth is encouraged; leadership that promotes a healthy other-care vs. self-care balance; social support from peers; receiving other-care from mentors; mentoring others; an emotional environment of respect, playfulness, humor, and joy.

Learning environment where practitioner growth is encouraged

What a compliment to practitioners – to realize that all of them are encouraged, supported, and challenged to keep growing. A major finding in the master therapist studies (Skovholt & Jennings, 2004) is the energy and vitality created for practitioners by working in a setting where the will to grow is present.

Leadership that promotes balance between caring for others and the self

We pay leaders more because they have the power to create a tone, vision, and direction in an organization. Let's hope that the leader has a symbolic sign that says, "Here, we care for the clients, students, and patients and also the practitioners." Such leadership makes a difference.

Professional social support

Many practitioners are social people by nature, and they seek out others. Within the social support research literature, Thoits (2011) found that social support from others can be a stress reducer. The support of one's colleagues can be quite powerful in reducing distress emotions such as depression and anxiety. The same principle holds for practitioners. When we can talk with our colleagues openly and honestly about our work, then the "universality of experience effect," a curative factor in groups (Yalom & Leszcz, 2005), can be a powerful force for our own professional vitality.

One source of self-care is the organizational and group atmosphere at work. Johnson (1994, personal communication), a graduate student in the helping professions, said:

> At my practicum site, I experienced and observed terrific support among staff members. This helped me feel as though I was a significant contributor and was a strong source of professional and emotional support. Through this experience, I better understand that this support is vital in the helping business in order to give the helper a sense that he or she is not alone, a feeling that can occur in this line of work where results are frequently hard to measure.
>
> (p. 8)

Another great source of practitioner vitality, a bedrock source of vitality, is the presence of close person-to-person work friendships. One of the most important aspects of these friendships is that, with a friend we trust, we are able to share our own real feelings about our work. For example, an article or book often communicates a certainty about a method of counseling vs. when we talk to a friend we can express our uncertainty and insecurities. Engaging in this giving and taking equally with another coworker can be so valuable. Michelle has experienced the power of close work friendships in deepening her work with clients and encouraging resiliency. Enjoying a close friendship in the workplace allows her to be willing to be vulnerable and take risks when consulting and have a place to process difficult therapeutic content.

Receiving Other-care from mentors, supervisors, or bosses

The mentoring literature has, of course, developed because of the power of these relationships. Levinson, Darrow, Klein, Levinson, and McKee (1978) describe the power of mentors in men's lives, just as Kram (1985) describes the importance of mentoring in women's lives.

Being nurtured from our work as mentors, supervisors, or managers

The act of mentoring, supervising, and managing others can be very positive in one's own self-care and professional development. For example, a psychologist in his 70s supervising new interns said, "They get brighter all the time. I feel that I learn as much from the interns as I teach them. They have become my teacher" (Skovholt & Rønnestad, 1992a, p. 92).

At work, learning how to be professional and playful, have fun, tell jokes, and laugh

We need to pump positive emotions into often-stressful helping relationships of clients bringing their disappointments, losses, betrayals, fears, and anger. One individual approached this task in the following way:

> I continue to try to find ways to make myself laugh and to do small fun things as a way to release tension and to feel more energized. Laughing seems to have a physiological effect. I can feel sad and begin to laugh, and the tension in my chest dissipates. I like to hear humorous stories from people's lives, I like to tease people and sometimes I like to be teased. I also keep toys at work to entertain me. I have a rainbow colored slinky that a friend gave me. I keep it on my desk. The colors

are fun and the slow, rhythmic sound it makes when I play with it is relaxing. I also have Play-Doh in my desk drawer. I use it in class as part of a topic on creativity and critical thinking. However, it also is fun to play with in my spare time. I find that kneading Play-Doh when I am tense can help relax me.

(S. Renninger, personal communication, February 1995)

Another did it this way:

She kept a tin noisemaker in her pocket, and two or three times a day, when no clients were around, she'd take it out and make a silly little "cricket" sound with it. Finally, curiosity got the best of me, and I asked her about it. "My biggest fault is seriousness," she said, "I need to remember that there's fun in the world, too. So I take out my little cricket and give it a couple of clicks, and it always makes me laugh."

(Help for Helpers, 1989, p. 147)

USING PROFESSIONAL VENTING AND EXPRESSIVE WRITING TO RELEASE DISTRESS EMOTIONS

Venting is cathartic, which is an old word out of the psychodynamic tradition. *Cathartic* describes the usefulness of talking about feelings. Professionals in the caring professions know that feelings are powerful. They are not surprised by the study findings that expressive writing, specifically expressing feelings and thoughts about an emotionally impactful experience, can change a person's mental and physical health (Frattaroli, 2006). In a scientific way, these researchers have documented what people already know and do. It is called venting, a wonderfully descriptive term for the process by which people use words and nonverbal communication to let go of distressing emotions. Venting means, by analogy, to let the air take away one's emotional distress, as through a vent.

Professional venting and expressive writing can be especially important for practitioners who attempt to help people in the human services, education, or health care. Practitioners hear stories of distress. They need to motivate individuals for change when internal motivation is limited, and they often work in an environment of loss, anxiety, and pain. At work, counselors, therapists, teachers, and health professionals live in an ocean of distress emotions. Their willingness to work in this ocean is a big part of why their work is valuable and rewarded.

Let us give you an example. One practitioner told of her job as an employment counselor for the unemployed. She worked for a government agency with a mandate to help clients move from being unemployed to employed. She described the work as very frustrating because of low client motivation.

She said that she was "saved" because she could vent to colleagues about the frustration of being unable to reach her clients.

We are describing venting and expressive writing as positive professional methods that help the practitioner stay in the work and continue with intense involvement within the Cycle of Caring. We are endorsing professional venting as a method of helping people do better work. This contrasts sharply with chronic complaining and negativity, which often have long-term negative consequences for practitioners, their colleagues, and the organizational climate. Professional venting improves work functioning; chronic complaining and negativity do the opposite. Negativity weakens one's ability to be hopeful for clients, students, and patients; offering hope is an important element of the practitioner's work.

THE "GOOD ENOUGH PRACTITIONER"

In workshops, presentations, and classes after each new edition of this book, the "Good Enough Practitioner" idea has produced considerable discussion and debate among practitioners. Some people really like the idea; others dislike it. Those who like it are often responding to their own physical, emotional, and spiritual exhaustion. Those who do not like the idea think of it as an excuse for doing shoddy work that is harmful to those who should be helped. What will be your reaction as you read this section about the "Good Enough Practitioner"?

Practitioners are often afraid of underperformance and want very much to perform at the 100% level, 100% of the time. This is impossible, however, and can lead to the dead-end experienced by an elementary school principal who told Tom, "I had to quit after 10 years because after I gave and gave and gave, there was nothing left." Now, after five years in moratorium and recovery, she is again trying to do the job, afraid of both underperformance and overperformance.

As a mentor in a program for new faculty members, Tom talked with these new, untenured assistant professors about avoiding maladaptive perfectionism as a teacher. Essentially, these five new assistant professors in music, chemistry, statistics, business, and history – talented, energetic, conscientious individuals – were facing an impossible job. The life of a university professor has no boundaries. There is always much more to do in the domains of the work: teaching; scholarship and research; and service to the university, one's profession, and the community. In addition, the tenure decision clock begins on appointment and, six years later, one either has a job or is fired.

Tom's formal job as a mentor was to help these new faculty members with their teaching. However, if they devoted all of their time to their teaching – reading, preparing, presenting, grading, and more – they could perhaps do almost perfect work. They could almost reach the practitioner's goal of 100% effort, 100% of the time. Yet, they would be perfect in only one element of the position, avoiding the other areas of research, grants, and service, which means they would eventually get fired. Tom has seen young professors take this route, a seemingly good choice that eventually leads to bitterness and an occupational dead-end. It has been hard to see talented, giving faculty members be hit by a toxin to their professional self. Knowing the seduction of the 100%-effort, 100%-of-the time fantasy, Tom suggested to these new professors that they entertain the style of the veteran athlete who knows when to sprint and when to jog.

The problem is that 100% performance, 100% of the time, is too exhausting to sustain in the work of the practitioner. For example, the paramedic must give all at critical times but perhaps not always. From the child development literature, there is a related concept, the "good enough mother" (Winnicott, 1965). The idea is that the child *very much* needs the parent to be good enough, but the child does not need the parent to be *everything* for *optimal* development of the child to occur. So perhaps our clients, students, and patients also need us to be "good enough," and anything less is unacceptable. Perhaps, however, they do not need us to try for that which we cannot sustain: a 100% effort for 100% of the time. It is a wonderful fantasy, but it also leads to the long-term dis-ease of occupational exhaustion and caring burnout, as well as a loss in creativity and growth. This is expressed by Kushner (1996): "If we are afraid to make a mistake because we have to maintain the pretense of perfection . . . we will never be brave enough to try anything new or anything challenging. We will never learn; we will never grow" (p. 85).

UNDERSTANDING THE REALITY OF PERVASIVE EARLY PROFESSIONAL ANXIETY

Fear of failure undermines altruism.

– C. Cherniss (1995, p. 7)

One of the most important findings in our research study of 100 practitioners (Skovholt & Rønnestad, 1992a; Rønnestad & Skovholt, 2013) is the high level of pervasive anxiety among beginners and the great reduction in this anxiety among seasoned veterans. Anxiety is the natural emotion an individual feels when threatened and out of control in an important situation. The novice–veteran contrast in pervasive performance anxiety was startling, and it affected many facets of the work. The high stress level of the beginning practitioner is supported by other research studies. Cherniss (1995) found an elevated stress level for first-year human service workers, and other researchers (Ackerley et al., 1988; Pearlman & MacIan, 1995) have found high stress with new psychotherapists.

Professional experience helps so much in reducing this anxiety because practitioners can increasingly rely on their own internalized experience base for professional functioning. The beginner must rely on the expertise of others, such as textbook theories, journal research studies, or the advice of a supervising senior practitioner. These sources can be invaluable. We all are indebted to useful theories and supportive supervisors: We appreciate Cognitive Behavior Therapy, empirically supported treatments, Carl Rogers, and other theorists, and we give thanks to our many excellent clinical supervisors. Unfortunately, external expertise often does not quite fit the situation, in the way that foreign language instruction in a college classroom often does not quite fit with the language usage of the people of a foreign country. Many Turks would get frustrated when Tom, as a visiting professor in Turkey, corrected their English, which they had diligently learned in class, with the comment, "That's really not the way Americans say it." With experience, internal expertise replaces external expertise and pervasive anxiety goes down. An elementary teacher told Tom that she got through her first year by every day asking a veteran colleague, "What should I do today?" Five years later, she never asked the question.

Relevant, fruitful, and illuminating work has been done about novice versus expert differences (Ericsson et al., 2006, 2007). Etringer, Hillerbrand, and Claiborn (1995) summarize the cognitive processing distinctions between novices and experts within the categories of memory and knowledge structures, declarative and procedural knowledge, pattern recognition, reasoning processes and goals, and problem structure. In summary, experts can understand more of the complexity of a situation, even if it is ambiguous or unique. They know how to use their more accurate judgments more efficiently; their knowledge is both more differentiated and integrated; and they recognize complex patterns more easily through sensing the most critical features of a problem, even if it is ill defined. Examples here include how an expert teacher can more quickly and accurately diagnose student mood level in a classroom and make quick instructional changes or how a nurse can understand the unique expression of a patient's changed pain level and respond with great skill.

This novice-versus-expert work in cognitive science can be highly useful to understanding how pervasive professional anxiety declines with experience because human work often involves complex, ill-defined, and difficult problem situations (e.g., how to introduce court-ordered treatment to a defensive person after a driving-under-the-influence arrest; assessing the maximum level of pain that a physical therapy patient will accept for healing without canceling appointments; finding a midlevel of instruction for a math class widely divergent in ability level). Working with people is so difficult because *Homo sapiens* are the most complex of all living organisms. As we have said in other places in the book, practitioners work constantly in ambiguous, confusing contexts. The veteran practitioner's hundreds of hours of experience can radically reduce daily pervasive professional anxiety.

INCREASING INTELLECTUAL EXCITEMENT AND DECREASING BOREDOM BY REINVENTING ONESELF

In Chapter 5, we discussed hazards that included cognitive deprivation and boredom, which can be a very negative force in the lives of veteran practitioners. Now, we discuss an antidote for the boredom.

Practitioners hear very directly from people about their lives. They can hear interesting human narratives. Swimming in this reality can be very stimulating for the practitioner. For example, a practitioner may wonder how to establish trust with a student client who is a guarded, defensive teenager. In time, he or she figures it out and creates a plan for such situations. The challenge, excitement, and rewarding qualities of the situation lessen. Now, if the practitioner often works with such teenagers, the intellectual challenge, over a long period of time, may decrease, and boredom can set in. Such a process often happens with teachers, health care providers, guidance counselors, and many others in relationship-intense professions who have, for example, a narrow set of client concerns, teach the same subject term after term, or administer the identical health procedure over and over again.

Some veteran practitioners do not get bored in their work domain. When Tom asked a 68-year-old veteran practitioner and beloved clinical supervisor about the challenge of sameness and boredom, she said, "I never get bored because every situation and every person has uniqueness. Like putting a complex puzzle together, the process is always somewhat different. So, this is the uniqueness that prevents the boredom" (H. Roehlke, personal communication, February 23, 2000).

Renewal is a word used to describe a process of refreshing. It is like an energy shot that animates the practitioner. Here, we focus specifically on the word *renewal* viewed as re*NEW*al. Meaningful new work tasks provide stimulation for the practitioner, and the stimulation, in turn, energizes the practitioner and makes for high practitioner vitality. How does the NEW work as an antidote and provide renewal? For us, one of the main issues concerns novelty. The key point is that novelty helps to animate the practitioner.

There is plenty of novelty for the novice practitioner! For the novice, the novelty provides so much stimulation that boredom is never a reality. In fact,

Table 8.1 Different ways experienced practitioners reinvent themselves

Ways to Create More Novelty, Challenge, and Energy	Examples
Changing the work tasks	Doing supervision instead of direct service
Changing the methods that one uses	Replacing group process with individual process
Changing the population with which one works	Working with adolescents instead of adults
Changing the time allocation	Doing some administration or research rather than 100% direct service

for the novice, there is more than enough stimulation. The novice worries more about being anxious and lost while trying to perform work tasks. For the experienced practitioner who works in a fairly narrow domain, the boredom threat involves too little novelty.

One of the satisfactions of the work is the cognitive challenge. Human beings are intricate, complicated, and convoluted. This is a major reason for the attraction to the field. For example, therapists talk of hearing the person's story and how engaging it can be to try to really understand the world of another.

Let us use the case of motivating the Other to show the excitement of the work. In all of the professional fields that we are addressing here – human services, education, health, religious/spiritual professions – motivating the client, student, patient, parishioner is a major practitioner challenge. How can a practitioner really motivate the other person to make necessary changes? How can the practitioner motivate the Other to become less angry, study harder, or continue with painful but important medical procedures? It is often a very challenging and intellectually stimulating dilemma.

This is the process whereby the NEW brings reNEWal. Experienced practitioners must keep reinventing themselves. This can occur through different ways (Table 8.1). The goal of all of this effort, of course, is to have the NEW provide renewal.

MINIMIZING THE AMBIGUITY OF THE WORK AND AMBIGUOUS ENDINGS

Tom remembers seeing a television documentary about an old, illiterate man who, earlier in his life, had a job making bricks one by one in a little machine. Then decades later, he was walking around his city with great pride, showing his grandson all the bricks that he had made. They were in buildings all over town and obvious for all to see. When watching the documentary, Tom felt pity for himself and others in the helping professions because the brick maker had solid evidence of his work of making bricks. The work was there for all to see. Where are your bricks? Where are the obvious, concrete signs of your labor?

The lack of closure and concrete evidence of success is a major ongoing stressor for many practitioners. One way to reduce this stressor is to acknowledge the lack of concrete evidence and this dimension of ambiguous endings. In Chapter 6, we described ambiguous endings as one of the five spears that stab at the practitioner's Caring Self. Here we look at solutions to this situation. We use this term, *ambiguous endings*, to describe the constant series of connections that the practitioner makes with the client, student, or patient that end without an ending. Awareness of this stressor can help us to acknowledge it to ourselves and gain support from colleagues. In addition, we can also try to have as many concrete endings as possible. Termination of the attachment relationship in a formal sense, no matter how brief, to give closure is often quite valuable for the practitioner's vitality.

At the University of Florida Counseling Center, the doctoral interns and the staff are captured in a yearly photo. The photos, year after year, are on the wall of the center in recognition of the training done by the senior practitioners. Year after year, these senior practitioners connect to a new group of enthusiastic and anxious interns. The interns leave at the end of the year and are replaced by a new group of enthusiastic and anxious interns. The product, the trained interns, are scattered throughout the United States. Where is the concrete evidence? It is there in the rows of photos of excited and proud interns and staff. What a great idea. What a great way to blunt the ambiguity of the work, especially the endings of helping relationships, which include clinical supervision relationships.

We all need lots of small ways of making the ambiguous concrete. This is the value of achievements that offer some visible, material evidence, such as a new title from a promotion or a new certification. Concrete activities such as professional writing can be helpful too. The key words are *tangible* and *permanent*.

The constant demand for helping professionals to attach, be involved, and separate over and over means that this process must be done in a way that is energizing to the individual practitioner. Ambiguous endings produce the opposite result; they drain the practitioner. Consider this description of ambiguous loss in a family and the resulting confusion and lack of closure:

> Who is psychologically in and who is psychologically out of the family system can block family reorganization and accommodation to chronic stress. . . . Caregivers have difficulty accepting the loss of their loved ones (because the loss is only partial) and they cannot grieve and move on to restructure the family as they could if the person were no longer physically present. . . . Caregivers' boundary ambiguity and sense of mastery are important correlates in understanding the development of caregiver depression.
> (Boss, Caron, Horbal, & Mortimer, 1990, pp. 246–247, 253, reprinted with permission from Wiley)

The lack of closure can be quite stressful for practitioners. Being sensitive enough to be affected by such experiences is, we contend, part of the "soft side of the turtle" issue. An exceptional capacity to attach demands emotional sensitivity and a vulnerability to the effects of ambiguous endings. Pauline Boss, the expert on ambiguous loss, suggests a way to manage the ambiguity, a way that can be applied to practitioners whose clients/students/patients 'disappear.' In an article titled "The Myth of Closure," Boss and Carnes (2012) write that often there is no closure to human loss. Carnes uses her own personal example of her husband sailing in the ocean and disappearing. They write:

> ambiguous loss with its lack of closure makes immense demands on the human capacity to cope and grieve . . . increasing our tolerance for ambiguity and unanswered questions frees us from the burden of needing to close the door on loss.
>
> (Boss & Carnes, 2012, pp. 457–458)

We endorse this idea of increasing our tolerance for ambiguity and unanswered questions as an important method to prevent the depletion of practitioner vitality.

LEARNING TO SET BOUNDARIES, CREATE LIMITS, AND SAY NO TO UNREASONABLE HELPING REQUESTS

> I'm glad that some of the lessons we must all learn as therapists came early in my career: that success and failure are relative, that progress is nonlinear, that there are limitations to what we can offer.
>
> – Sanger (2010, p. 74)

As described earlier, learning to set limits only after becoming exhausted is a normative experience for counselors, therapists, teachers, and health professionals. Stone (1988) described this process in "The Heroic Syndrome." Veteran practitioners, like veteran athletes, learn to pace themselves, always being ready at critical moments but pulling back some at noncritical moments. For some practitioners, finding the appropriate level of letting go is a major struggle.

SUMMARY

In this chapter, we have presented a number of ideas for you to consider in sustaining your professional self. Table 8.2 lists factors that practitioners have told us are important in sustaining or depleting the professional self.

Table 8.2 Factors that sustain and deplete the professional self

Factors That Sustain the Professional Self	Factors That Deplete the Professional Self
Joy in participating in others' growth	Feeling unsuccessful in helping the Other
Feeling successful in helping others	Professional boundaries that allow for excessive other-care and too little self-care
Closely observing human life (creativity, courage, ingenuity, tolerance of pain) and meaningful human contact	Low peer support
Finely tuned professional boundaries	Low supervisor support
Peer support	High organizational conflict
Supervisor support	Excessive seriousness in purposes and style
Low level of organizational conflict	Little attention to long-term professional development
Sense of humor and playfulness	Inability to accept any ambiguous endings or normative failure
Constant focus on professional development and avoidance of stagnation and pseudodevelopment	Neglecting the importance for self and others of a positive closure experience at the time of professional separation
Tolerance of some ambiguous endings and normative failure	Insufficient salary and benefits (or educational credits, if the practitioner is in training)
Attempting to have a closure experience at the time of professional separation that is positive for both parties	No distinguishing between idealism and realism
Sufficient salary and benefits or educational credits if the practitioner is in training	

SELF-REFLECTION EXERCISES

A variety of ideas were mentioned in this chapter. They comprise a bag of tricks of the trade. These tips come from seasoned practitioners and the literature on professional functioning.

1. Which of these ideas do you already use in your own work? Perhaps you have a refined and improved version of one of these ideas. If so, please describe it.

_____

_____

_____

_____

_____

2. Are there any new ideas in the chapter for you? If so, write about one or two that may offer something to you as a practitioner. How do you imagine these idea(s) might be helpful in your life?

_____

_____

_____

_____

_____

_____

_____

_____

_____

_____

_____

9

SUSTAINING THE PERSONAL SELF

Sustaining the personal self is a serious obligation because the work, *giving of the self*, cannot successfully proceed without it. Many practitioners in the caring professions struggle with feelings of selfishness when they think of trying to meet their own needs. Their own conflicts about feelings of selfishness versus needing some self-focus can be very intense. You may be one of these people.

Our goal here is not to increase a person's capacity to be self-centered. The goal is to help the practitioner, over decades of work, to be able to engage in caring for others. *Maintaining oneself personally is necessary to function effectively in a professional role.* By itself, this idea can help those in the caring fields feel less selfish when meeting the needs of the self.

There are many methods of personal renewal. In this chapter, we suggest some of them. You may have developed others.

CONSTANT INVESTMENT IN A PERSONAL RENEWAL PROCESS

Constant renewal is essential so that our "pond" does not become stagnant. Being fed by "springs" and "streams" is important so that we can continue to attach/connect professionally as practitioners who assist others with emotional, educational, and physical needs. Self-care means finding ways to replenish the self. The result is more important than the method. The point here is to find ways to produce constant self-renewal.

A major goal for professional self-care is to develop attitudes and activities that serve as natural endorphin boosters and stress hormone reducers.

By this, we are suggesting that personal self-care should focus in part on producing feelings of zest, peace, euphoria, excitement, happiness, and pleasure. One major word in our inventory at the beginning of the book is *vitality*. All of these feelings serve as endorphin boosters.

AWARENESS OF THE DANGER OF ONE-WAY CARING RELATIONSHIPS IN ONE'S PERSONAL LIFE

Individuals in the caring professions are experts at one-way caring. People in their personal sphere, especially when distressed or suffering, are attracted to them because of their expertise and caring attitude. Consider a doctor who is asked to diagnose a mysterious ailment in the middle of a festive party: What to do? One therapist decided to shed two friendships that were too much like work to her; she was the giver in these one-way caring relationships. A teacher made sure that the caring was two-way in a friendship by assertively telling the Other his problems while also being a good, supportive listener. As an overall self-care strategy, we suggest caution about the number of one-way caring relationships in practitioners' personal lives. It is important for us in the caring professions to have a distinction between our personal relationships and our professional relationships. The hope is that caring goes back and forth in our personal lives; as other people care for us, we, of course, want to care for them. As others discuss their personal dilemmas, we discuss ours.

NURTURING ONE'S SELF

One could describe the self as composed of parts, with each part needing nurturing by the practitioner. Here, we describe the parts as the emotional self, the financial self, the humorous self, the loving self, the nutritious self, the physical self, the playful self, the priority-setting self, the recreational self, the relaxation/stress-reduction self, the solitary self, and the spiritual or religious self. Each of these elements of the personal self can use nurturing for ongoing sustenance.

Nurturing the emotional self

> Problems do not go away. They must be worked through or else they remain, forever a barrier to the growth and development of the spirit.
> – M. S. Peck (1978, p. 30)

> When I do not know myself, I cannot know who my students are. I will see them through a glass darkly, in the shadows of my unexamined life – and when I cannot see them clearly, I cannot teach them well. . . . The

work required to "know thyself" is neither selfish nor narcissistic. Whatever self-knowledge we attain as teachers will serve our students and our scholarship well. Good teaching requires self-knowledge; it is a secret hidden in plain sight.

– P. J. Palmer (1998, p. 23)

We need to acknowledge that what is good for others is good for ourselves. Psychotherapists have led the way in emotional self-care through the concept of "therapy for the therapist." Geller, Norcross, and Orlinsky (2005) explore this topic in their book *The Psychotherapist's Own Psychotherapy: Patient and Clinician Perspectives*. In an earlier study by Pope and Tabachnick (1994), 476 psychologists described their own therapy, and the vast majority of this group (86%) found it to be very or extremely helpful. Many reported positive changes in self qualities such as awareness, understanding, esteem, and confidence. Because helping professionals often use the self as the work instrument, these positive changes are notable. Perhaps psychotherapists, in their use of therapy and supervision for themselves, are setting a valuable self-care example for other helpers, teachers, and healers. Yet, it is even difficult for therapists, according to senior practitioner E. Nightengale (personal communication, 1995), who said, "Too many therapists fail to take the 'medicine' they prescribe for others." Here we have an example of the famous saying: The shoemaker has no shoes.

Another concept that is helpful in caring for the emotional self is developing practices that foster self-compassion. Self-compassion is defined as "being kind and understanding toward oneself in instances of pain or failure rather than being harshly self-critical; perceiving one's experiences as a part of the larger human experience rather than seeing them as isolating; and holding painful thoughts and feelings in mindful awareness rather than over-identifying with them" (Neff, 2003, p. 1). The practice of self-compassion promotes the ability to forgive oneself and understand that imperfection is a part of the human experience. Neff, Kirkpatrick, and Rude (2007) and Hall, Row, Wuensch, and Godley (2013) found in their research that self-compassion is linked to psychological well-being. Developing a sense of self-compassion can help us respond more productively to the highs and lows of the work.

Nurturing the financial self

Culture can have a profound effect on the causes of happiness by influencing the goals people pursue as well as the resources available to attain goals . . . selecting compatible goals may be a critical aspect of achieving [subjective well-being].

– Diener, Suh, Lucus, and Smith (1999, p. 285)

How does the practitioner manage the stress that comes from a modest-level salary while living in a consumption-saturated culture? This is our question in this section.

For many of its citizens, the United States is a place of affluence (e.g., there is only one person in most cars). The percentage of consumption of the world's resources vastly exceeds the United States' percentage of the world's population. Living, however, within a cultural bubble of unending messages to consume more means that most people do not feel wealthy. The unrelenting saturation of advertisements and pleas to buy are powerful. See *The Overspent American* by Schor (1998) for a description of this reality.

In America, many people spend all that they make. The irony is that in a rich country "the personal savings rate is zero. In the aggregate, Americans are spending every dollar they take home" (Cassidy, 1999, p. 88). A note to students: Beginners usually feel that, after school is over, they will have money and save it. The record, however, is different. Usually spending increases with more salary, resulting in an even dance of money in, money out. When they get money, many people spend all of it, and with credit, they spend even more.

In the United States, consumption is a major value that drives many decisions. What is called the Great Recession of 2007–2009 brought hardship to many and altered some of this behavior. Yet, having lots of good, new stuff is a basic value for many.

Why, you may ask, do we speak here about this issue? We do so because the helping professions pay well, but not in cash. The pay comes in the immense satisfaction and pleasure one gets from the work at the deeper level of human existence. The pay comes from making a significantly positive difference in the lives of many other people. It is the joys, rewards, and gifts of practice effect we discussed in Chapter 2.

A major practitioner stress factor comes from being paid modestly yet living in a consumption-saturated culture. Controlling this dominant cultural voice is a key to sustaining the financial self. Most jobs within human services, education, and health pay modestly. The starting salary gets the attention of most beginners. That number is often low, but it is not the really important statistic; salary range is more important. High-paying occupations can start low but have a large range. Low-paying occupations start low and have a narrow range. The range is more important because a narrow range means a person will never be paid a lot. Of course, there are some helping professions with wide ranges, like psychotherapists for the wealthy, industrial psychologists consulting for large corporations, professors with lucrative consulting contracts, and physicians in many specialties. These, however, are exceptions. Most practitioners work in jobs that start low and cap within a narrow range.

For practitioners, the key to developing the financial self is to spend less and invest more. It is impossible to do this if one is strongly influenced by the intense advertising propaganda in the culture.

Three factors can help mitigate this effect. Living in a developing country gets one out of the cultural bubble and makes it easier to really see the wealth in the developed world. There, one can see that many in the United States live "high on the hog." Knowing that one is already high on the hog makes for less motivation to live higher and higher on the hog. To aspire to higher consumption levels makes less sense. Because of the power of the cultural bubble, a person in a developed country is usually encapsulated and feels that overconsumption isn't overconsumption – it is just normal behavior. Outside of the bubble, it seems less sensible because the person can see the situation differently.

A second factor is the literature, which shows that an individual's financial well-being has a stronger association with modest spending and moderate risk investing than it does with high income. It is common to think that one's income is, by far, the most important determinant of financial prosperity. This focus is misguided. Some good academic research on this topic is described in *The Millionaire Next Door* (Stanley & Danko, 1996). The central finding of this academic study is a surprise because it violates two basic ideas of the American ethos – that millionaires are very different from the rest of us and that buying a lot now and paying with credit is a reasonable thing to do. The central premise is that millionaires are often people who live next door to the rest of us and are wealthy in part because they live well below their means and make good investment decisions with the difference.

A similar thrust comes from the simplicity movement. Dominguez and Robin (1992) argue in *Your Money or Your Life* that frantically living to pay for overspending, which they say is the basic American approach, is a very unwise use of time, which they call a person's most precious resource. Their book title spells out this option – chasing money for spending or having time for a life. Their answer is found in the charts they use, where they offer evidence for how low consumption and high savings can lead, at midlife, to living off one's investments. This, they suggest, then dramatically reduces the time and energy one needs to work to pay the bills. Instead, they say, people can use their time for richly meaningful life activities . . . and for us in the helping professions, that could mean a deeply meaningful job, with low pay.

One other factor is worth mentioning concerning the financial self of the counselor, therapist, teacher, or health professional. In these jobs, the pay is usually mediocre, but sometimes it is even more mediocre than necessary because the practitioner has poor assertiveness skills regarding money. Let us tell you a story. We know of a person who worked at a university on a 9-month contract. Usually he found work in the summer. One summer, it was especially important because his salary had to support two adults and four children. He was told that there would be summer work, but he was passive about the whole process. Then, a few weeks before summer was to begin, he was told that there was no summer money. It was a good lesson for him. He told himself that it would never happen again and that he had to be more active and assertive about financial needs. The point of this story is that financially unassertive practitioners in the low-paying human services, education, and health jobs can become particularly demoralized because of financial stress. They must take time to actively plan financial self-care.

If a practitioner has poor money skills or is financially unassertive, and also has been seduced by the consumption culture, then the financial self can be highly stressed. In time, this can affect the practitioner so that he or she can no longer make the necessary emotional connections with clients, students, or patients. If that happens, competent work in the relationship-intense professions is no longer possible.

Nurturing the humorous self

Study: Laughing puts brain in mock-meditative state
— Healy (2014, p. 12A)

Maintaining a sense of humor was the number-three career-sustaining behavior (behind spending time with partner/family and maintaining balance between professional and personal lives) in a study of professional psychologists' coping strategies (Stevanovic & Rupert, 2004). Actively laughing, being playful, telling jokes, and being humorous are very positive activities for individuals whose work environment is often filled with serious human problems. How then does one laugh in a serious environment? It takes time to learn the "art and science of laughter" at work. Students in training often lose their sense of humor because they worry that it will be perceived as unprofessional. In time, one's sense of humor often emerges from hiding, and gradually there is, in the best situations, a proper place for humor in the environment of the caring professions. Laughter sustains practitioners. Learning how to be playful and have fun can help sustain the self.

Nurturing the loving self

Here we address the problem of *the nurturer has no nurturing*. Affection in the practitioner's personal life can be such a powerful source of professional vitality, enabling the practitioner to sustain himself/herself amid significant professional stress. Over and over again, year after year, popular songs speak to this human need. For many people, this means a strong primary relationship with one other person who is loving, affectionate, nurturing, and fun to be with. It often means having and raising children. For many practitioners, a family is a very rich source of the best ingredients of self-care. For others, loving and being loved takes a different form. The overall effect, however, is a sense of well-being that radiates from the practitioner's personal life.

Those in the caring professions are occupational experts at addressing the needs of others. Often, they have a long personal and professional history of successfully nurturing the mind, body, soul, and heart of others and getting praise for doing so. They may also have hopes, fantasies, and dreams of others anticipating and addressing their own needs. The nurturing dream often involves a sense of anticipation by the Other and may sound like this: "The other will know what I want and gracefully – in timing, method, and style – care for me." The dream may end with a sense of frustration and resentment because no one seems to notice. Where is he or she *or somebody or anybody* for the professional nurturer? Too often the dream ends with a disappointing reality.

When nurturers have no nurturing, it is like the shoemakers who have no shoes; they can make shoes for others but not so easily for themselves. In moments of reflection, they realize that their feet are bare. Part of the conflict for practitioners is their own ambivalence about putting their own needs versus the needs of others under the spotlight. Perhaps it is important to realize that, according to the attachment process described earlier as an essential element of practitioner success, care of the self is a sacred responsibility. Being loved by another, or others, is a wonderful method of self-care for those in the helping professions. Being cared for in one's personal life can be very sustaining and is often greatly appreciated by the practitioner.

Two recent studies of thriving practitioners found these individuals had rich, positive, loving personal lives. Hou (2015) in his study of highly resilient therapists found they had a strong web of vibrant connectedness. Nissen-Lie et al. (2015) found the most succesful practitioners had personal lives with strong positive attachment and love for self. Point here: to give love upi have to get love!

Nurturing the nutritious self

Psychologist and performance specialist Kate Hays (1999) addressed practitioners at a "Taking Care of Yourself" symposium. There, she provided eight nutritional recommendations for high performance. The commentary under each one is from us. Though written over 15 years ago, her basic recommendations still apply.

1 *Happiness is a steady rhythm of blood glucose* – This idea speaks against skipping and binging patterns of eating, such as "sugar hits," and supports regular eating. The idea of eating small meals combined with snacks (Schafer, 1996) is one way to maintain a steady glucose stream. Consultation with a dietitian can

be a valuable way to discover what combinations of foods provide you with a steady glucose stream.

2 *Provide yourself with a regular routine of eating* – Routine provides structure and stability, and encourages planning. Planning helps us to avoid the impulsive eating that serves as admission to the paved-with-good-intentions, filled-with-traffic, road to (low blood sugar) hell.

3 *Breakfast is the one meal a day not to skip* – In a world of mixed, contradictory, and confusing messages about nutrition, this one is consistently recommended. Why? It seems that breakfast is used as gasoline to get the body going. Without food early in the day, the body runs out of gas late in the day and screams for food. Large amounts of food eaten late in the day tend to go into storage, perhaps forever.

4 *Your body needs water* – Back to the basics. Water, and lots of it, seems to be one of the top nutritional secrets. Because over 70% of the body is water, it makes sense that the hose should keep running. On this note, Balch and Balch (1997) state, "To keep the body functioning properly, it is essential to drink at least eight 8-ounce glasses of quality water each day" (p. 30). Products containing water, such as cola and coffee, are not part of the secret because the caffeine acts as a diuretic, draining water from the body.

5 *Befriend food and be flexible* – Eating disorders are at war with food when they use and abuse food to serve other gods and goddesses. It is better to enjoy the friendship of food, just as one enjoys, but does not abuse, other friends. Flexibility speaks to the failure of fad diets whose inflexibility means that they desist rather than persist. Flexibility also means that small indulgences can be allowed for long-term success.

6 *Learn how to distinguish true hunger signals from other bodily or emotional signals* – Bad feelings such as anxiety, loneliness, anger, fear, confusion, hurt, and sadness trigger eating for lots of people. The problem is that people reach for food when they are not hungry, and often it's the nutritionally emptiest of foods and beverages, so they wind up consuming not only too many calories but also too little nutrition.

7 *Learn for what your body is hungry and thirsty* – Self-awareness can be a valuable people skill. Listening to oneself can provide lots of important information. Knowing the language of hunger and thirst can lead to efficient responses to the messages of the body rather than responses in another language –emotional hunger, for instance – which may be telling the person to eat unnecessary foods.

8 *Develop a long-term perspective with regard to eating habits* – Eating is forever, and for most people, that is a long time. This means that all kinds of short-term schemes (e.g., losing 20 pounds before the reunion) don't cut the mustard. Going from a bad relationship with food to a good one is more than adding a little veneer. Sometimes it's a major remodeling job. The payoff is that, after major remodeling, one has something lasting.

In a review of studies focusing on the outcomes of calorie-restricting diets as a treatment for obesity, Mann et al. (2007) conclude that diets don't lead to lasting weight loss. Smith and Hawks (2006) offer intuitive eating ("an anti-dieting, hunger-based approach to eating"; p. 130) as an effective tool for weight management.

The aforementioned nutrition recommendations give the practitioner another attractive piece of fabric for creating the "sustaining the personal self" quilt.

Nurturing the physical self

The vast majority of studies examining the role of exercise on psychological well-being and mood support the notion that exercise will improve well-being and mood states such as anxiety, stress, depression, tension, and fatigue.

– T. G. Plante (1993, p. 362)

Exercise has so many benefits in combating depression and improving brain chemistry that the following advice – while true – may sound like a cliché: Find a form of vigorous movement that appeals to you, practice it three to five times a week for twenty to forty minutes, and watch your mood improve.

– Henry Emmons, MD (Emmons & Kranz, 2006, p. 93)

We repeatedly hear that we are supposed to get exercise. Often, this is said as a way to improve general physical health; however, we are bringing up this topic for a different reason. As Emmons says in the quote above, there is strong evidence that vigorous physical exercise is beneficial in regulating mood (Penedo & Dahn, 2005). It is only a short step to suggest that intense physical activity is an antidote for the emotional toxins in the practitioner's work life. Given the benefits of exercise, it is easy to speculate that, if it came in pill form, exercise would be *the* most popular pill taken on a daily basis.

The work in the caring professions is emotionally demanding and draining. Remember that the term *burnout* originated in these professions. For a reminder that practitioners' work is stressful, we ask you to look again at the content in earlier chapters: "The Cycle of Caring: Core of the Helping Professions," "The Elevated Stressors of the Novice Practitioner," and "Hazards of Practice." These chapters, read together, present a view of the work as overwhelmingly difficult. For example, there is the hazard of living in a world of distress emotions. Each of us needs methods to combat the depression, anxiety, and pain that the practitioner feels when closeted with the distressed client, student, or patient. This is why helpers, teachers, and health professionals must seriously consider intense physical activity as a piece of the "sustaining the personal self" self-care plan.

In addition to knowing that intense physical activity is good for us, we also know how hard it is to maintain a highly active physical life. Why is it so hard for practitioners? For one thing, competent practitioners in the caring fields tend to put the needs of others before their own. It is an occupational characteristic. A great example occurs in the practitioner's personal life when he or she is a parent. Of course, good parents do focus on the needs of their children; however, the result is a reality where the practitioner's needs get squeezed. Then, there is the time problem in modern life – or shall we call it the lack-of-time problem? Also, there is the way that we have starched out almost all physical activity from modern life. This happens in building design (the elevator is available, but where are the stairs?) and attitude (at the health club, people try to park close to the door).

It seems that one of the greatest self-care challenges for many practitioners is the challenge of creating and maintaining a highly active physical life. Research suggests that physical exercise can be highly effective in combating the emotionally stressful parts of the work. Unfortunately, it does not come in pill form.

In addition to exercise, sleep is an essential component of overall health. According to research compiled by the National Sleep Foundation (2006), lack of sleep is linked to decreases in cognitive performance and mood difficulties such as anger, anxiety, and sadness. The amount of sleep a person needs varies by individual, though researchers tend to agree that adults need between seven and nine hours per night. As practitioners in the helping or caring professions, you are likely aware of strategies that promote healthy sleep, often referred to as "sleep hygiene." If not, try these simple strategies to help develop a more regular sleep schedule: (1) go to bed at the same time each night and wake at the same time each morning to help your body develop a routine; (2) develop an evening routine that encourages your body to relax and prepare for sleep; (3) reserve your bedroom for sleeping and intimacy and refrain from using the room for other activities, such as doing work.

Knowledge of sleep science has even shaped how practice times are determined for players on some teams in the National Basketball Association (NBA), Beck (2009) reports in *The New York Times*. In consultation with Harvard Medical School sleep expert Dr. Charles Czeisler, the director of the Division of Sleep, some teams have opted to cut their morning practices (called morning shootarounds) in favor of allowing players to get more sleep. Czeisler recommends 8.2 to 8.4 hours of sleep per night for players, to promote the ability to learn new information and perform their best. If sleep is important for basketball players' performance and learning, it is equally as important for practitioners to care for themselves in this way.

Nurturing the playful self

Practitioners are serious people trying to do good work under stressful conditions. To have a long, happy career, there is a seemingly paradoxical prescription for these serious people. That prescription is play. Listen to these words: "The world of play favors exuberance, license, abandon. Shenanigans are allowed, strategies can be tried, selves can be revisited. In the self-enclosed world of play, there is no hunger. It is its own goal which it reaches in a richly satisfying way" (Ackerman, 1999, p. 6). The emotional world of the practitioner is filled with words like *earnest, hard, stressful, challenging*, and *serious* and more intense words like *sad, anxious, fearful*, and *angry*. The words of play are different. These words include *fun, zest, relish, delight, enjoyment, gusto, enthusiasm*, and *exuberance*. The paradox: The world of play helps make the world of work possible.

In transactional analysis (TA), it is the child ego state that does the playing. So how does one nurture this part of the self? In popular language, it is called babying oneself. What does it mean to baby the self? It usually means to attend to, to pamper, to be tender. Why is this important? Because it is the self of the professional that must work very hard. So how can the practitioner baby the self? Lots of ways: taking bubble baths and eating chocolates, playing golf or watching a great basketball game, walking aimlessly in the woods, lunching with girlfriends, and on and on. The choices are endless. Finding something that babies the self and doing it are the essentials.

In her book *Deep Play*, Ackerman (1999) describes deep play as an ecstatic form of play. She says that there is an unconscious engagement with the world and an exalted zone of transcendence. In the book, she travels through multiple examples: scuba diving, mountain climbing, wearing a mask, studying animals in the wild, and visiting exotic sites. Describing one form of deep play, she says, "While cycling, I tend to commune with nature, feel life's elements, and repeat a simple mantra of sensations that I experience separately: blue sky, white clouds, green trees, apple scent, bright sun, warm breeze" (p. 33).

Her discussion of the Grand Canyon reminded Tom of his own deep play nine-day rafting trip on the Colorado River through the Grand Canyon. At the time, he was very tired from all the intense work demands over many months. Every day, he sat on the raft and watched the beauty unfold all around. It was so much fun! Looking through this kaleidoscope of color, shape, and form brought pleasure and peace. He was just sitting in this big raft going down the river through the Grand Canyon! Sitting there doing nothing but transcending the reality of the work life and being renewed. One member of the raft group found out after a few days that he was a psychologist and asked Tom if he was observing the group process. Tom said: "Are you kidding? What group process? I'm on vacation watching the water and the rocks!"

May we invite you as a practitioner to inventory your playtime. Perhaps it is there; perhaps it needs to be added.

Nurturing the priority-setting self

Let's start with this premise: There is always too much to do. Why is it so? Modern life is a decent answer, with information overload (it comes from the north and south, east and west, from everywhere); the disappearance of work boundaries; and constant accessibility by cell phone, e-mail, text messing, video conferencing, and social networking. The "Berlin Wall" of our lives has disappeared, a blessing and a curse.

We must make our own boundaries around our work and lives. Where is the compass for this task? It is our own values, job and boss demands, and personal lives. It is important for all of us to set priorities for our time – an irreplaceable, precious commodity. If we can set priorities, there is more of a chance that each of us will get to the primacy, our own hot center of importance, and never have time for the flotsam of our life. This can be a good outcome.

Setting priorities and time management are, first of all, a recognition that there is always too much to do. Secondly, they are a realization that the locus of control for the person's agenda can be internal or external. As they say in Alcoholics Anonymous (AA), "Who is driving your bus?" The task can be difficult for those in helping occupations who readily want to assist the Other. The struggle to stand upright and follow one's own compass gets hard on the slippery floor of trying to be there for the Other. The bells and whistles of time management – put an A next to the important tasks for the day – are more easily mastered when the bigger issue of setting priorities is directly faced and managed. Good luck. We are still working on it!

Nurturing the recreational self

Hobbies can be great for self-care because they have so many elements of renewal. An element of this is what C. Wambach (personal communication, 1989), a college teacher of high-risk students, calls "positive significant distractions." We control the involvement and outcome; the domain is manageable; and the task is fun, interesting, and absorbing.

Being a collector – of whatever – captures so many of these positive elements, and it is concrete – one can see and feel results. Concrete is the opposite of the practitioner's world, where multiple realities and unclear patterns of results are central in the work. Is it any wonder that collecting is a popular activity in the stress-filled world of other-care practitioners? E. Nightengale (personal communication, 1995), a senior Veterans Administration hospital psychologist, responded to these comments by saying, "The value of a hobby, with concrete results, clear beginnings and finished 'products,' is important for the helping professional. The need for completion, for progress, and success can be channeled or 'found' by these kinds of activities." One of our friends, a counselor in a day hospital depression treatment program, collects rocks. For her, it is a low maintenance, concrete hobby with no care or watering needed; even after a long Minnesota winter, the rocks left outside emerge from the receding snow undamaged. She can look at them, touch them, move them around, and add to her collection. No nurturing is needed. The key with collecting or other hobbies is to be taken away from the focus on one's own professional work demands. The result can be a healthier perspective on work, the world, and oneself. There are so many possible hobbies and fun activities – gardening, photography, movies, playing music, building birdhouses. These are the enjoyable activities of some practitioners we know.

Nurturing the relaxation/stress-reduction self

Do practitioners manage stress by using techniques developed from their own professions? Sometimes. Many of us in these practitioner fields are familiar, through our professional work, with stress-management methods such as relaxation training, meditation, mindfulness, biofeedback, yoga, and self-hypnosis. Yet, we often do not personally practice these methods to reduce our own physical body response of overarousal, although we know that physical – emotional – cognitive overarousal is the key to many current lifestyle-type physical problems and diseases.

There are many work sources of stress that lead to overarousal. There is the constant need for practitioners to focus on the needs and acute suffering of the Other. There are, of course, other sources of stress, such as organizational politics and policies that may greatly affect the individual practitioner, who often has little voice in major decisions. Big bureaucracies can be difficult places to feel control over one's professional life. Electronics and technology can be so great and also so frustrating. For example, many physicians in 2016 report great frustration that they now need to do electronic record-keeping while interacting with their patients. Some have solved this by hiring scribes to work the keyboard.

Another source of stress is internal in the practitioner's own thoughts and appraisal of self in a variety of contexts. For the practitioner's cognitive distortions, Martha Teater and John Ludgate (2014) offer a CBT solution in their book, *Overcoming Compassion Fatigue*. If CBT can help our clients, how about ourselves? It offers another version of other-care/self-care.

A century ago, overarousal was termed the *fight or flight response* by Cannon, a professor at Harvard. Cannon suggested that, in response to threat, the human body goes into an emergency mode to either attack the threatening object or escape from it. The attack mode produces physical changes in the body that can help in the attack or escape. Modern life produces the same physical reaction but within a different context – for example, a traffic jam. The long-term consequence is the onset of stress-related disease turning into a disease. Current diseases that sometimes have a stress component include high blood pressure, heart disease, depression, cancer, arthritis, and gastrointestinal system disorders.

Nearly one hundred years after Cannon, another Harvard professor, Herbert Benson (1975), stated that the best antidote to overarousal is a simple procedure he called "the relaxation response." The Benson-Henry Institute for Mind Body Medicine (2010) states that relaxation, as an antidote to the chronic overarousal of modern life, can be done through two simple steps. Within a context of quiet and comfort, and a period such as 20 minutes, the individual is to:

1   Repeat a word, sound, prayer, thought, phrase, or muscular activity.
2   Return to number 1 whenever other thoughts or activities intrude.

These two steps, along with slow, deep breathing, are the elements of the relaxation response. Benson (1999) states that increasing oxygen consumption is a powerful yet easy part of stress reduction. He also maintains that all of the world's major religions have incorporated these elements into their religious prayers, rituals, and practices.

Learning through practice and overpractice to reduce the stress response of overarousal can be of great value in the practitioner's personal and professional life. *The Relaxation and Stress Reduction Workbook*, by Davis, Eshelman, and McKay (2008), is one of many sources of useful techniques. Some of the stress-reduction methods they emphasize are body awareness, breathing, progressive relaxation, and visualization. They describe body awareness as a first self-assessment step and breathing as a central part of stress reduction. They say, "Improper breathing contributes to anxiety, panic attacks, depression, muscle tension, headache, and fatigue. . . . Breathing awareness and good breathing habits will enhance your psychological and physical well-being, whether you practice them alone or in combination with other relaxation techniques" (p. 23). They emphasize the importance of deep abdominal (diaphragmatic) breathing as opposed to shallow chest (thoracic) breathing.

First developed by Jacobson in 1929, progressive relaxation is an old method of relaxing the body. It has been a central part of therapist-directed anxiety management for many years. It essentially consists of tightening and then relaxing different muscle groups in the body. The theory is that a person cannot be tense and relaxed at the same time. By relaxing, the person is teaching the body to respond differently during periods of overarousal.

Visualization is the practice of seeing something in the mind's eye. It is a way of using one's imagination and creativity to enhance one's life. Similar terms are *imagery* and *guided fantasy*. Skovholt, Morgan, and Cunningham (1989) have described the use of visualization in career and life planning. In managing stress, Davis and colleagues (2008) say that guided visualization begins when you imagine a place where you can be very relaxed. For many people, this involves an outdoor scene, such as the ocean, a lake, or the wilderness. The individual can develop this picture in the mind and then imagine it during high-stress times.

Mindfulness

> From the outset of practice we are reminded that mindfulness is not about getting anywhere else or fixing anything. Rather, it is an invitation to allow oneself to be where one already is and to know the inner and outer landscape of the direct experience in each moment.
>
> **– J. Kabat-Zinn (2003, p. 148)**

Mindfulness is defined as "paying attention on purpose, in the present moment, and nonjudgmentally to the unfolding of experience moment to moment" (Kabat-Zinn, 2003, p. 145). Mindfulness takes many forms in therapeutic offerings. Namely, programs such as dialectical behavior therapy, mindfulness-based stress reduction (MBSR), and acceptance and commitment therapy teach mindfulness as the key component of the therapy. Mindfulness has been shown to be an effective intervention for issues such as treatment of chronic pain (Kabat-Zinn, Lipworth, & Burney, 1985), depression and anxiety (Reibel, Greeson, Brainard, & Rosenzweig, 2001), and chronic stress (Chang et al., 2004).

In addition to having clinical significance, mindfulness is a useful tool for practitioner self-care. For example, the practice of mindfulness meditation (MM) is based on a simple strategy of bringing mindful attention to the present moment experience. Formal practice of mindfulness mediation involves focusing on the breath as an entry to the practice.

You may wish to try these simple instructions for mindfulness meditation. Sit in a comfortable position in which your body is alert and relaxed, allowing the breath to flow freely. Take a deep inhalation through the nose and a deep exhalation through the mouth. Often people have a tendency to breathe into their upper lungs; thus, only the chest rises and falls as they breathe. Consider an image of a baby sleeping: You see her belly rising and falling as she breathes. Hold this image in your mind as you work to breathe into your belly. You may choose to bring attention to your belly by placing your hand there and watching it move as you begin to learn this breathing. The mind will naturally wander onto other thoughts; you can bring your awareness back to the sensations of the breath. Each time the mind wanders, simply return to your breathing.

Another helpful practice, taught through the MBSR program, is the body scan. Participants in the course are taught to bring awareness to different parts of their bodies and notice any bodily tension or tightness, pain, lack of sensation, or relaxation. This practice is typically done lying down and in a quiet space. Busy practitioners can get at the essence of the body scan by working to develop more awareness of how the body feels throughout the day. For example, in between meeting with clients, patients, or students, simply take a moment to scan your body from head to toe and notice any sources of tension or strain; mindfully relax these parts of the body.

MBSR programs offer formal training in mindfulness meditation, body awareness (through the use of the body scan), and gentle hatha yoga. As a practitioner, participating in such a program can be a useful self-care endeavor. Michelle has participated in an MBSR program as both a student and a co-facilitator. She found that the practices had a powerful impact on her life both personally and professionally. Additionally, Michelle's dissertation research explored the effects of participation in a 12-week MBSR course on college students' psychological well-being, psychological distress, self-compassion and health status (Trotter, 2009).

Another therapist writes of how mindfulness practices promoted self-care (Christopher, 2010):

> Mindfulness practices also provided me with a way of taking care of myself and preventing burnout. I learned through meditation that I could just allow experiences to move through me. I do not mean "moving through" in the sense of moving through to get rid of. Rather, moving through in the sense of not resisting, not putting up walls around seemingly negative experiences and emotions, but giving them space and being a good host, to use the mystic poet Rumi's metaphor from "The Guest House" (Barks, 2005). At the end of those days or sessions that felt tiring, burdensome, deadening, I would allow myself some time for the residuals that seemed stuck in my body to manifest themselves and to have access to my consciousness. Often this would be accompanied by tears, but then a sense of having been cleansed, of the heaviness lifting. Through yoga I learned when I was "efforting" or unnecessarily expending energy or tension to accomplish something. Noticing the state of my body when sitting with clients gave me indicators of when I was becoming tense, when I was trying too hard in session, when I was getting attached to a particular outcome.
>
> (p. 39)

Yoga

For her dissertation research, Anna Roth conducted a qualitative interview study in 2014. Her research participants were 14 licensed doctoral psychologists who were also registered yoga teachers. This is the first research study of dual-trained psychology–yoga practitioners in the helping professions. This unique sample makes the study quite valuable. These research participants were asked to describe the psychological benefits of yoga.

This is such a good topic for us because our own psychological health is so important. We are entrusted with helping others combat their sadness of the soul. These participants told Roth in the interviews that yoga can help with psychological growth if people are open to it. Of course, this is true for most methods of helping oneself; maybe with yoga there is a special need for openness because of its Eastern roots, which may feel foreign to some in the West. Here we are summarizing some of the results of the Roth study.

Benefit #1: Breath

When we think of the stress level endured by practitioners in the helping fields, in their work and in their personal lives, the core value of deep, slow breathing seems of great value.

Other methods such as meditation and biofeedback offer deep breathing, too, but here we offer descriptions of how breath is central to the benefits of yoga from psychologists/yoga teachers:

> Anybody who's doing yoga, everything starts with the breath. You can go a couple of weeks without food, you can go a couple of days without water, but you can't go more than a couple of minutes without breathing.
>
> (Roth, 2014, p. 48, permission granted by the author)

> Yoga teaches us how to rest. I believe all true healing happens when we are rested and calm, to actually teach someone how to be still. We don't do that in our culture. I think that is extremely healing for people. They are being given permission for rest . . .
>
> (Roth, 2014, p. 48, permission granted by the author)

Benefit #2: Mindful observation of the self

The second component deemed essential by participants was engaging the observing self via the practice of mindfulness/meditation:

> Mindful awareness, learning how to stop being at war with one's experience and bring a kind, accepting attention to what's happening while it's happening . . . engaging the observing self.
>
> (Roth, 2014, p. 49).

Bringing a kind, accepting attention to one's own experience – what a beautiful way of saying don't fall into the 'shoemaker has no shoes' problem. Give the same acceptance to oneself as one gives to clients, students, patients. Years ago,

Carl Rogers (1961) in *On Becoming a Person* passionately communicated the same message of self-acceptance.

Benefit #3: With practice on the mat, a person learns distress tolerance

Yoga practice involves stretching oneself, and while holding certain positions, a person can practice abiding and managing a variety of uncomfortable feelings – physical, emotional, mental. Imagine how well this can translate for the helping practitioner who is a witness to human pain and suffering. For example, clients in despair will sometimes talk about suicide with their therapist; listening deeply to these client words without getting overwhelmed requires practice in distress tolerance.

Benefit #4: Active healing of one's relationship with oneself

Here are direct words from Anna Roth: "Participants expressed feeling the dissemination of yoga philosophy as tremendously healing as it encourages greater self-acceptance, self-compassion, and relating to the self in gentler and more attentive ways" (2014, p. 50). Again, we are talking about the importance of practitioner emotional well-being being essential for the work. We as practitioners need great vitality in order to continually engage in the Cycle of Caring with others in the I-Thou relationship. Learning self-acceptance and self-compassion through yoga can be a very positive way of doing it.

Benefit #5: Putting in the time on the mat

So many self-improvement activities involve a lot of time and effort. Tom played three competitive sports in high school and one in college . . . two hours a day five days a week for 300 days a year for 12 years. Putting in the time! Michelle did this with acting and speech competitions in high school – so much so that her brother and parents would also memorize lines from the speech or play. In AA, there is a saying for the new person, deep in denial: "Keep coming back." Grinding away at self-development may not sound fun or romantic, and often it isn't. In terms of putting in one's time, a research participant told Anna Roth (2014):

> What happens physically on the yoga mat becomes a metaphor for what the person experiences cognitively, and psychologically, and then a yoga instructor can help articulate those lengths, so that the person can bring their experience on the mat and transfer those experiences into personal things that happen off the mat. It all becomes a metaphor, just like in a therapy session how the transference/counter-transference is

a metaphor for all type relationships – what the person experiences on the yoga mat is a metaphor for what they experience in the rest of their life.

(p. 51, permission granted by the author)

We have outlined above five psychological benefits from yoga from the perspective of dual-trained, licensed psychologists/certified yoga teachers. There is much more in the dissertation to explore. Regarding the physical stress-reduction effects of yoga, Anna Roth reviewed many research studies and concluded:

the strongest evidence for yoga's effect is in relation to the **endocrine system** – particularly lowering cortisol. Lowering cortisol has been associated with decreasing perceived stress, anxiety and increasing feelings of wellbeing. Enhanced serotonin production, oxytocin release, and increased melatonin were noted as other potential effects of yoga in this area. The second strongest area of evidence was found in relation to yoga's impact on the **nervous system** via direct influence on the sympathetic and parasympathetic activity in the autonomic nervous system. Reviewed studies found a reduction in sympathetic activation, increases in levels of GABA, and improved regulation of the HPA axis to improve outcomes in mood disorders, anxiety, stress, and wellbeing.

(Roth, 2014, pp. 9–10)

Nurturing the solitary self

It is a difficult lesson to learn today – to leave one's friends and family and deliberately practice the art of solitude. . . . I feel a limb is being torn off, without which I shall be unable to function. And yet once it is done, I find there is a quality to being alone that is incredibly precious. Life rushes back into the void, richer, more vivid, fuller than before. It is as if in parting one actually did lose an arm. And then, like the starfish, one grows it anew; one is whole again, complete and round – more whole ever than before, when the other people had pieces of one.

– **A. M. Lindbergh (1975, p. 42)**

Solitude as an antidote to people intensity can be important for professional givers of the self. Solitude can nurture us in a profound way. Learning to enjoy solitude can be a difficult process for practitioners. Solitude is increasingly difficult to find and nurture. There is so much media in our everyday lives and, increasingly, many of us around the world live in population-dense cities. Lots of television viewing has become central to most people's lives. There is so much about the technology of television that is deeply appealing to people.

Conversely, television is so overstimulating that solitude becomes even more foreign and uncomfortable.

Solitude means removing oneself from the known channel of life (e.g., being plugged into the electronic world, intense contact with others in need) to an often unknown channel (silence, no human voices, aloneness). Those in the caring professions often have to fight through the disquieting elements of the quiet – the loneliness, the self-focus, an alienation from nature. They need to learn how to change loneliness into solitude. In time, however, the sounds of the natural world, the wilderness, can fill up the self in a way that refreshes. So, too, can just plain quiet. We suggest reading more on this topic in *The Singing Wilderness* (Olson, 1997), a wonderful book.

A negative byproduct of technology has been noise pollution; noise is everywhere. The cell phone is wonderful, as are texting, Skype, Facebook, and other ways of connecting. The phone rings; cars drive by; people are talking all around. The life-enhancing machinery around us, such as loud lawn mowers, also produces noise that gradually becomes the new normal. In solitude, silence is the gold. Spiritual and religious practices also offer a bed for solitude. One can meditate and pray alone, with the focus often being the connection between the self and the universe.

The typical K–12 teacher is exposed on Monday through Friday to overwhelming numbers of living, breathing, needing students. Was it a genius who invented a professional teaching year of nine months? This permits a teacher to recover and be ready again after being away for three months from the people intensity. Maybe the nine-month–three-month cycle of intensity and distance was created by a very wise scholar of professional development rather than by the agrarian pattern of early American life. We prefer to think that the calendar came from someone who knew, decades ago, that the Cycle of Caring demands an ON and then an OFF of human contact. After the phases of empathetic attachment with the new children in the fall, active involvement during the school year, and then the felt separation of May and June, there is the summer of time away. This is the solitude of the re-creation phase, so necessary so that when the children fill the school again in the fall, the teacher can vigorously enter the empathetic attachment phase.

Yes, of course, teachers do not go from nine months of work to three months of hermitlike existence. In fact, many take classes and work during the summer. However, at least the occupation is structurally set up to permit removal from the intense human contact at work. The nine-month–three-month rhythm permits something else that is very valuable. It permits the felt separation phase to occur within the structure of the occupation. Listen carefully to elementary teachers talk about their work. They often use the words "my children" when describing their students, and they often describe end-of-the-year rituals that they say are to help the children make the transition to summer. We hope that the rituals are also for the teachers to help them grieve the loss of their caring attachments – attachments that will change forever.

Positive loss experiences permit a new round of attachments for teachers when August and September come again. With too many unresolved and painful losses, we cannot attach again in our personal lives. With too many unresolved and painful losses at work, we cannot continue to attach in our professional lives. Unlike K–12 teaching, most careers in the helping professions do not have an involvement–distance structure built into the occupation.

We emphasize the importance of getting away, from both the noise of our technology-filled lives, and also from extensive people contact in the relationship-intense professions, to solitude and quiet. Please remember our main point here: *Getting away* permits us to *come back* with vitality to the helping relationships, the core of our work.

Nurturing the spiritual or religious self

The mystery of life, cloaked so guilelessly in day and night, makes the search for God the enduring human drama. We know so little, we feel so much. We have only the shape of our lives, experienced in the cycle of light and dark, to guide us toward meaning.

– P. Hampl (1995, p. xxvi)

Friends have said that *The Denial of Death* by Ernest Becker (1973) is the most profound book, the one with the greatest depth, they have read. In the book, Becker describes death as the great human fear, a fear so great, he says, that people construct their whole lives to manage its intensity. Becker suggests that denial of death's reality is a central coping strategy for this intense fear.

It seems to us that the reality of death is a major motivation in the human quest for a spiritual or religious life. This quest is both cross-cultural and historic. In many houses of worship, Tom has celebrated the sacred and God's presence – with Muslims in Turkey, Buddhists in Thailand, Lutherans as a child growing up in Minnesota, Catholics at the Vatican, Jews when his father was a resident of a Jewish nursing home, Chinese Baptists in Singapore, and recently, while giving a workshop in Norway, he listened as his second cousin preached at his church in Oslo. He has also experienced the power of the Christian God in the beautiful wilderness of Minnesota's canoe country.

A spiritual or religious life can be an important part of how one sustains the personal self. This has many meanings for different people. For us, there are two reasons why being active spiritually or religiously is important. First, an active spiritual or religious life acknowledges the reality described by Becker. Death can be terrifying, and facing the reality directly through a spiritual or religious life is a reaction of more depth than the use of denial. An active spiritual or religious quest addresses the central mysteries of life: What is the meaning of life? Is there an active divine presence? What is God's plan for my life? Are people basically good or evil? How does one achieve forgiveness, atonement, and peace? What moral rules should govern my life? Is there eternal life?

Second, workers in the caring professions are actively present in the drama of human tragedy, disappointment, and pain. Examples include a counselor hearing of betrayal of one person by another, a teacher seeing a student try but fail, or a nurse watching while a severely injured person struggles with intense pain. An active spiritual or religious life can help the practitioner search for meaning in and understanding of these painful human realities seen at work on a daily basis. For example, it can be important to ask questions such as: Why does God permit acute human pain and suffering? An active spiritual or religious life seems for many practitioners to be an important part of sustaining the personal self.

SUMMARY: KEEPING IN FOCUS ONE'S OWN NEED FOR BALANCED WELLNESS – PHYSICAL, SPIRITUAL, EMOTIONAL, AND SOCIAL

Professionals in the caring fields need to be assertive about their own wellness. One way of conceptualizing this involves four dimensions of health and the balance among them (Figure 9.1). The diamond and its four dimensions help one to see the need for a focus on the dynamic interplay between them. The diamond symbolizes the reality that the whole is greater than the sum of the parts. Yet, the whole is strong only by attending to each dimension.

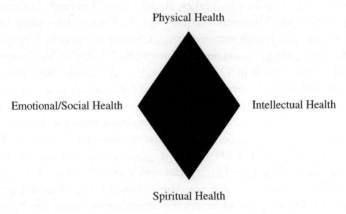

FOUR DIMENSIONS OF HEALTH

Physical Health

Emotional/Social Health   Intellectual Health

Spiritual Health

Figure 9.1 Four dimensions of health

SELF-REFLECTION EXERCISES

Here, versions of the personal self were considered. In terms of a self-care action plan for you, which parts of the personal self are in "good shape" in your life, which ones need a "tune-up," and which ones need a "major overhaul"?

1. Parts of the personal self in good shape:

_____

_____

_____

_____

_____

_____

_____

_____

2. Parts of the personal self in need of a tune-up:

_____

_____

_____

_____

_____

_____

_____

_____

3. Parts of the personal self in need of a major overhaul:

_____

_____

_____

_____

_____

_____

_____

_____

10

THE EYE OF THE STORM
MODEL OF PRACTITIONER
RESILIENCY

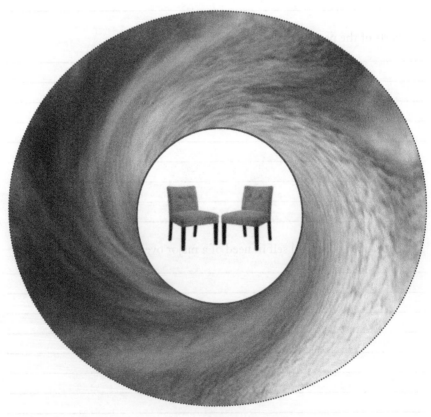

Figure 10.1 The helping relationship within the Eye of the Storm

W hat makes a practitioner a resilient practitioner? In the thicket of all the definitions of human resilience, a simple but accurate one comes from the Latin word *resilire* and can be summarized as *the ability to bounce back*. We explored some of the history of the word *resilience* in Chapter 7 by first going back to the two pioneer psychology researchers, Werner (Werner et al., 1971) and Garmazey (1971). We also note the scholarship on resilience by the British psychiatrist, Rutter (1985). Here, in this chapter, we will cite some of the valuable research and theory on practitioner resilience and then move on to a three-part model of practitioner resiliency.

Fletcher and Sarkar (2013) examined many definitions of resilience and found two essential components: struggles and positive coping. There we have the resilient practitioner. David (2012) has done insightful work in investigating how resilience can help those helpers and healers who work with traumatized clients. Harrison and Westwood (2009) also contributed an important piece with their article outlining protective practices for those working in mental health. An earlier contribution to the positive side (resilience, burnout prevention) vs. the negative side (burnout, vicarious traumatization) was written by Coster and Schwebel (1997). They shined the light on wellness, or what they called at the time *well-functioning*, in professional psychologists. (See also Chapter 12 in this book, in which Mullenbach describes "Burnout Prevention and Self-Care Practices of Expert Practitioners.") In addition, Hou (2015) completed a dissertation on the topic of highly resilient therapists. He found a sample group, interviewed them, analyzed the data, and then developed a composite description that will be described later. Here, now is the:

EYE OF THE STORM MODEL

The practitioner sits in the Eye of the Storm on a three-legged stool of a High Vitality Index, Expertise in the Cycle of Caring, and an Intense Will to Learn and Grow. The resilient practitioner dwells in the Eye, sitting together in the quiet with the Other. Within the language of storms, the Coriolis Force deflects the life-churning powerful winds that are so dangerous outside of the Eye. The suffering of the Other goes on around the resilient practitioner, often with the power of gale force winds.

The resilient practitioner and the Other: The Other is another human being, just like the resilient practitioner. The Other is also called a client, patient, student, supervisee, mentee, parishioner, or similar help-seeking person. The resilient practitioner has other names too: counselor, psychotherapist, teacher, physician, nurse, physical therapist, dentist, family law attorney, case worker, clergy, clinical supervisor, professor, academic advisor, rabbi, minister, imam, and the possibilities go on. Resilient practitioners, as often said in many places in this book, belong to the *helping professions, human service professions*, or *caring professions*. An even bigger occupational term is the *relationship-intense professions*, a new term that captures the essence of the work: relationship-intense.

In the quiet, they sit together, just as Buber (1970) describes the I-Thou relationship. In the Eye of the Storm, the quiet of the safe space is guided by professional ethics in the helping fields of *benevolence*, acting to help others; *nonmaleficence*, not inflicting harm on others; and *respect*, valuing the Other's worth.

ONE LEG OF THE STOOL: *THE RESILIENT PRACTITIONER HAS A HIGH VITALITY INDEX*

Outside the Eye, all around the resilient practitioner and the Other, is the storm of human suffering experienced by the Other. This suffering may take an acute form of one of the distress emotions of depression, anxiety, or anger. Behind the distress emotion there may be a deeper human story of life being lived with both triumph and despair. The Other may have a "seemingly unsolvable problem that needs to be solved," an inability to take in valuable feedback that can be useful for growth, a lack of realizing that often "love is a hell of a lot of work," acute or chronic attachment loss, or one of many other very human versions of despair, dilemma, loss of direction, or need for love.

Frank and Frank (1991) describe all of these client emotions as versions of demoralization, an acute and often chronic level of discouragement. In the Eye, the client demoralization is met by practitioner vitality. Human demoralization meets human vitality. An essential part of the helping fields is to match negative client affect with our positive affect, their hopelessness with our hope, and their pessimism with our optimism.

This is one leg of the Eye in the Storm Model of the resilient practitioner. Vitality means exuberance. It means having deep purpose. It means having the power to live and grow. Take a look at the resiliency inventory at the beginning of the book. (Remember this is only an inventory for your self-reflection; it has not been validated for psychological assessment and prediction.)

There are eight inventory questions about Professional Vitality (e.g., I find my work as a practitioner or as a student to be meaningful) and eleven questions about Personal Vitality (e.g., I feel loved by intimate others). What are the sources of your vitality? This is a very important question. As mentioned earlier, Hou (2015) interviewed validly selected resilient practitioners. He developed a composite description of them. At the center of the composite, there is a Strong Web of Vibrant Connectedness, tied to four parts, one in each direction posess a Core Values and Beliefs Framework, Actively Engage with the Core Self, Desire to Learn and Grow, Drawn to Strong Interpersonal Relationships (p. 139).

Using the Hou research, we could call these four wells for the practitioner's vitality "water."

In the Eye, client demoralization meets practitioner vitality. In addition to sources of vitality, the resilient practitioner actively reduces sources of stress. Of course, this is easy to say, often hard to do. In the inventory, there are nine sources of professional stress (e.g., I have found a way to have high standards for my work yet avoid unreachable perfection) and 10 sources of personal stress (e.g., there are different ways I can get away from stress and relax). To have high vitality, we have to continue to whack away at stress while finding energy, optimism, hope, and joy so that we can go toe to toe in the quiet of the Eye with the Other's despair.

A high vitality index is present when Personal Vitality and Professional Vitality greatly exceed Personal Stress and Professional Stress.

THE SECOND LEG: *THE CYCLE OF CARING PROCESS AS THE CORE OF THE PRACTITIONER'S WORK*

The Cycle of Caring is described in detail in Chapter 3. Here is a snapshot of it as one leg of the three-legged stool of the resilient practitioner.

How can the practitioner and Other sit in the Quiet of the Eye while around them are the swirling dangerous winds of the Other's suffering? How can the practitioner not get caught up in the swirling winds of the Other's suffering, which we define as conditions like burnout, compassion fatigue, and vicarious traumatization? The Cycle of Caring offers a powerful key (Skovholt, 2005, 2012a). The practitioner is only responsible for her or his part of the equation – not both human sides of the equation. Of course, we want positive outcomes for those we intensively try to help, and that are often tied directly to evaluations of our own performance. The practitioner often feels joy when the Other improves. A veteran of many years of teaching in New York public schools, Frank McCourt (2005), in his book *Teacher Man*, expresses both highs and lows of teaching tied to student outcomes. He says:

> Sometimes [the students] they'll tell you that was a pretty good lesson and you're on top of the world. That somehow gives you energy and makes you want to sing on the way home . . . There are other classes you wish would take the ferry to Manhattan and never return.
>
> (p. 77)

These are examples of how whatever happens to the Other directly impacts the practitioner.

The Cycle of Caring offers a different view. One way of understanding this is with our paradoxical concept of Boundaried Generosity. To preserve the practitioner's Self for the long-term, there needs to be both generosity and deep self-care: self-care for the long term, to be able to continue to give. Without a self to give, the realities of burnout, compassion fatigue, and/or vicarious trauma emerge.

If you look at Figure 14.1 in this book you will see two job stress dimensions: control and demand. The quadrant of low control and high demand is considered the home of high job stress; the quadrant of high control and low demand is the home of low job stress. Our focus here is on the dimension of control (not demand).

The Cycle of Caring offers the practitioner high control over the tasks she or he can actually control; that lowers job stress and helps produce the quiet within the Eye of the Storm. This idea is expressed well by the Serenity Prayer. Theologian Reinhold Neibuhr described the AA adoption of the prayer he wrote as: "God give us the grace to accept with serenity the things that cannot be changed, courage to change the things that should be changed and the wisdom to distinguish the one from the other" (Brown, 1986, p. 251).

In the helping professions, we often focus on what we DO to the Other, as in a method, procedure, technique. Workshops and trainings are often about that. For example, in counseling, a DO could come in the form of a technique or method such as CBT, DBT, Mindfulness Training, EMDR, or Two Chair Dialogue. The variety of intervention methods of helping expand as the helping professions continue to develop. This is true of all the helping, caring, relationship-intense fields – and sometimes the DO is very important. For example, a family law attorney has a DO of valuable, specific legal advice to give. However, here we are focusing on process success. Success is *engaging* in The Cycle of Caring.

Beginning practicum students in counseling often are thrilled by obvious client improvement or client appreciation, sometimes expressed to the practicum counselor with the equation of *client gets better = I am a good counselor* and *client does not get better = I am not a good counselor*. This kind of counselor thinking increases the urge to do something to make the client better and causes the counselor to feel very stressed when the client does not show improvement relatively quickly. With the Cycle of Caring, success does not depend on client outcome, success is determined by the practitioner engaging in the four-phase Cycle of Caring. Effective counseling depends in part on the client's self-healing properties being engaged.

The Cycle of Caring involves deep involvement in Phase 1: Empathetic Attachment. Here the work is to develop a positive working alliance with the Other. Phase 2: Active Involvement is the longest phase in terms of time. This is when the hoped-for growth and development of the Other takes place – often there is a version of reduction of distress emotions and an increase in human coping. Practitioner knowledge in one of the helping fields – knowledge, methods, techniques, suggestions, ideas – is used here. Phase 3: Felt Separation is the time when the human connection between the practitioner and the Other ends. Phase 4: Re-Creation: Here the process work for the practitioner is to re-new the self and prepare for a new Cycle of Caring with a new Other. One example of the four phases of the Cycle of Caring is the life of the elementary school teacher, saying hello in the fall, working together with students during the school year, saying good-bye in the spring, and then resting and renewing in summer. A crisis counselor or emergency room physician may do the first three phases in one meeting, with a short Phase 4 before beginning again. Expertise in the Cycle of Caring for the practitioner is doing the four Phases well and doing them again and again with new clients/students/patients at a high level of functioning.

In the quiet of the Eye, the practitioner does the four Phases. The practitioner hopes for client, student, patient change and improvement . . . but the practitioner does not control whether this actually happens. The concept of work satisfaction experienced as Flow, as described by Csikszentmihalyi (2008), corresponds with satisfaction in Cycle of Caring work. Orlinsky and Rønnestad (2013) have a concept of Healing Involvement that also seems to correspond in terms of practitioner well-being. They wrote, "about 50% of the nearly 5,000 therapists we had studied experienced much Healing Involvement and little Stressful Involvement, a practice pattern that we designated Effective Practice" (p. 268). Although these ideas came from different places, it seems both the concept of Flow and the concept of much Healing Involvement can be present when the practitioner does her/his side of the relationship-intense human equation.

THE THIRD LEG OF THE RESILIENT PRACTITIONER STOOL: *THE INTENSE WILL TO LEARN AND GROW*

From our earliest studies of counselor development described in Skovholt and Rønnestad (1992a) to the continuity of those studies highlighted in Chapter 11 of this book and in Rønnestad and Skovholt (2013) to the latest research on high-level performance via the master therapist studies (Jennings et al., in press), the intense will to learn and grow shows up as a defining attribute.

Why is the intense will to learn and grow so important? And how does it become one of the legs of the Eye of the Storm model of practitioner resiliency? We will explore these questions here.

The core of the helping professions is paradoxically both very easy and extremely difficult to master. Easy because in every corner of the world people today are talking to each other in informal helping relationships – for example, best friends talking and listening and supporting and giving advice to each other. Parallel to the easy version is the hard version. When we stop using the epistemology of our own lives to understand the Other and actually try to approach the Other from inside of them emotionally at their own 'Hot Center,' and take in the complexity of the Other, we can get flooded with data.

The poets, playwrights, and theologians struggle to understand human nature. Why would it be any easier for those of us using a relationship-intense method in the helping professions?

Based on our research, the beginning student in the helping fields is flooded with data: "Six data bases constitute significant sources of influence for the individual; theories/research, clients, professional elders (professors/supervisors/mentors/therapists, one's own personal life, one's peers/colleagues and the social/cultural environment" (Skovholt & Rønnestad, 1992a, p. 24). Just one of these six sources of data is like a bountiful garden, offering so much. For example, consider the life's work of 28 researchers as summarized in the final chapter of a book titled *Bringing Psychotherapy Research to Life* (Angus et al., 2010).

In an understatement, one beginner said, "It is harder to be a counselor than it first appeared" (p. 25). If you look at the Model of Development in Chapter 11, created primarily by Helge Rønnestad through his clinical supervision research, our joint research, and his research with David Orlinsky, you will find the entrance to the world of helping relationships in the model is fraught with experiences of difficulties/challenges. This leads to reflection (e.g., Why did I feel lost in the session? Did the client get better? Maybe I am not any good at this work? Is the theory too global to help me understand?) Questions, questions, questions.

This overwhelming sense of ambiguity and uncertainty in the work can really tax the developing practitioner who is trying to get it right. In Chapter 11, we discuss three themes of professional development that fit here: an intense commitment to learn propels the developmental process, professional development is a lifelong process, and for the practitioner there is a realignment from self as hero to client as hero. Taking risks to stretch oneself within ethical boundaries and staying open to new learning increase one's ability level within the helping fields. The culture of clinical supervision is so positive for development. Within this culture, we are all encouraged to be open to feedback. Professional growth is not linear. Development can be cyclical, periods of moratorium can be positive, and critical incident/defining moments can be catalysts for sudden bursts forward. When formal school is over, the practitioner is now in charge of her or his own development. There are many years to work on optimal development. During these many years, an increased sense of ability paradoxically also raises the sense that the client is in charge of her or his own growth. This idea is reflected in the theme of the hero changing from the practitioner to the client.

The intense will to learn and grow relates to six markers of professional development for mastery: Rage to Master, Deliberate Practice Over Many Years, Open to Feedback but Not Derailed by It, Humility, Deep Coaching Attachments, and Boundaried Generosity (Skovholt, Vaughan and Jennings, 2012, p. 231–239). Each of these markers moves the development process. For example, humility seems to increase openness to input from others about one's performance. Here is an example of the humility of experts. Bain (2004) studied dozens of great college teachers and found humility to be a core attribute. Bain wrote of an award-winning professor at Northwestern University who "often attributed his own success as a teacher to 'how slow I am'. . . . A similar humility marked others in the study" (pp. 142–3).

The result of the intense will to learn and grow over a long time is a high level of competence, as described in the Jennings CER model of the master therapist (Jennings & Skovholt, 1999), with these experts being high on Cognitive, Emotional, and Relational Characteristics. A newer version of master therapist characteristics, an examination of 72 practitioners around the world, can be found in Jennings et al. (in press).

The critical factor in the will to learn and grow is the resulting increased competence. In general, in our lives a new sense of accomplishment often leads to more confidence and that can lead to more energy for the work. We found this in the master therapist studies. The increased competence serves as one source of vitality, and vitality is the first leg of the Eye in the Storm Model of practitioner resiliency. Vitality can come from many sources. Here we are discussing how a strong self-directed development process with the will to learn and grow can serve as one leg of the stool.

SUMMARY OF THE EYE OF THE STORM MODEL OF PRACTITIONER RESILIENCY

The storm of human need, distress, misery, and despair offers frightening realities for practitioners, such as burnout, compassion fatigue, and vicarious traumatization. There can be a high cost to caring. In reaction, like a vaccination, the three legs of vitality, the Cycle of Caring, and the will to learn and grow support the practitioner as she or he sits with the Other in the Eye of the Storm. Outside, the storm swirls; inside the Eye in the quiet the practitioner and the Other are working together in the helping relationship. The Coriolis Force, in the language of storms, produces the quiet. May the Eye be a wonderful place for human hope and restoration!

11

THE EVOLVING PRACTITIONER FROM EARLY CAREER ANXIETY TO LATER – USUALLY – COMPETENCE

Thomas M. Skovholt and Michael H. Rønnestad

This chapter describes the development of the practitioner. We, Tom and Helge, are happy to offer it to you. It has been rewarding to research the topic of practitioner development! We began this research in 1985 when we met and decided to work together on this topic. Now it is 2016 and 31 years later, and we are still writing, thinking, researching, teaching, and presenting on this topic. Perhaps the most gratifying reaction to our work, over all of these years, is the comment from Professor Hadas Wiseman, current President of the Society for Psychotherapy Research, who said we were "the inventors of the study of therapist and counselor development."

We first met as doctoral students in 1971 at the University of Missouri, where we were trained to be practitioners, researchers, and teachers in psychology. Our advisors were Norm Gysbers for Helge and Joe Johnston for Tom. We have maintained these advising relationships for all of these decades. What a blessing for both of us. Norm and Joe are experts in career development and career psychology. They were instrumental in our tilting toward a research focus on the career development of counselors and therapists.

After graduation from Missouri, Helge returned home to Norway and a position at the University of Oslo, and Tom went first to the University of Florida for four years and then returned home to Minnesota and the University of Minnesota. For both of us, those early career years were full ones, with new families and new jobs. Both of us were teaching new courses, practicing as counselors and therapists, writing for journals, and presenting at conferences on a variety of topics, such as clinical hypnosis, counseling men, clinical supervision, guided imagery in career counseling, and cross-cultural counseling.

When we began our research on practitioner development, we benefited from Helge's exposure to qualitative methods, which have a strong standing in European psychology. These methods were seldom used in American psychology in the 1970s and 1980s. We began by interviewing 100 American counselors and therapists, from beginning graduate students to practitioners with 25 years of post-doctoral experience. In total, we did 160 interviews with this sample group. Both of us, along with a group of graduate students in Minnesota, conducted the interviews. It took many years to do the interviews and write up the results. At the same time, we were intensely involved in many other rewarding activities, such as becoming fathers. We published a book on the results, *The Evolving Professional Self*, in 1992. And we kept working on the topic, both together and with others.

Helge began a fruitful collaboration with David Orlinsky and a large global network of other collaborators. Using a questionnaire, they obtained results from a large international sample. This work resulted in a book, *How Psychotherapists Develop: A Study of Therapeutic Work and Professional Growth* (Orlinsky & Rønnestad, 2005). Helge is the initiator of a Norwegian psychotherapy process-outcome study of psychotherapy in which therapists who are also psychotherapy teachers participate (Rønnestad, 2008; Rønnestad, et al., 2014). He is also chair-elect in SPRISTAD, the Society for Psychotherapy Research Interest Section for the Study of Training and Development, a study that has enlisted the collaboration of more than 40 training institutions throughout the world.

During the time when Helge was working with David Orlinsky, Tom started working with doctoral advisees in studying master therapists. This resulted in a book: *Master Therapists* (Skovholt & Jennings, 2004). Tom also branched out into the topic of practitioner resiliency with two previous editions of the current book, *The Resilient Practitioner* (Skovholt, 2001; Skovholt & Trotter-Mathison, 2011). Tom also has been an examiner for over 50 oral exams for Board Certification by ABPP, a licensure for psychologists that is higher than state level. This enabled him to witness many talented practitioners interview clients. In this context, a high level of the working alliance, conceptual style, cognitive complexity, and affective engagement – all essential parts of mastery in the helping professions – was demonstrated.

All of this professional work mentioned above, plus much more, such as Helge's clinical supervision workshops in the Nordic countries, has been funneled into our latest book. We have incorporated the additional work of the international survey study, the master therapist interview studies, and the work on practitioner resiliency with our original N=100 qualitative interview study to form the book *The Developing Practitioner: Growth and Stagnation of Therapists and Counselors* (Rønnestad & Skovholt, 2013).

Now, in this present chapter, we will present this research with an emphasis on the re-analyses and revision of the results of the original study. (Note:

As with other chapters in this book, although we have focused our research on counselors and therapists, we also apply this research to a broader group by using these terms: *high-touch career fields* vs. *high-tech career fields*, *helping professions*, *practitioners*, *clinicians*, and *caring professions*; most recently, we have used the term *relationship-intense professions*. The common ingredient in these career fields is the strong focus on being helpful to the Other in an interpersonal way.)

One metaphor we use for the development of the practitioner is a journey on a path. This metaphor is not complete because professional development also can be described in other ways, such as through (1) periods of loops, (2) moratorium, and (3) sudden bursts caused by critical incidents or defining moments. Yet, we come back to the path metaphor because it captures some of the long, textured, journey-like reality of practitioner development.

For the beginner there is often, as described in other chapters of this book, a hope-prayer-wish that it doesn't take great effort and time to really get someplace in a complex domain. We wish this were so. Tom has often told novices that he wishes he could give them an injection of 10 years of experience to take away so much of the early confusion and distress. However, as you can see looking at the flow chart of development vs. stagnation in Figure 11.1, difficulties and challenges are – paradoxically – key to learning and growing in the relationship-intense professions.

Ah, one of the great human urges is to have the wisdom of the old, while still young! However, we know from our own lives as athletes, Helge on the Norwegian national alpine ski team and Tom as an American college basketball player, that complex skill development takes time and has no simple formulas. So that is what we promise here. Nothing simple, nothing quick, but a map of practitioner development . . . and we all know how great it is to have a map of the place you are searching for (via smartphone or other means).

We start the metaphor with a vision from American history. Ellis Island is an important place in American history. Situated near the Statue of Liberty, Ellis Island is where the early immigrant entered the new land. The immigrant had to first leave the homeland– often a painful decision. After finding and entering Ellis Island, the new immigrant would explore the land to find a place to live. For some, this meant a long road across the American landscape to a place later called home.

Entering a career in helping, teaching, or healing is like the immigrant experience. Who am I? Where do I fit? What do I want? What can I do well? What provides opportunity? These immigrant questions are also the questions for someone considering a caring profession. And like the new immigrant, the person seeking to enter a field cannot envision or understand the whole picture. Walking along a path, in life or in a career, is like a long hike on a challenging trail. It is step by step. As research colleagues, we have tried to describe the steps along the long hike.

This chapter is divided into three two sections: a section describing themes of professional growth, another describing phases of practitioner development, and a third mainly from Helge's work in graphic form. Earlier versions of this chapter were published in the first and second editions of this book.

THEMES IN PROFESSIONAL DEVELOPMENT

Organizing content according to phases, which we describe later, has advantages and disadvantages. One disadvantage is that the phase concept, although not as much as the stage concept, seems to communicate breaks between time periods; however, in real life, change is more gradual, like with seasons. To combat the disadvantages of phases, we have also organized the content according to themes, which comprise this section of the chapter.

Theme 1: Professional development involves an increasing higher-order integration of the professional self and the personal self

How do I improve and get better at the work, you may ask? First, we can ask how competence develops. There are many ways: watching practitioners develop, reading the research literature, working as a practitioner, teaching novices, and supervising them – all of these activities, and more, are part of the slow evolutionary growth that leads to practitioner competence.

If we were to hike together on the long, textured career path, we would come across experienced hikers, each with his or her own style of hiking. The stride, pace, body slope, and use of a walking stick could vary greatly among hikers. With time and experience, a hiker develops an individual style. So do practitioners. It is, in fact, the process of developing an individual style that is so important to practitioner identity. The embracing of a unique, individual style can, we believe, be an important factor in career vitality. Let us mention the long career of the great painter Georgia O'Keeffe. Her work changed as she changed, and with it, her originality emerged (Lisle, 1987). In its optimal expression, integration involves a process akin to Rogers's (1957) concept of congruence, where experiences are consistent with the (professional) self-concept.

Although it may seem simple and painless, the winnowing of the professional self can be difficult. It involves the merging of one's values, theoretical beliefs, and skills. It involves shedding values, beliefs, and skills that no longer fit and adding others. Like hiking, this individuation process requires constant effort. This individuation process is done through a two-sided process of aloneness and connection and is similar to the work of Grotevant and Cooper's (1986) individuation process. Their definition includes both the "qualities of individuality and connectedness" (p. 89). Recent work on individuation is from Blatt (2008), who described the two polarities of experience as relatedness and self-definition.

In our research interviews, we have observed numerous expressions of movements toward better integration. Examples include therapists and counselors who have changed their theoretical orientations. The older method, perhaps very well known, is discarded or radically modified to fit with the practitioner's emerging identity. There may have been significant and transforming events in their personal lives. As a result, professional and personal identity is altered, with a necessary integration between them.

Theme 2: The focus of functioning shifts dramatically over time, from internal to external to internal

There are three parts of this theme that describe changes over time in the practitioner's development:

1   *Pretraining* – The conventional mode. Just as hikers hike without instruction, so do untrained helpers, teachers, and healers, who operate according to conventional and nonprofessional ways of helping, teaching, and healing. Natural rules and personal experience govern role, working style, and methods used.

During this period, the individual operates from a commonsense base. Behaviors and conceptions of helping, teaching, and healing reflect each individual's interpretation of effective ways; ways that are fueled by both personal dispositions and popular ways of doing it. For example, for the lay helper, some characteristics of conventional helping in our culture are to define the problem quickly, to provide strong emotional support, to provide sympathy as contrasted to empathy, and to give advice based on one's own experience. There is a personal base of helping that contributes to helping being experienced as authentic and natural.

2   *Training* – The external, rigid mode. Suddenly, the path meets a bridge between the lay world of high-touch work and the high-touch professions. On the other side of the bridge, there are experts in professional hiking who strongly believe in only using certain methods, skills, attitudes, and approaches. These experts teach people to be qualified for practitioner fields (such as counseling, advising, social work, psychotherapy, human resource development, elementary and secondary teaching, college teaching, nursing, physical therapy, and medicine). All of these fields attempt to help people, although the focus may vary greatly.

After basic training, Marine recruits are suddenly enveloped by the right way to do things. So too are recruits to the high-touch professions after they cross the bridge. The recruit's reaction to criticism of lay methods is to try to do everything correctly according to professional standards. We call this the external, rigid mode. The novice helper, teacher, or healer is often trying desperately to do things the correct way to pass through gates and jump over hurdles on the training part of the path. This is an exhausting process that takes much of the person's energy.

Behavior becomes less natural or loose and more rigid. The use of humor may be seen as an index of this movement from natural and loose/flexible in pretraining to nonnatural and rigid during training and back to natural and flexible with more professional experience. Use of humor typically disappears for the student practitioner, to reappear later with the professional self-confidence of the experienced practitioner.

3   *Posttraining* – The loosening, internal mode. *Commencement* celebrates the end of school, but the term really means the beginning. Now, the practitioner begins the self-directed professional development process. During this long period after training, which lasts decades, there is a moving away from prescribed ways taught during the externalizing period. There is shedding and adding as part of the sculpting of the professional self.

Theme 3: Continuous reflection is a prerequisite for optimal learning and professional development at all levels of experience

Learning from experience, a powerful possibility, is not always a reality. Professional experience does not always increase expertise. Why, you may ask. There seem to be two routes on the path. The practitioner can have years of experience – rich, textured, illuminating, practice-changing professional experience in a helping, teaching, or health occupation. Or a person can have one year of experience repeated over and over. This happens because feedback from the work with clients, students, or patients is not used to transform practice.

As will be described in more detail later, the ability and willingness to reflect upon one's professional experiences in general and on challenges and hardships in particular is a prerequisite to avoid the stagnant process that ensures a mismatch between competence and task. A stimulating and supportive work environment, including informal dialogues among colleagues and informal supervision, impact the reflective capacity and adaptive handling of the challenges encountered. The concepts of scaffolding (Wood, Bruner, & Ross, 1976) and proximal zone of development (Vygotsky, 1962) may inform us of the supportive and relational conditions that stimulate reflection, learning, and development at all levels.

In our view, valuable learning from experience, a wonderful part of the practitioner years, only occurs when three conditions are present:

1   *Professional and personal experience* – Researchers of expertise development (Chi, Glaser, & Farr, 1988) studied chess players, taxi drivers, and physicians and concluded that experience is essential to develop expertise in a domain.

So one ingredient of increased competence is experience in the domain. Some teachers in a domain (e.g., counseling, teaching, health care) also practice. Others do not and risk teaching in a way that is not effectively honed by practice.

2   *Open, supportive work environment* – A dogmatic work environment, one where certain truth is already known, does not permit the essential searching process. The novice in such an environment quickly learns that certain answers are better than others. Whereas some certainty and structure are helpful in sorting out the complex, ambiguous data of the work, too much leads to a process that we call pseudodevelopment. Administrative and supervisor support for an open work climate is an important feature. In such a setting, the practitioner can bring in the data from the work and dwell with it.

3   *Reflective stance* – "Dwelling with it" is called reflectivity in the literature on professional development (Neufeldt et.al, 1996). This dwelling means thinking about, pondering, considering, and processing the reality of the profound experience of meeting with a client, student, or patient. The reflective stance is well described by Benner and Wrubel (1982):

> Experience is necessary for moving from one level of expertise to another, but experience is not the equivalent of longevity, seniority, or the simple passage of time. Experience means living through actual situations in such a way that it informs the practitioner's perception and understanding of all subsequent situations.
>
> (p. 28)

One challenge to the dwelling is the frantic work pace for many practitioners. If one is so busy doing, there is no chance to be. Yet, it is the being that produces the chance to learn. The clinical supervision process, if done right, also provides an environment for reflection. Later in this chapter, you will see that reflection has a pivotal position in a revised model of therapist and counselor development (Rønnestad & Skovholt, 2013). In our revision, we are also extending Schön's (1987) concepts of reflection-in-action and reflection-on-action, by adding reflection-pre-action, the preparatory planning activity that precedes therapy/counseling sessions.

Theme 4: An intense commitment to learn propels the developmental process

The practitioner's own motivation to grow professionally is an important fuel that propels professional development. Hiking along the professional path depends on the hiker actually doing the hiking. Most of our research informants, whether students or practitioners, impressed us with an attitude of reflective awareness and an eagerness to learn and develop. Trying new ways of hiking, going down side routes to explore and try to improve – these are important for professional growth. Commitment to learn and willingness within ethical boundaries to take risks and to be open to new learning are building blocks of increased professional functioning.

Our informants told us of periods of moratorium, times when they needed to stop and rest, to not keep going forward. We came to see these rest periods – these times of moratorium – as positive. Although the achievement culture of training programs and the professions focus on excellence and lots of it, there is also an important place for dwelling in a place for a time before going on. The sequence of hiking–rest–hiking–rest–hiking is well known to those who make long-term progress on the trail. We also learned of periods of stagnation and decline, but most reports conveyed a message of an urgency, commitment, and intensity in motivation to develop professionally.

Research and writing on master therapists (Jennings et al., 2008; Jennings & Skovholt, in press; Kottler & Carlson, 2014) has shown a continual motivation to grow professionally for these colleague-nominated experts. This is also the case with an international sample of practitioners. Research within the Collaborative Research Network (Orlinsky et al., 1999) has shown that therapists' sense of currently experienced professional growth did not decline as a function of years in practice. Survey responses of therapists with two or more decades of professional experience also reported a sense of growth characterized by experiences of improving, becoming skillful, and feeling a growing sense of enthusiasm about doing therapy. The researcher interpretation of the results was that "therapists' sense of currently experienced growth reflects a renewal of the morale and motivation needed to practice therapy, a replenishment of the energy and refreshing of the acumen demanded by therapeutic work" (Orlinsky et al., 1999, p. 212).

Theme 5: The cognitive map changes; beginning practitioners rely on external expertise, seasoned practitioners rely on internal expertise

A wonderful reality gradually emerges for the practitioner as he or she hikes down the path over the years. Instruction books on hiking are gradually discarded as the practitioner discovers a self-developed method that works. Over a long period of time and great effort, lessons from the instruction books are combined with the rich knowledge gained from one's own hiking.

You may ask what has happened. We contend that external expertise has been replaced by internal expertise. It is a positive change in a practitioner's professional life. Experience-based generalizations and accumulated wisdom have replaced global theory developed by others. There is a rich literature in the study of expertise, which helps us understand the path from novice to master (Ericsson, 2007; Ericsson, Charness, Feltovich, & Hoffman, 2006) with Colvin (2010) and Gladwell (2008) writing more popular books on this topic. Expertise entails a "rich structure of domain specific knowledge" (Glaser & Chi, 1988, p. xxi). The practitioner now has this expertise after hundreds of hours of practice in a domain and the active use of reflection about that practice. Using Winston Churchill's words from a more extreme situation, it has come from "blood, sweat and toil."

Dreyfus and Dreyfus (1986) describe this progression from external to internal expertise as:

> the progression from the analytic behavior of a detached subject, consciously decomposing his environment into recognizable elements, and following abstract rules, to involved skilled behavior based on an accumulation of concrete experiences and the unconscious recognition of new situations as similar to whole remembered ones.
>
> (p. 35)

From looking for external guidance to looking for internal guidance, this is one of the most profound ways that the hiking of the practitioner is altered during the long time on the path. Another way of saying this is that there is movement from received knowledge toward constructed knowledge. Belenky, Chinchy, Goldberger, and Tarule (1986) have formulated a model for understanding the evolution in knowledge development that we have observed. Anchoring their model in Perry's (1981) model of cognitive meaning and development, they described seven levels of ways of knowing. Received knowledge is the entry level, and constructed knowledge is the highest of seven levels of knowing. Beginning practitioners, as new students, seem to fit the entry level: "While received knowers can be very open to take in what others have to offer, they have very little confidence in their own ability to speak. Believing that truth comes from others, they still their own voices to hear the voices of others" (Belenky et al., 1986, p. 37). Senior practitioners seem to fit the highest level.

> All knowledge is constructed, and the knower is an intimate part of the known. . . . To see that all knowledge is a construction and that truth is a matter of the context in which it is embedded is to greatly expand the possibilities of how to think about anything . . . theories become not truth but models for approximate experience.
>
> (Belenky et al., 1986, pp. 137–139)

This movement from external expertise to internal expertise profoundly affects the practitioner's functioning.

Theme 6: Optimal professional development is a long, slow, and erratic process

Lewis and Clark had quite an adventure in their journey across the American frontier. Ambrose (1996) describes this adventure of making a path through the wilderness. Sometimes things went well for these explorers; other times there was great uncertainty and danger. Hardship could always be around the next corner. A route would appear and then disappear, and it took so much time for them to progress. In the end, however, they traversed the American continent.

Each practitioner, like Lewis or Clark, encounters a similar long, slow, and erratic trek on the professional development path. It takes a long time to make real progress. The development of expertise in the complexity of difficult human work takes hours. Understanding the reality of the long journey can help pale the coupled novice feelings of frantic insecurity and lusting for quick competence. The practitioner generally experiences professional development as a continual increase in competence and mastery. Our data suggest that this process may at any point in time be barely noticeable but appear as substantial in the retrospective view.

The practitioner's pace through his or her own developmental wilderness is also erratic. Sometimes the change process is slow, other times rapid. For example, there are recycling loops of anxiety, self-doubt, and feelings of dejection that come and go. Critical incidents (Skovholt & McCarthy, 1988) or defining moments (Trotter-Mathison, Koch, Sanger, & Skovholt, 2010) often produce rapid development. Piaget (1972) calls the overall change in cognitive complexity "assimilation" followed by "accommodation."

Theme 7: Professional development is a lifelong process

This theme follows closely on the previous one. Commencement is thought to be an end. Actually, the word means the beginning. And this is true for professional development. When formal school is over, one is now in charge of one's own development. The postgraduate years are crucial for optimal development. The importance of the postgraduate years was a notable result of our research – so much literature concentrates on student growth. It reminds us of human development models that emphasize the early years without much attention to the events of adult life. For example, Freud's last stage covered all events from adolescence to the senior years.

Many models of development within the counseling and therapy professions are in fact models of student development. "Little is known about the postgraduate counselor . . . Such studies are necessary for a complete understanding of counselor development across the professional life span" (Borders, 1989, p. 21).

Major changes in many aspects of work and the professional self happen after graduation. Practitioners improve their competence, handle difficulties and challenges more adequately, and become more skillful in regulating responsibilities. In addition, senior activities such as being a mentor, supervisor, or teacher fuel professional growth.

This concentration on student growth makes it appear that most of the path is walked during those days; however, the reality is more like Lewis and

Clark. In the first weeks of their trek across the American continent, they got started, but that was about it. The cold winter of 1805 was ahead, as was dysentery and a grizzly attack. So was seeing, for the first time in the same week, the grandeur of the great falls of the Missouri River and the beauty of the Rocky Mountains (Ambrose, 1996). If the practitioner trek is more a marathon than a sprint, it is important for those who want to achieve higher levels of competence to understand it this way, as a lifelong process.

Theme 8: Many beginning practitioners experience much anxiety in their professional work; over time, anxiety is mastered by most

Like tiny seeds prudently sown and nurtured, professional experience in helping, teaching, and healing can lead to a rich harvest. The harvest brings a competent practitioner who can skillfully perform multiple professional tasks. One result of the harvest is a major decline in performance anxiety from novice to senior practitioner.

Many elements combine to increase performance anxiety in the beginner. Examples are a lack of professional knowledge, the high achievement expectations of the academic culture, and the fear of being unsuited for the work ("imposter syndrome"). One practitioner, looking back, told us he was so scared he barely heard what the client was saying. The anxiety of the beginner has been discussed by many authors since Robinson's description of social work trainees in 1936 (as cited in Gysbers & Rønnestad, 1974). With increasing experience and an accompanying sense of mastery and expertise, anxiety levels diminish markedly. One greatly respected senior informant told us in the research interview: "In time you are no longer afraid of your clients." (Skovholt & Rønnestad, 1992a, p. 96). Describing the underpinnings for the decline in anxiety and increase in confidence, Martin, Slemon, Hiebert, Halberg, and Cummings (1989) say that the work "equips seasoned practitioners with efficient sets of schema that they consistently draw on . . . These schemata probably have tremendous practical advantages in both economy of time and energy and felt confidence" (p. 399).

Theme 9: Clients, students, or patients serve as a major source of influence and serve as primary teachers

It may sound strange to talk of the client as teacher. The practitioner is the teacher, not the other way around. So, you may ask: "What does this mean?" Here we are talking about the professional relationship between the practitioner and the Other. In their interactions, the client, student, or patient constantly gives feedback. This is the source of "teaching by the client" for the practitioner. As one experienced practitioner told Tom, "If you really listen, you can really learn a lot from those you are trying to help about what helps." In fact, our sample group emphatically told us that their clients served as primary teachers. This is also supported by other research such as a study of therapists from 20 countries (Orlinsky, Botermans, & Rønnestad, 2001). In this study, experience in therapy with clients was rated as the most important source of influence for professional development.

By extension, students and patients serve the same primary role. People-oriented practitioners usually do not talk about learning so directly from the Other in the high-touch professional interaction. Of course, the learning has to be in an ethical context. The reaction of the client, student, or patient, however, continually gives data for reflection.

Openness to the feedback, especially when the data is part of the "series of humiliations" experienced by all practitioners, is critical. Otherwise, the Other is a mute teacher, and nothing is heard.

A common major crisis, often in the beginning years, involves the use of a major, highly valued approach in the field. The novice works hard to learn the approach and then energetically applies it. The result is often disappointment, not success. The practitioner senses the poor result because the client, student, or patient does not change. As part of growing, the practitioner must struggle with this stressful information. This is an example, often painful but valuable, of how the client, student, or patient serves as a primary teacher.

The counseling/therapy room, the classroom, the doctor's office – these are all laboratories for learning. Client, student, or patient reactions continually influence the practitioner. Through the close interpersonal contact, the feedback provided adds intensity to the learning process. Negative feedback can impact how practitioners understand what is working and what is not.

Although often difficult, learning to listen to negative client, student, or patient feedback is especially important in order to fully use the client as teacher for professional development. Of course, positive feedback from the client, student, or patient is valuable, too. And how nice and empowering it is to get this kind of feedback.

Theme 10: Personal life is a central component of professional functioning

How do we know? Where does the knowledge come from? In professional fields like psychotherapy and counseling, teaching, and health care, knowledge is said to come from empirical research studies. And it does. However, there are other powerful areas, too, including, as mentioned, clients, students, and patients as teachers. Now with the present theme, we are discussing another source of knowledge, another epistemology. In these high-touch human fields, the practitioner also learns from her or his own life.

In the people-oriented fields, the practitioner's own personal life is highly influential. Motivation for entering the work, for example, often has a personal part. Many novices are inspired by someone close to them, such as a relative. Some also receive assistance from a caring and competent practitioner in therapy, education, or physical health at a critical point. Examples here are the college student, at a point of emotional anguish, greatly helped by a skilled therapist; the junior high student awash in an unstable home empowered by a towering teacher; and the child elevated from illness by a dedicated nurse. Motivation to enter professional training may also come from personal pain, like those borne by people who have witnessed the devastation of parental alcoholism or seen acute physical illness steal life away from a loved one.

These examples concern just one personal element – motivation for work in the helping professions. Throughout one's career, personal life keeps swirling around the practitioner. Bountiful lessons come from the practitioner's normative life events, such as one's personal aging march through life. Each decade provides so many lessons about emotional, intellectual, or physical development. Equally instructive are the unusual realities, such as acute loss (e.g., job loss) or glorious success (e.g., an award for competence). For optimal professional development, the practitioner illuminates, reflects on, and uses these ongoing personal realities in a highly instructive, nonbiased way to improve his or her work.

The impacts of personal life on professional functioning were clearly demonstrated as we interviewed the most experienced therapists for the second time, when they averaged 74 years old. Two of the learning arenas that we identified and described were in personal life domains. They were profound impact of early life experience and profound personal experiences in adult life (Rønnestad & Skovholt, 2001). Adversities and crises in adult personal life were seen to exert an immediate negative influence on professional functioning. Sometimes personal suffering increases professional sensitivity. In our work, we found this to be particularly so for suffering in the adult years. Examples of intense personal experiences that in the long run were instructive include death of spouse and children, physical disability, or severe psychological impairment of members of family. Examples of positive consequences were increased ability to understand and relate to clients, increased tolerance and patience, heightened credibility as a model, and greater awareness of what is effective helping. Marriage was often described as highly sustaining, with supportive and caring spouses convincingly portrayed as impactful. Reports of life and marital satisfaction were associated with the way therapists related to clients. The generality of these findings is supported in a recent study of Norwegian therapists (Nissen-Lie, Havik, Høglend, Monsen, & Rønnestad, 2013). This study documented a significant relationship between the quality of therapists' personal life and both clients' and therapists' rating of the working alliance (p. 483):

> It seems that patients are particularly sensitive to their therapists' private life experience of distress, which presumably is communicated through the therapists' in-session behaviors, whereas the therapists' judgments of alliance quality were positively biased by their own sense of personal well-being.

Theme 11: Interpersonal encounters are more influential than impersonal data

In the people-oriented professions, where intense people contact and caring about the Other are central, it is not surprising that the drama of human contact is a great teacher. In fact, we were told many times by our sample group that interpersonal encounters were more instructive than the theory and research of the profession. Meaningful contact with people was the catalyst for growth. People most often mentioned were clients, professional elders (i.e., supervisors, personal therapists, professors, mentors), professional peers, friends, family members, and, later in one's career, younger colleagues.

When interviewing our informants and examining the impact of different sources of influence at different levels of professional functioning, strong human relationships emerged as more important than impersonal data. When asking in the interviews about the impact of theories and research, we thought that theory and research would be perceived as of central importance for subjects' development. However, in the interviews, the subjects kept telling us most about person impact and least about empirical research results.

For our informants as a group, person impact in the work context occurred in this order: clients as most impactful, then professional elders, then peers, then being a professional elder for others. Of course, there is a great variety across individuals in their ranking of person impact. In time, being a professional elder can also be very impactful for the individual. Theory and research is often mediated through these individuals, and in this way, both people and theory/research are of importance.

Theme 12: Newer members of the field view professional elders and graduate training with strong affective reactions

Professional elders are of extreme importance to new members in any helping, teaching, or healing career field. Beginners are often dependent on more established members (i.e., clinical supervisors, professors, mentors, more experienced peers) of the field for career advancement and feel vulnerable to their judgment. Students are continually scrutinizing and evaluating professors, teachers, and supervisors. Students want to learn from and model seniors they see as competent. Professors and supervisors are seen as having the power to control students' entry into the profession.

This sense of power difference and vulnerability contributes to tendencies by the novice to either idealize or devalue more senior members. Students admire practitioners who are more advanced and have characteristics such as intellectual brilliance, strong therapeutic skills, outstanding supervision ability, unusual emotional support for beginners, and the modeling of professional values in personal life.

Our research showed that negative reactions to professional elders were just as common and intense. Students tend to devalue some seniors with the same intensity that they idealize others. Being in a dependent and relatively low power position is the fuel that propels the sometimes strong reaction. Professional elders are devalued if they possess behaviors perceived as highly negative. These include individuals such as a supervisor who is perceived as unfairly critical or a professor who teaches content but seems unable to practice it.

In time, and with more experience and less dependency in the novice, seniors are viewed with less affective intensity. In time, the younger practitioner, usually years later, may go through normative transitions in the way most regard parents: from idealizing the parent as a child, through devaluating/criticizing parents as an adolescent, to seeing the parent as a person with all the ordinary humanness of people in general. Beyond graduate school, professional elders are idealized and devalued less, and their humanness (ordinariness, strengths/weaknesses, uniqueness) is more clearly seen.

Training programs also receive intense scrutiny by students of the helping professions. The student's roller coaster of feelings often starts with a peak of excitement and idealization, leading to a valley of strong disappointment later in training. This disappointment often occurs when the beginner feels unprepared for the rigors of performing (i.e., a first clinical practicum in counseling, the first days of practice teaching with classes of eighth-grade students, having an appointment with patients as a new medical resident).

Most practitioners experience some disillusionment regarding their graduate education and training. Participants report a strong expectation to be taught specifically and concretely about how to do the work, an expectation that is often not met. A common question from students, often seasoned by frustration, when newly trying to teach, give health care, or counsel is: Why didn't they train us better for this?

Here we are addressing the classic gap between theory and practice in all the relationship-intense professions, where there is intense human interaction and helping of the Other as a core activity. If the work were simply doing something to the Other, like using a can of spray paint to change the color of an object, precise instructions could be delineated. However, in the people-oriented professions, there is interaction with the Other that is like a complex multiple-person art form. Theory cannot translate directly to practice. It takes time, lots of time, to learn how to do the work. Professors know this painful gap is one that all students go through, just as they themselves did. Disappointment and disillusionment come to the student when the theory–practice gap is experienced. Good clinical supervision seems to buffer against the student confusion caused by the theory–practice gap. Long after graduation, the roller coaster hills and valleys usually diminish and are replaced with a more objective – some good parts, some not so good – evaluation of graduate training.

In a more general way, how can we describe the commonalities where students struggle with the theory–practice gap? Here we are talking of fields that are very different yet very similar, such as nursing, addiction counseling, medicine, elementary school teaching, physical therapy, and the ministry. One analysis of the characteristics of these people-oriented professions suggests some common aspects. These aspects are (1) the process of change takes place in a *relationship* between the professional, student, or patient; (2) the process of change can be conceptualized as *communicative practice*; (3) the process of change can be conceptualized as *emotional practice*; and (4) the professional practice requires the professional to exercise an *ethical responsibility*. There is reason to believe that these commonalities make it particularly demanding to acquire, maintain, and develop a high level of professional competence within these professions (Rønnestad, 2008). These four characteristics help explain why students cannot simply and directly apply theory in their work and why there can be so much frustration for students as they struggle to become competent.

Theme 13: Extensive experience with suffering contributes to heightened recognition, acceptance, and appreciation of human variability

With the passing of professional and personal time and all the experiences life brings, the practitioner usually becomes less judgmental of others. The practitioner has been a witness to so many intense lived moments with clients, students, or patients. The practitioner has seen many attempts by the Other and many resolutions to make improvements in the domain (emotional, intellectual, or physical) needing change. The practitioner's own life has also been a school in which the lessons have usually produced a more understanding stance toward self and others.

Contributing to wisdom is an awareness of the unpredictability of life, uncertainties as to the best way to handle difficult life situations (Baltes & Smith, 1990), and increased tolerance for human variability. Research on the development of wisdom suggests that the self-evaluation and self-acceptance that follow the inner-directed life review process contribute to wisdom (Hartmann, 2001). Interviews with our research informants suggest that insight, introspection, and reflection contribute to the development of wisdom as conceptualized by Erikson (1950). Our informants, especially when we interviewed senior informants a second time when they were in their 70s, told us of the varieties of personal and professional experiences that have combined to influence them in unique and diverse ways (Rønnestad & Skovholt, 2001).

Theme 14: For the practitioner, there is a realignment from self as hero to client as hero

Practitioners in the helping professions enter the fields of helping, education, and health to positively impact the Other. It is a central motivation for being drawn to these occupations. Entering the work world, the new student is unsure of the amount of emotional, intellectual, or physical improvement there will be for the client, student, or patient. Drawn to the field, some new students make an error in believing that the work can bring change more quickly and more completely than is realistic. It takes a long time for the practitioner to sort out the realistic from the ideal. This error is often coupled with a belief that one may possess a strong helping impulse – one that can really make a difference, meaning a belief by the practitioner that he or she can be an instrument for wondrous change. In time, there is a more textured understanding of the change process, with the practitioner being only one part of success.

With experience of both failures and successes with a large variety of clients, students, and patients, there is a gradual shift in understanding the change process. This change can be formulated as a movement from practitioner power to client power. This shift in attitude parallels the emphasis in the contemporary psychotherapy literature of the heroic client by Duncan and Miller (2000). Although practitioners feel more confident and assured as professionals with the passing of time, they also experience a "series of humiliations" that contribute to increased realism as to what can be accomplished in professional work. If these "blows to the ego" are processed and integrated into the practitioner's self-experience, they may contribute to the paradox of increased sense of confidence and competence while also feeling more humble and less powerful as a practitioner. This general movement is also similar to how Skovholt and Jennings (2004) describe master therapists.

Commentary

In a reformulation of a conceptual model of therapist and counselor development that includes themes of development, (Rønnestad & Skovholt, 2013), we have collapsed some themes and added another (Not All Therapists/Counselors Develop Optimally), and we have suggested ways to understand why some therapists develop optimally and others do not. In a revised model, three potential *trajectories* may be taken by individual therapists as they move through each developmental phase. How challenges are met decides movements within and between developmental phases, which will be described below. These movements are largely determined by the therapist's capacity for and engagement in *reflection*, which requires capacities such as tolerance for ambiguity, cognitive complexity, openness to experience, and ability to process negative affect. Productive reflection facilitates *functional closure*, which in turn fuels continued development. This involves organizing relevant information hierarchically, in a way that enables therapists to respond effectively to their clients. Alternatively, *premature closure* and *inadequate closure* result in stagnation. *Premature closure* is a defensive process that sets in when therapists' competencies are insufficient to handle the challenges they encounter. Characteristics of

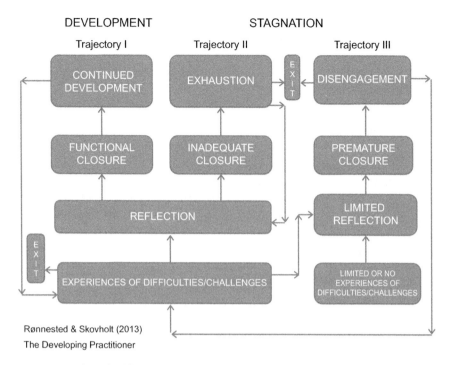

DEVELOPMENT   STAGNATION

Trajectory I   Trajectory II   Trajectory III

CONTINUED DEVELOPMENT   EXHAUSTION   EXIT   DISENGAGEMENT

FUNCTIONAL CLOSURE   INADEQUATE CLOSURE   PREMATURE CLOSURE

REFLECTION   LIMITED REFLECTION

EXIT   EXPERIENCES OF DIFFICULTIES/CHALLENGES   LIMITED OR NO EXPERIENCES OF DIFFICULTIES/CHALLENGES

Rønnested & Skovholt (2013)
The Developing Practitioner

Figure 11.1 A cyclical/trajectories model of counselor and therapist development

premature closure are (a) misattribution (e.g., the therapist may unjustifiably define client drop-out as the client not being motivated for therapy), (b) distortion (e.g., therapist misunderstands the client), or (c) over-simplification of phenomena when difficulties are encountered. *Inadequate closure* refers to therapists' inability to integrate and synthesize their experiences sufficiently to arrive at an understanding of the client that makes possible a constructive therapeutic response. This involves a lack of capacity to differentiate essential from inessential information, and thus an inability to organize information hierarchically.

Figure 11.1 shows a graphic description of development vs. stagnation, which is more fully described in Rønnestad and Skovholt (2013).

PHASES OF PRACTITIONER DEVELOPMENT

One way to understand human development is to think in stages, such as the classic stages described by Freud, Piaget, and Erikson. Usually, the stage perspective describes changes that occur suddenly and sequentially. Many stage models are not suited to capturing changes that occur gradually, continually, or chaotically; however, for many human realities, there are no sudden shifts as suggested by stage models. Stage models have strengths and limitations.

In our first formulation, we did use the stage concept. In our reformulations (Rønnestad & Skovholt, 2003), we have been using the term *phase* to indicate less abrupt changes. We hope that the following descriptions of the phases in our model will be of use for you in understanding your own development as a practitioner.

Phase 1: The lay helper phase

In roles as parents, friends, sisters, brothers, grandparents, children, colleagues, and volunteers, people help other people. Looking at this picture through a historic and cross-cultural lens, we see patterns of counseling, therapy, teaching, and healing where kin, rather than professionals, fill these roles. For generation after generation, people have cared for each other emotionally and given guidance and advice, usually through relationships of blood, marriage, or friendship. In these worlds, parents, older siblings, and other relatives are the primary teachers of children. Health care, as in first aid, is also given by those close to a person.

In recent years, in a variety of countries, as kin relationships have loosened, professional helping, teaching, and healing occupations have grown. Also, volunteer and paraprofessional relationships of giving through helping, teaching, and healing have increased. These are not primarily blood related. In the United States, for example, most adults volunteer in the community in one capacity or another. Across cultures and across time, there have been different patterns of non-professional caring. Here, we attempt to describe this pattern of helping, teaching, and healing in the lay helper phase.

The central task in the lay helper phase is to use one's abilities and skills to be helpful to the Other. The lay helper often identifies the problem quickly, which contrasts with the expert in the helping fields, who often takes considerable time to identify the problem. It may be that the expert is processing so much data about the problem that it takes longer to really understand it. Quick problem identification for the lay helper is often accompanied by strong emotional support and advice.

Although individuals without professional training in helping populate this phase, the goal is still quite close to that of the caring professions – giving to the Other emotional, educational, or health help. Perhaps this is because of kinship obligations, close relationship connections, or a sense of wanting to be a successful volunteer.

Usually there is sympathy toward the Other and an interest in assisting the Other. The sympathy of the lay helper, a feeling sorry for the Other, may have a component of overidentification with the Other and a getting lost in the sympathy. Sympathy can feel enveloping for the lay helper.

This is in contrast to the empathy of the professional helper. Empathy consists of a temporary identification with the Other. One definition of empathy is from Bohart et al. (2002): "The therapist's sensitive ability and willingness to understand the client's thoughts, feelings and struggles from the client's point of view" (p. 85). One is not the Other; there is more of an as-if quality rather than being lost in the sympathy. This as-if formulation from Rogers (1957) suggests the separation of the self from the Other. Regulating emotional engagement is a characteristic of professional empathy.

Sometimes the lay helper does not have an emotional investment in the helping of the Other. There is more of a distance than an overwhelming connection to the Other's problems. The advice will come from the lay helper's own personal life. Knowledge, perspective, and approach come from what life, in one way or another, has taught a person. For example, a young woman who is having trouble with her boyfriend turns to a female friend for help. Often, the friend will give advice based on her own life experience. It is a kind of "based on my life, here is what to do" approach. As much as the friend's life offers useful help, then the lay helper phase approach is useful. It also has limits, however, because the friend's helping method and solution, based on her own life, may not be a "glove that fits." The same principle of competence to assist another coming from one's life experience governs other helping efforts, such as teaching a child to read, helping an adult to be happy, or offering spiritual guidance.

It is common, without professional training in the helping fields, to project one's own experiences and one's own solutions on to the life of the Other. The lay helper often gives answers, and these can have a base in the notion of common sense. There will usually not be a self-consciousness or reflectivity about the helping process. Rather, there will be a naturalness in the whole process. For example, when a person is unsure whether to take one path or another, the lay helper may say, "This is what I did. Try that," or give romantic advice like "You are better off without him," or "Keep trying."

At the lay helper phase, there is usually less self-awareness of the concerns that students in professional training programs have, like "Am I doing this right?" or "Am I any good at this work?" At the beginning student phase there is often an acute self-consciousness about performing in a helping role in a professional way. Here, there is a more relaxed, commonsense approach to both the work method and evaluation of success.

Phase 2: Beginning student phase

The people-oriented professions are marked by an unusual paradox. The core work of these careers is reserved for only a few yet open to all. For example, the psychotherapist consoles a person enveloped in intense grief. So does the sister, father, or friend. An essential reason for the large overlap between exclusive and inclusive is the core work of caring for the Other. The career essential of caring for the Other is the occupational glue in the people-oriented professions.

Of course, caring for the Other is also the glue that marks the human bond in families, friendships, and volunteer activities. There is the overlap.

The beginning student phase is the bridge from a land of the known lay helper phase to the land of the complex professional world of intense training and exacting standards. By entering the beginning student phase, the student is crossing the bridge to the professional field. By doing so, the person is volunteering to give up old ways of thinking, acting, and feeling in order to learn the professionally correct methods, whatever they are. In this phase, there is a movement from open to all to reserved for just some (from inclusive to exclusive). These movements are exemplified by teaching a child to count (open to all) to teaching linguistic theory to university students (reserved for some). This phase is marked first by the transition from the known to the unknown. The known is the conventional way that the lay helper functions as a helper, teacher, or healer, and the unknown is the prescribed ways of a profession, such as mental health counseling, secondary teaching, or nursing.

While crossing the bridge, the professional novice-to-be is often filled with excitement and enthusiasm. The person has chosen this field for advanced training, perhaps in part because of positive volunteer experiences, and looks forward to learning new skills. There is also worry about an unpredictable and unknown future.

The approach to this phase and the movement through it and other phases are influenced by age and life experience. An older person with experience in a people-oriented profession will move through the training stages faster than a younger person with less life experience. A 40-year-old explained how she was different than a 23-year-old when beginning a graduate training program:

> Perhaps part of this is a function of being older and already having two careers which have been rewarding and engrossing for me: teacher and mother. From these I have brought the knowledge that I could work effectively with people . . . I also have the notion that in any field there are many theories and that I can comfortably pick and choose and combine elements.*
>
> (Skovholt & Rønnestad, 1992a, p. 25)

When school begins, the new student is exposed to theories, ideas, perspectives, facts, approaches, and visions. This formal schooling brings new information cascading onto the student. Two elements, self-assessment of skill level and theoretical approaches, absorb the novice's time and attention. What is first welcomed quickly becomes overwhelming. Suddenly, there is so much to learn and know. One student said, "There was too much data, too many conflicting ideas, and the techniques learned in class seemed kind of wooden and sometimes made things worse."

> (p. 27)

Having a first client is a sign of moving from the known of the lay helper role to the unknown of the professional role. The student often feels the chasm between theory and practice. Questions such as "How do you keep talking for a whole hour?" are very important at this point. The beginning student can be preoccupied with trying to apply classroom methods to actual practice and finds it difficult to do so.

Two influential groups in training are one's teachers and one's peers. Both of these groups begin to exert a strong influence on the beginning student. In addition, both the new ideas and the new people serve as catalysts for the novice's life review. The past begins to be examined through a new lens. This is especially true for some occupations such as family therapy, where one's family of origin is examined in new ways, and teaching, where one's own teachers are examined as models of teaching.

In trying on the professional role, a person is often eager but unsure. One student said, "I was very motivated to be in the right saddle but didn't know what that saddle felt like" (p. 26). Another said, "If I don't have success I get disillusioned with myself" (p. 29). In time, the transition to professional immersion is not as raw and new.

The counselor, therapist, teacher, or health professional is now into professional schooling, which provides so much new information – research, theory, technique, skill, and approach – that the student is swimming in it, swimming in a swirling pool that is rising and growing in strength. The possibility of drowning in the professional newness can be a suddenly felt threat. In reaction, the helping professional-in-training often searches for a life vest to use in the swirling water, turmoil, and confusion. Two popular life vests are (1) modeling oneself after an expert and (2) searching for an understandable theoretical model that explains the confusion about human beings. Questions can be: How do people develop problems? What approaches are the best in improving human life in areas like counseling, teaching, or health care?

One of the central tasks at this phase is to grab onto a life vest and use it to keep from drowning, while realizing that authentic practitioner development means that eventually one must swim without a life vest. Translating the metaphor, this means that the challenge for the student is to remain open at the metalevel while making tentative choices at the microlevel. These choices are about what to embrace in terms of theory and practice. Making tentative choices provides a temporary relief from the anxiety that can threaten the student. The anxiety arises from not knowing. There has been an increase in understanding the complexity of the professional world, like recognizing the difference between what emerges when one is looking at a leaf from a distance and under a microscope. If the anxiety of not knowing is too strong, the student may retreat. Leaving the field or rigidly clinging to one way of understanding reality (one theoretical approach) are two retreat styles that reduce anxiety but, unfortunately, also reduce the capacity for cognitive complexity, a long-term key to senior expertise.

If a life vest is used, the anxiety of bewilderment gives way to temporary relief and calm; therefore, searching for a life vest has the built-in motivation of a teachable moment. The student is ready and often frustrated when a life vest is not available.

Life vest #1 is to use a senior practitioner as a model. One counseling student stated this simply: "I wanted to absorb from the counselors I observed" (p. 31). Students of teaching watch their teachers teach, students of medicine watch their teachers interact with patients, and teachers of counseling are intensely observed while demonstrating a client interview. The style, mannerisms, thinking method, and approach of positive models – national or local experts and even admired peers – are readily adopted. It is a quick way to feeling more competent. Video or live demonstrations are popular. For example, the American Psychological Association Systems of Psychotherapy video interviews, edited by Jon Carlson, feature many practitioners demonstrating methods of therapy and counseling.

Negative models are also used to cut down the complexity of choice. If something can be eliminated, then confusion can be lessened. Negative models, usually more advanced practitioners judged harshly by the student, provide a picture for the novice of "things I do not want to do." A classic example is the teacher of teaching methods judged to be a poor teacher by the student of teaching. A more general negative model in the caring professions is the senior practitioner who no longer seems to care about the client, student, or patient. Such a practitioner, perceived to be burned out, is sternly judged and avoided. There is a strong factor in the negative view; the student fears, "I may end up like that."

For *life vest #2*, the search is on for a theoretical approach to lessen the confusion. Here is one student's description of this process:

> I'm putting together a jigsaw puzzle. First I pick up a piece to see how it fits with another. I turn it around and try to get it to fit. I try lots of different combinations. If a piece fits, I keep it and it becomes a natural part of the puzzle. If it doesn't fit, I keep trying to find a place for it. Eventually with no place, it gets dropped.
>
> (p. 33)

The life vest is an easily learned method that suggests "pay attention to this" and "do this." How, for example, should the nursing student provide care to an elderly patient during a routine health visit? The theoretical model, read in a text or heard about in class, suggests a few key variables. In the mental health professions, students quickly grab a theoretical model, such as versions of basic helping skills or cognitive therapy. A simple cognitive approach, for example, suggests that, in the great complexity of the human being, one can be an effective helper by just paying attention to faulty thinking patterns with a goal of correcting "stinking thinking."

If neither of the two life vests is available to students in ways that meet their needs, they usually begin criticizing their training. The initial excitement of being in school turns to disappointment and frustration, feelings most often voiced to one's peers. Without a life vest, rather than being more prepared for the work, the student feels more vulnerable. One person expressed it this way: "The intensity of the anger comes from the next set of challenges. The person must perform at a consistent level and often feels unprepared" (p. 35).

A central task here – being open to professional complexity while finding safety in temporary solutions – continues as the student enters the next phase.

Openness to new learning is important for the student at this point. Yet, the openness presents a problem that has been described as "trying to drink from a fire hose." There is so much to think about and decide about. So, as we stated, one or more life vests can be valuable. Openness to new learning means a willingness to recognize that professional work is complex. It can be disconcerting to become aware that the circle of not knowing grows about as fast as the circle of knowing. This realization runs counter to the reason to go to school: to feel more competent, not to feel that confusion and clarity are neck to neck in a professional development race.

In spite of the struggles between confusion and clarity, too much of a closed attitude fosters professional stagnation. Conversely, accepting the slow process of professional development and an acceptance toward oneself as a learner in a learning community helps the professional development process.

The complexities of professional work need to be addressed. But, how to do it? We think that the developmental approach has an accepting quality and that it is a process that takes time. It has an exploring, active, searching, trying-out quality and is understood, at least somewhat, by the novice as a long-term project.

The nondevelopmental (eventually stagnant) approach attempts to limit the confusion by focusing not on exploration but rather on fitting all the data into one way of understanding the client and one way of proceeding. It has an experience-limiting, defensive, anxiety-reducing quality with impression management (Goffman, 1967) being the focus. Here, looking good is more important than being open about the struggles that accompany long-term professional development.

The impression management route is attractive because of the accumulative impact of a variety of forces. First, the training program is usually part of the intense achievement culture of a university. Perfection is the goal and doing well at everything is expected. The normative struggles of the novice period do not get support in such a culture. There is also the power differential between the supervisor or instructor and the student in practicum, internship, or field placement. This power differential is exaggerated by the evaluative function of the educational system. Last, during those times when the novice hits the tidal wave of confusion and low self-efficacy, the student is likely to engage more actively in impression management.

Students vary in how confident and competent they feel while in training. Some, because of previous work experience in the helping professions or related fields, such as teaching, have more confidence. Life experience and personal maturity fuel a sense of professional confidence. Others trace the learning curve in their practitioner work with the learning curve of another area where they started with no skill and then gradually got much better. Students in our graduate classes have made analogies to skills such as learning to be a debater, learning to be proficient at the piano, learning to play baseball, learning how to integrate complex and diverse knowledge arenas, learning how to live in a foreign culture. Each of these involved early attempts that were helped greatly by a positive teacher or mentor. These first attempts led to increased practice with feedback that improved performance. Some in the beginning student phase seem to be a natural fit with the role. They may be wired by biological inclination or early family role as mediator or helper to the practitioner role. These are all situations where there may be less student anxiety in the early practice days.

It is more common for students to feel threatened and anxious in the early student days (Rønnestad & Skovholt, 2003, 2013). Student anxiety during the early practice days seems to be present across countries and cultures. These results are from the most extensive international survey ever done of practitioners from student to senior level: the International Study of the Development of Psychotherapists (Orlinsky & Rønnestad, 2005). From this research, we know that inexperienced therapists in many countries frequently feel overwhelmed and highly challenged in client sessions. Compared to functioning at later phases of development, Norwegian therapists (Rønnestad & von der Lippe, 2002) reported more frequently to experience the following difficulties: (a) lacking in confidence that you can have a beneficial effect on a client, (b) unsure how best to deal with a client, (c) in danger of losing control of the therapeutic situation to a client, (d) distressed by the powerlessness to affect a client's tragic life situation, (e) troubled by moral or ethical issues that have arisen in your work with a client, (f) irritated with a client who is actively blocking your efforts, and (g) guilty about having mishandled a critical situation with a client.

Also, research on supervision within counseling/therapy confirms how threatening training experiences may be for students. The works by Gray, Ladany, Walker, and Ancis (2001); Moskowitz and Rupert (1983); and Ladany, Hill, Corbett, and Nutt (1996), in particular, have demonstrated the counterproductivity that may result from a non-optimal supervision relationship.

Phase 3: The advanced student phase

The many people-oriented professions (e.g., university counseling, elementary teaching, physical therapy) differ in many important ways. As an occupational core, however, focus is on caring for the Other, which occurs within the practitioner role. The most intense practitioner training usually occurs in this stage. Here, the practitioner-in-training needs supportive guides for the long, challenging, difficult career path. The supervisor as guide does not do the work of the novice or carry the novice along the path; however, the supervisor does watch as the novice struggles while hiking and may point out hazards and pitfalls on the path, suggesting alternative methods of hiking during arduous parts. When a person hikes with a guide for the first time, it goes by different names, such as field placement, internship, externship, practicum, student teaching, clerkship, and residency.

The central task here is to look, act, think, feel, and perform at a basic established professional level. Many students, however, have higher aspirations for their functioning and want not only to avoid making mistakes but to excel in their work. This takes enormous amounts of student energy, time, and effort. Many feel pressure to do things more perfectly than ever before. The advanced student usually has a serious and cautious approach to role and function. They are typically not relaxed, risk taking, or spontaneous. Years later down the practitioner path, the task is to shed aspects of this narrow professional role. Now, however, the task is to show professional gatekeepers that one has what it takes to pass through the gate.

The internalized high standards for professional functioning for many students contribute to the tendency toward excessive and misunderstood responsibility. A female student at this phase said: "I do a good job of letting myself feel responsible for everything." Another said: "I thought I could and should help everybody," and a third expressed it this way: "Every single request for consultation I wanted to do. I wanted to learn things and to prove to the director of training that I could do the job."

Supervisors are both guide and evaluator. This dual role of guide and evaluator can contribute to student ambivalence toward gatekeepers at the advanced student phase. Most loved are the wise and expert gatekeepers who adroitly teach the trade with large doses of emotional support and small doses of evaluation fear. Most despised and feared are the opposite – incompetent practitioners who unfairly evaluate the student as inadequate. The student dream is for the former. Most supervisors/gatekeepers fall in between these extremes.

When novice practitioners have critical supervisors and clients who do not seem to improve, the situation is ripe for what Orlinsky and Rønnestad (2005) call "double traumatization." This, like other critical events early in one's career when the experience base is fragile, such as a client suicide, can be very harmful to the naturally slow evolutionary growth of practitioner competence.

If the reference point for evaluating one's own competence changes to that of the seasoned professional, the advanced student realizes there is still much to learn. The advanced student as practitioner may still feel vulnerable and insecure, and actively seek confirmation and feedback from seniors and peers. There is still considerable external dependency.

The reaction of the client, student, or patient lies at the center of the drama at this point. The person at the advanced student phase uses the indirect and direct feedback from the client, student, or patient to judge one's own practitioner self. A common self-assessment question and a very important one: Am I any good at this work? Other questions are: Can I do it? Will the person I am trying to help think that I am good at this? How about the view of my peers and my supervisor? Do they think I can be a very skilled practitioner? The variable confidence at this phase is expressed by these individuals. One said, "There weren't many times I felt highly competent. I questioned, am I in the right place, is this what I should do?" Said another, "I've gone from being petrified to being comfortable." Another stated, "I'm less afraid of losing patients than in the past."

At this phase, the practitioner-in-training is most interested in pragmatic information that can immediately help the novice with the current client, student, or patient. The social work student with the teenage client suffering from a psychotic break wonders, "What can I read to help me interview her?" The secondary teacher-in-training eagerly seeks out a method to keep order in a class of 35 highly distractible students. Before stitching a wound for the first time, the medical student, like a dry sponge, eagerly soaks up lessons given by the supervisor. Practical, useful information is valued; confusing, impractical theory is read only when there is the external, anxiety-based motivation of a class assignment.

Supervision of beginning practicum students can be a powerful source of influence for the advanced student. One female, reflecting on her internship, said: "It was a concrete realization of what I had learned. It was really valuable. The contrast between them and me helped me see my own style and how far I had come in my development" (p. 44).

Practicing like a professional makes the person eager to move beyond the student role to the world of professional practice. It is, in fact, the act of graduating and leaving school that ushers in the next phase of the long practitioner road.

Phase 4: The novice professional phase

At commencement, the ritual of graduation celebrates the end of school, and students are happy because they are escaping from the demands of formal training. The novice professional phase is a time of freedom for many. It is the dawn of a new time, a time for discovery of a new part of the novice to senior practitioner path. The central task of this phase is searching onward beyond what the individual has already successfully explored.

The novice professional phase encompasses the first years after graduation, although individual paths vary. For most practitioners, these years are experienced as intense and engaging. There are many challenges to master and many choices to be made.

In the novice professional phase, there is a sense of being on one's own. In addition, there is a continual process of reformulating, a process of "shedding and adding" at the conceptual and behavioral level. There seems to be a sequentially ordered change that occurs during the first years following graduation. First, there is a period where the practitioner seeks to confirm the validity of training. Second, when confronted with professional challenges inadequately mastered, there follows a period of disillusionment with professional training and self. Third, there is a period with a more intense exploration into self and the professional environment.

The new practitioner is excited to finally leave the student role and be a professional in the world of helping, teaching, and healing. The person is eager to use all the new skills that were gleaned through hard work during the stress and grind of student life. We call this the confirmation subphase because the new professional is eager to confirm the usefulness of one's formal training and the status of the school or university.

In the preceding phase, the practitioner had supervisors and teachers as guides. The supervisor and the built-in structure of the practicum, internship, or clerkship are there to help ensure a positive learning experience. Helpful and instructive developmental supervision is part of this equation. The ideal does not always happen. Sometimes the guides and the structure of the training experience are not ideal. Now, with the freedom of the novice professional phase comes the path without the guide, which is often confusing and dangerous. The long dreamed-about freedom may also produce a surprise reaction of anxiety, loss, and confusion. Three individuals at this phase commented revealingly. One said, "Having less guidance from professors and supervisors was scary." Another said: "People weren't protecting you from taking on too much anymore." A third had the following reaction:

> I didn't anticipate all of this. I was concerned all the time that things wouldn't work if I didn't finish [my degree]. I used to think that my doubts about me and my despair would go away with the degree . . . It is a disorienting process because I don't know any more now except that there are more expectations . . . I didn't expect the formal training would lead to feeling adequate until I felt inadequate and then realized how much I expected to know by now. My professional training was over and I lacked so much.
>
> (pp. 51–52)

Many will look for workplace mentors who will offer guidance and support, thereby easing the transition to autonomous professional functioning.

The realization that one's schooling was not enough usually comes to the practitioner while performing work tasks. The person starts getting hit with challenges that he or she is not prepared to meet. This most often happens when the feedback from those served – clients, students, and patients – clearly tells the practitioner that his or her work is not totally successful. This may come through what we call "a series of humiliations" that are painfully experienced by the practitioner. The painfully experienced element comes because there is a demand to succeed at helping, teaching, and healing and because the vast majority of people-oriented professionals are highly motivated to provide service to the Other. Failure is distressing.

Here is an example of disillusionment: An individual with a math and science undergraduate degree entered a graduate program with a strong research-based empirical approach. As he applied what he had learned, an approach with an emphasis on precision and rationality, to patients with spinal cord injuries, he was overwhelmed by the emotional anguish and pain of these patients. He said: "Sometimes you feel like you were trying to fight a forest fire with a glass of water."

The realization that one's training has been insufficient brings on the disillusionment subphase. This realization of inadequacy often accompanies anger at not being better prepared. One female looked back and said: "I realized that graduate training had real gaps. There was much I had to cover that was not offered in graduate school. I remember writing letters to the director of the program, pointing out things that should have been addressed." Others point the finger inward and go through painful self-examination of the inadequacy.

The novice professional is typically experiencing an increased sense of the complexity of practitioner work and is recognizing more profoundly how important the therapeutic relationship is for client progress. As the novice professional is focusing more attention on understanding and mastering relationship issues, the practitioner is also becoming more skillful in defining work roles and regulating boundaries.

The developmental challenge is to continue down the path with self as the primary guide. The key is to be open and searching, to use the reflection process to learn, and to continue to rely on peers for support and professional elders for guidance. Practitioner development is a long process. The novice professional phase practitioner who embraces this reality continues the step-by-step process of growth.

Phase 5: The experienced professional phase

By this phase, the practitioner is highly experienced. Formal schooling occurred years ago, and the hiking boots have now racked up many miles on the career path. The central task on this part of the path is the development of a more authentic, genuine professional self. This means creating a role that is highly congruent with the individual's self-perceptions (including values, interests, attitudes), which makes it possible for the practitioner to apply his or her professional competence in an authentic way. Expressing this authentic self, one research participant at this phase used a music analogy when saying:

If I know my pieces really well I can then play them individually with ease. Played well together there is a unifying and coherent quality that is difficult to achieve but is beautiful when it occurs.

(p. 68)

Major sources that we have found to influence professional development (theories and research, clients, professional elders [professor, supervisors, mentors, therapists], peers and colleagues, one's own personal life, and the social and cultural environment) continue to play an important role in professional functioning. Increasingly, the experienced practitioner reports understanding human behavior through professional literature in related fields such as anthropology or religion; or through reading prose, poetry, and biographies; or through movies, the theater, and other artistic expressions.

A shedding and adding process is the key to forming and shaping an authentic professional self. Consolidation is a major part of the shedding and adding. Examining the professional life of the famous Norwegian painter Edvard Munch shows strong evidence of this shedding and adding process as part of developing the authentic professional self (Berman, Heller, Prelinger, & Munch, 2006). One practitioner at this stage called it "throwing out the clutter" (p. 62). Other research participants said it in the following ways:

There was a time I had an investment in one approach in part due to training but exposure to clients, other approaches, and my own therapy led me to change.

(p. 64)

One person expressed it this way:

I learned all the rules [practice guidelines] and so I came to a point – after lots of effort – where I knew the rules very well. Gradually I modified the rules. Then I began to use the rules to let me go where I wanted to go. Lately I haven't been talking so much in terms of rules.

(pp. 66–67)

Another said:

I'm more loose than I used to be in my approach to the work. Sure, everything must be done ethically and professionally. That's a given. I'm just not so frantic about answers or even questions. Now I really feel there isn't a right way to do it, although there is a right process for me.

(p. 67)

This personalization of the professional self lets the practitioner express the helping, teaching, and healing self at a higher level of creativity. In sharp contrast with earlier functioning, techniques and methods are not applied in a conforming, rigid, external, or mechanical fashion, but can be used in a personalized and flexible way. Expressions of this are seen in the active formulating of a conceptual system and the active developing of a working style that fits the individual. Increasingly, there is little tolerance for lack of close fit and a strong tendency to search for a work environment experienced as compatible with self, a movement consistent with the underlying premise in Holland's (1997) theory of vocational choice. Data to shape the professional self has been coming to the practitioner from a variety of sources for a number of years. The early disillusionment of the previous phase has been replaced by active building of the professional self. The adding and shedding process occurs through trying out a wide variety of methods, approaches, and techniques; insights from direct and indirect feedback from clients, students, and patients; learning from a variety of supervisors and other professional elders; and learning from admired peers.

The practitioner must continue moving forward toward more professional maturity while dodging hazardous elements on the path (the dangerous branches, rocks, and roots): becoming stale, exhausted, and apathetic. One element that makes self-awareness of stagnation versus development difficult is the recycling of older concepts, methods, and techniques under new terms. In the people-oriented professions, attention is paid to that which is new, revolutionary, successful, and highly impactful. Researchers get credit for publishing something new, not replicating something old. Practitioners, especially new practitioners, are not drawn to "old ideas that sometimes work." However, the experienced practitioner can sense the "old fish in a new wrapper," and a cynicism can emerge. One person said: "I've recently stopped going to workshops. They seemed to be geared to 'Freshman English' and to be old stuff" (p. 78). Is this burnout or the wisdom of experience? It can be difficult for the practitioner to assess this accurately.

The great challenge at this phase is to both settle into a consistent style of walking along the path while also pushing oneself to explore more and develop further. Together, these two forces combine to form the central task of deeper authenticity and individuation.

The practitioner, years after continual interaction with professors, mentors, and clinical supervisors, is no longer guided on the path by these professional gatekeepers. As a source of influence for the practitioner, these professional elders have receded from the illuminated part of the developmental path and are now in the background. The experienced professional phase requires the practitioner to continue to develop professionally with self as director. Life is different, and the experienced professional phase practitioner is now in the front of the professional parade. This does not mean, however, that one's own professional elders are absent. No, they have just been internalized and live on in that manner. Concerning the influence of John, who was a supervisor 20 years before, one practitioner said, "I have running around in my mind words, phrases, quotes that I periodically pull back to . . . and sometimes I say to myself, how would John handle this situation?" (p. 79). These "internalized mentors" were often recalled with great fondness and appreciation by our research participants.

This professional development process is analogous to a similar process in personal human development. Here is one description:

> [I was] talking with an elderly man who was explaining to me that his wife, whom he cared for deeply, wasn't really dead because the pleasure of their time together lived on inside him. While he spoke these words, . . . I began to feel that all the people I'd ever known who had died or left me had not in fact gone away, but continued to live on inside me just as the man's wife lived on inside him.
>
> (Golden, 1997, p. 427)

The learning process at the experienced professional phase is highly self-directed. The pace, the direction, the focus, and the content are all self-directed. Continuing education requirements must be met, but they usually are structured in a very conventional method of "seat time" with a formal, one-way distribution of information. In contrast, highly impactful continuing education such as critical incidents and defining moments in the practitioner's life are broader in method and focus. Serious learning may also come through watching movies, an intense cross-cultural experience, having personal therapy, teaching a class, or making pottery. As described in the following quote, the key part for development versus stagnation is an ongoing, self-directed effort.

> With a new client I think about cases I've had. I think about how they have gone. Themes come in a case and this stimulates a memory in me. The memory is in the form of a collection of vignettes, stories and scripts. It isn't fully conscious but new cases do kick off the memory – the memory of how things went before provides a foundation to begin the current case.
>
> (p. 77)

A strong source of influence is the practitioner's personal maturation and life experience. This is a high-impact arena because the high-touch occupations are, by their nature, focused on human themes of emotional, intellectual, and physical development and health. In addition, the practitioner at the experienced professional phase has now lived more years and has more personal history data on which to draw. For example, becoming a parent – a powerful personal experience – can potentially affect any helper, teacher, or healer in how he or she does their work. Another example is the death of a close relative or friend and the resulting profound mourning. These are examples from the two ends of a central arena of human development: the attachment–loss process.

As we interviewed our research participants with more experience, we increasingly heard stories of the interrelationship between adult personal and professional life. Although some talked about how the fatigue from over-burdening work could negatively influence family life, or how professional knowledge and competence could be transferred into one's personal life, there were more tales of "traffic" in the other direction, that is, of how personal life was seen to influence professional functioning. One said: "You learn a lot from your kids just like you learn a lot from your clients" (p. 65). Another talked of her divorce being the most difficult experience of her life. She found it forced her to see herself as a separate person and not a daughter or wife in relation to others. She said: "It really shocked me to my core. I had to tap into some dark places and look at things about me" (p. 65). The whole experience, she said, increased her connections with human pain, made her more intellectually curious, and ultimately helped her be a better therapist. We heard many similar stories of the long-term positive influence of adverse experiences in therapists' and counselors' adult personal lives.

The immediate influence of adverse personal experiences is often negative. One senior therapist told us a story that moved us deeply. She told us that after losing her husband and her only child, a daughter, within a two-year period, it took another two years "before I could breathe again." It was not until after a long period of intense grieving that she could use the traumatic experience constructively in her work. This kind of shocking loss reminds us of the evoca-tive, intense prose of Joan Didion when she wrote of her husband collapsing in front of her and dying while her one child, her daughter, was in the hospital. The shock changed her perceptions, as described in her book *The Year of Magical Thinking* (2007). For those individuals in the relationship-intense professions, intense personal grief affects professional functioning in a variety of ways.

As previously described, there were several stories from our research infor-mants of negative experiences in early childhood and family life exerting an adverse and not positive influence on professional functioning (Rønnestad & Skovholt, 2001). This was surprising as it runs counter to a common percep-tion of "the wounded healer" (Henry, 1966), where healed early wounds are understood to contribute to the formation of a more effective helper. Early wounds are not necessarily healed, and may find their expression in adult pro-fessional functioning. However, from our interviews, there were several stories indicating that wounds acquired late (i.e., in adult life) can, if they are reflected upon, understood, and assimilated (see Stiles, 1997), contribute to more effec-tive helping. We may add that research within the International Study of the Development on Psychotherapists (ISDP) has shown that the relationship between early family experiences and later therapeutic functioning is positively moderated by therapists' personal therapy (Orlinsky & Rønnestad, 2005).

Yes, it is true that the personal human development of a practitioner of human development – emotional, intellectual, or physical – is quite natu-rally a source of influence. Yet, paradoxically, some practitioners are not very self-aware or reflective about the impact of personal life on work. Georgia O'Keeffe seemed to be in this camp regarding her flower paintings. She denied that the lush flower paintings had a sexual component although they were painted during the most intensely romantic part of her life (Lisle, 1987). Others are quite aware of the power of personal life. One practitioner stated:

> Certainly my experience has been an important factor. . . . My experience in the Peace Corps for a few years has taught me . . . a sense of relativity of this culture. Raising children I think is so important. I got a chance to go back through development with my own children, and to be able to see what it felt like to be them.
>
> (p. 79)

An expression of authenticity is more use of one's own professional experience as the epistemological base for one's work. The truth about how to do effective helping, teaching, and healing now comes predominantly from one's own experience-based generalizations and accumulated wisdom. Practitioners at this point voiced this.

> I think that the more you [work] . . . you find out more ways of what works. So I think with experience, what you end up doing . . . you do, with all your experience, what you know works, what has worked in the past. . . . It leaves you with a model that you developed, that fits your personality, and also from your experience, you know that it works. You start out with a theory and you eventually modify it.
>
> (p. 75)

A significant finding in our qualitative study is reflected in this quote above. Early practitioner experiences seem to be most deeply embedded for the experienced practitioner. And these early experiences form a cognitive schema for doing practice in the high-touch fields. The power of early practice experiences is evident in a collection of defining moments in counselor and therapist development edited by Trotter-Mathison et al. (2010). Defining moments, like critical incidents, are powerful events that shape one's professional identity and style. Of 87 defining moments, most of the authors describe events in early practice, such as a client experience or an experience in clinical supervision.

Later in practice, it is not every client, student, or patient that dramatically affects the practitioner. It tends to be those who are on the extremes – those who do really well or do really poorly. The practitioner at the experienced professional phase is typically deeply moved if one of their clients, students, or patients experiences a profound event, either positive or negative, when they are working together.

To get to an often deeply satisfying professional level, the practitioner must have moved far down the path. First, there is the absorption from professional elders, and theory and research in the field; then there is the agony of early practice when the novice is lost and confused; then comes the shedding and adding and, most of all, listening to the lessons from experience. There is also the research and theory in the field obtained from workshops, professional reading, and clinical supervision, including the great value many find in peer group supervision. With the lessons from practice and the active use of reflection, deeper professional personalization occurs, as described in the previous quotations.

Satisfaction is a common practitioner emotion at this phase. It seems to result from the effort over the years that has now formed a practitioner who feels competent at many complex professional tasks and is paid, at a modest level or above, for the work. Yet some are not doing so well. From the international survey research, a conclusion is that a minority of therapists report rather substantial difficulties in their practice in combination with a sense of professional decline (Orlinsky & Rønnestad, 2005). Thirteen percent of therapists, including many who had practiced for decades, experienced "distressing practice." Earlier, we mentioned a theme we recently began to explore: "Not All Therapists/Counselors Develop Optimally." It is important for us to note that the path from being a novice to a highly experienced practitioner is not a path that always leads higher and higher to levels of senior bliss! There is a lot of variability just as there is in human development in general. For example, 10 babies in the maternity ward end up with great variability at age 80!

Yet, in line with what we found in our qualitative interview study, the majority at the experienced professional phase seem able to regulate their emotions and handle the professional challenges they encounter. The majority also feel they are growing professionally. The earlier study found that 87% did not experience "distressed practice."

Now, practitioner joy relates in part to realistic expectations. Those who have entered the career field to "change the world" either have left the work out of frustration or have modified their expectations. Wanting to have a big impact may be a good way to begin a heroic occupation – that is, one that aims to reduce human suffering. Yet, in time, veteran practitioners see these strivings as dangerous, foolish versions of perfectionism and grandiosity. Thus, in a paradoxical way, the reduction of expectations makes satisfaction and sprinkles of joy more possible.

With experience, as goal setting has become more realistic, with increased awareness of strengths and limitations, and with a clearer definition of and differentiation of responsibility, it is more likely that the involvement level has been fine-tuned in a professional way. The practitioner is typically good at regulating involvement and identification with clients. A male therapist said: "I have a better sense of personal boundaries and blame myself less if things don't work out well" (p. 85). Another said: "When the session is over I can leave it there" (p. 93). This process of letting go of "overresponsibility" is likely a prerequisite for the regulation of emotions and attitude expressed when the practitioner is able to be totally absorbed in client work and then, when the session is over, is able within minutes to refocus attention and subsequently engage in work with another client. When this is successfully and ideally mastered, the practitioner can end many workdays more refreshed and stimulated than exhausted and depleted.

Paralleling realistic outcome replacing ideal outcome and improved regulation of professional boundaries, the experienced professional has learned how to separate the professional role from roles such as that of a friend, parent, or spouse. One female reflected back to her graduate school years when this was more of a problem. Laughing, she said that her daughter gave her useful feedback when she said: "Mother, will you quit being a damn social worker and just be my mother" (p. 69).

Phase 6: The senior professional phase

Practitioners, at this phase, have practiced about 25 years, some more, some less. Many are approaching retirement. This group, the most experienced in our sample, averaged 64 years of age when we interviewed them the first time, and 74 when we interviewed them again. This second set of interviews especially gave us the opportunity to learn about experiences and reflections of practitioners in the very mature professional years. Some at this senior level welcome this change in status, whereas others are not so positive about it. One talked about supervising younger interns and said: "They get brighter all the time: I feel that I learn as much from the interns as I teach them. They have become my teacher" (p. 92). Conversely, another said: "Suddenly I was seen by others as a leader, but I didn't see it that way. I didn't feel I belonged" (p. 80).

From our research, we have concluded that the central career task at this phase is *integrity*, defined as maintaining the fullness of one's individuality. We have framed this central task within the terms of the famous psychologist Erik Erikson (1968), who said that the psychological focus at this point is integrity versus despair. Integrity is often expressed by an alignment of values, much professional experience, high competence, and an integration of the professional and personal selves. A quiet joy seeps out into the work. The idea here at this phase, within the metaphor of the long, textured path, is for the senior practitioner to keep on trekking, using the individual style that the senior practitioner has developed during decades of practice. Yet, as much as there can be a positive flow to the work when a person is at the senior professional phase, we also heard objections to the glamorization of being older. For example, one male therapist said: "I think the golden age is not best by any means. As far as I can tell, being old and wise is not better than being young and innocent and energetic" (Rønnestad & Skovholt, 2001, p. 183).

While practicing within the ethical standards of the profession, this phase represents a profound acceptance and full expression of the self. As one senior practitioner said, "I think I am more myself than I have ever been" (p. 87). This full expression by the practitioner requires a chiseling of the professional self over the years of all the postgraduate phases; the novice professional phase, the experienced professional phase, and now the senior professional phase. With self as director, there has been shedding of unwanted exterior influences while other influences have been added.

Acceptance, a predominant senior practitioner emotion, comes from the fruit of one's labor. Related emotions are serenity, security, humility, and confidence. One senior practitioner described it this way: "The longer I've been at it the more I've become accepting of my limitations. That is just the way it is. Some things I do well, other things not so well" (p. 88). Secondary emotions are excitement about the work and regret, which is related to time gone and the missed opportunities.

Performance anxiety is greatly reduced from the early years. The practitioner does not have the dreaded feeling of not knowing what to do or the strong dependence on professional elders as guides. A major contribution to reduced anxiety is the internalization of expertise. After thousands of hours of experience, knowing what to do no longer comes from others such as textbook and guidebook authors, clinical supervisors, professors, and mentors. The big problem for the novice in using the ideas of others is that they are often generalizations that the novice must customize to the individual client. The senior practitioner does not have that problem because the knowledge base is mostly internal and more easily sculpted to the individual client than with the external expertise of the novice. For the senior, it is experience-based generalizations and accumulated wisdom that now form the autopilot that guides the work. A senior professional phase practitioner expressed this feeling when saying, "Almost never do I feel anxious about my work. I've done everything before and it has turned out all right" (p. 88).

The cascade of influences for the novice practitioner – theory and research; clients, students, or patients; professional elders; and peers and colleagues – is different now. These sources of influence are not absorbed during the senior phase with the same straw-gulping urgency of a thirsty novice who is drinking in the professional knowledge base. Drinking a cold milkshake too fast can lead to an intense feeling in a person's head; this is often the experience of the novice practitioner when being overwhelmed by so much data from so many places.

Now, at the senior phase, things are different. Why is this? Many of these influences have been internalized. They now reside internally and are forceful in role and working style in that way. The senior practitioner tends to get less excited about new ideas in the field. For year after year over decades, he or she has already been exposed to an avalanche of new ideas. For the senior phase practitioner, the similarity of new ideas and old ideas is seen more than the discontinuity. New, revolutionary professional ideas and practices are less often perceived as absolutely better than the old. This does not mean the veteran practitioner is stuck in the old, but rather that there is more adding to what is already there. As one practitioner, at this point, said:

> By the time a person reaches the end of one's work life, he/she has seen the wheel reinvented so many times. . . . Old ideas emerge under new names and it can be frustrating . . . to see people make a big fuss about something he/she has known for years. This contributes to cynicism for the person.
>
> (p. 95)

One source of influence has expanded, which is from the classes of the school of hard knocks. Perhaps of most significance is the depth and wisdom gained from losses. For example, almost all mentors and models have gone away in one way or another and peers are often no longer a strong influence. There is also a loss of innocence about the work, whether it be teaching, physical healing, counseling, or a related field. There has been a fading of illusions and increased sense of reality in terms of what can be accomplished professionally.

These losses can be instructive for a practitioner in a people-oriented profession. The practitioner must, however, do his or her own grief work and get to a point of resolution (Rønnestad & Skovholt, 2001). Then he or she can speak from this depth and wisdom, as described by the leading character in *Memoirs of a Geisha* who said, "I don't think any of us can speak frankly about pain until we are no longer enduring it" (Golden, 1997, p. 419). So this source of influence, using the depth and wisdom gained from enduring profound human loss, can be of great value to the senior practitioner in helping, teaching, and healing.

The seductions for practitioners at the senior professional phase are the intellectual apathy and boredom that can come from routine tasks completed over and over again, experiences that can reduce engagement in high-touch work. This is very dangerous because much of the power of the work comes from the human engagement with the Other – that is, accessing the powerful I–Thou relationship while avoiding the I–It relationship, to use Martin Buber's (Kramer, 2004) language. Researching psychotherapists Orlinsky and Rønnestad (2005) and their colleagues found that most of their sample avoided this disengagement and continued to be committed to growing professionally.

Many forces converge to make the work satisfying for numerous senior practitioners. Performance anxiety is greatly diminished; there is often a strong feeling of competence in the work and control in the work setting. New energy is not needed for miles of hiking on the path, yet the work brings success with clients, students, and patients. One senior professional phase practitioner stated it this way:

> With diminished anxiety, I became less and less afraid of my clients and with that came an ease for me in using my own wide repertoire of skills

and procedures. They became more available to me when I needed them. And during those moments it became remarkable to me that someone would have the willingness to share their private world with me and that my work with them would bring very positive results for them. This brought a sense of immense pleasure to me.

(p. 96)

We see in this quotation the joy of practice described in Chapter 2 of this book. Now, at the senior professional phase, the most dangerous hiking elements – tree branches, steep incline, dangerous overlooks, and sharp-edged rocks – have been managed. The end is closer and the professional hiker can enjoy being very present during these miles of the long, textured path.

NOTE

* All quotations throughout the rest of this chapter are from Skovholt & Rønnestad, 1992a unless otherwise cited.

12

BURNOUT PREVENTION AND SELF-CARE STRATEGIES OF EXPERT PRACTITIONERS*

Mary Mullenbach and Thomas M. Skovholt

We are excited to present the results of this study in this chapter. To the best of our understanding, this is the first and only resiliency study that has investigated validly chosen expert/master therapists. Peer nomination methodology, a method that has good validity and reliability data, was used to find these experts. This method is excellent in finding those described by Kottler and Carlson (2014, p. 218): "The most creative practitioners work in relative obscurity, uninterested in notoriety and too busy to broadcast their ideas to a larger audience." These experts often do not actively advocate a new approach or speak charismatically to an audience of novice practitioners – those most in need of the certainty of method/tips/procedures while experiencing the uncertainty of professional work. Rather, expert practitioners often just keep working in direct client care and clinical supervision, satisfied by being able to directly respond to human need and suffering.

This method of peer nomination to find experts or master therapists, followed by qualitative interviews, has been used in more studies in recent years. These studies did not directly focus on resiliency patterns for these practitioners, but they did study characteristics, defined broadly. Studies of master therapists outside of the U.S. include those in Canada (Smith, 2008), Japan (Hirai, 2010), Korea (Kwon & Kim, 2007), Portugal (Carvalho & Matos, 2011a, 2011b), and Singapore (Jennings et al., 2008).

The focus of the current chapter is on the methods used by one group of practitioners in the helping professions in order to maintain professional vitality. The ideas presented here can be of use to a wide variety of practitioners across the rainbow of the many helping professions, caring professions, and relationship-intense professions. This is a big group of helpers, healers, teachers, clergy, human resource professionals, and attorneys in areas such as family law and immigration.

Practitioners encounter stressors that originate from both internal and external sources (Baker, 2003; Freudenberger, 1990; Norcross & Guy, 2007). Both have a direct effect on the practitioner. Burnout is especially prevalent in helping professionals. Practitioners are expected to engage in an ongoing series of professional attachments and separations, as discussed in Chapter 3. The stress of attachment and separation is often intensified by a lack of client success, nonreciprocated giving within the counseling relationship, overwork, difficult client behaviors, discouragement as a result of the slow and uneven pace of the helping process, the practitioner's existing personal issues that emerge in response to involvement in the counseling process, isolation, and administrative demands from agency and managed care organizations (Dupree & Day, 1995; Farber, 1990; Figley, 2002; Kassam-Adams, 1995). Burnout occurs when the practitioner is continuously depleted from this intense process of engagement.

The debilitating effects of the helping role on the practitioner have long been recognized as an occupational hazard with far-reaching effects (Freudenberger & Robbins, 1979; Smith & Moss, 2009). Based on his research, Farber (1983) concluded that counseling work can have a substantial negative impact on practitioners' self-identity, behavior, and attitudes, both within and outside of the work setting. Historically, studies in this area have primarily focused on identifying work-related stressors.

As mentioned in the beginning of this chapter, this is the first, and to the best of our knowledge, only study of the resiliency patterns of validly chosen expert practitioners. In 1996, a research program was started with 10 peer-nominated mental health practitioners. The purpose of the initial study was to identify the components of mastery among this group of expert practitioners. Since that time, the research program has been expanded. The current study identified components relevant to wellness and professional resiliency in this group of practitioners. In this study, a qualitative design was utilized as a means of drawing a store of rich information from the sample group. Data were collected through the use of a semi-structured interview format, with questions cultivated from existing research focused on stressors among mental health practitioners. The questions were designed to identify stressors and to access information pertaining to the emotional wellness and professional resiliency of these practitioners. The data analysis relied on an inductive approach that allowed for an in-depth exploration. Two interviews were completed with each of the participants. An analysis of a second data source obtained from a previous study with this same group of participants was used to supplement the findings. The total amount of research time, most clocked by Mary Mullenbach (2000), was in the hundreds of hours. Quality qualitative research often takes a lot of time! The selected findings presented in this chapter focus on high-level stressors and self-care strategies identified within this group of practitioners. The quotations from the participants are often very meaningful for readers of this research. We hope this is true for you too!

This chapter presents 20 themes within five categories that originated from the data analysis. The five categories are (1) professional stressors, (2) emergence of the expert practitioner, (3) creating a positive work structure, (4) protective factors, and (5) nurturing self through solitude and relationships. A summary of the information is in the list below.

CATEGORY A: PROFESSIONAL STRESSORS

Category A contains four themes that identify stressor areas that are confronted by the participants in their work.

Category A: Professional Stressors

Participants are stressed by issues that challenge their competency.
A frozen therapy process is highly stressful for participants.
Breaches in peer relationships are stressful.
Intrapersonal crises negatively impact the professional role.

Category B: Emergence of the Expert Practitioner

Participants learned role limits and boundaries.
Over time, participants experienced less performance anxiety.
With experience, participants moved from theory to use of self.
Participants view attachment and separation as a natural process.
Participants understand human suffering at a profound level.

Category C: Creating a Positive Work Structure

Mentor and peer support was critical at the novice phase.
Participants have ongoing and enriching peer relationships.
Multiple roles are a protective factor.
Participants create health-promoting work environments.

Category D: Protective Factors

Participants directly engage highly stressful professional dilemmas.
Participants confront and resolve personal issues.
Highly engaged learning is a powerful source of renewal.

Category E: Nurturing Self Through Solitude and Relationships

Participants foster professional stability by nurturing a personal life.
Participants invest in a broad array of restorative activities.
Participants construct fortifying personal relationships.
Participants value an internal focus.

Theme 1: Participants are stressed by issues that challenge their competency

Participants reported an array of issues and events that challenge their sense of wellness. Sometimes, as in the case of a suicidal client, these experiences represented unpredicted critical incidents for the practitioners. Other, less intense events and issues were chronic in nature and occurred on an ongoing basis. Regardless of the specific experience, a commonality that ran through was the participants' experience of feeling "tapped out" in regard to their level of competency or comfort. One participant discussed the emotional impact of a client who committed suicide during a hospitalization.**

> I know that she ended up in the hospital; I arranged it. . . . So I took care of her safety, I felt. And I don't know what the heck they did; she was suicidal, and they weren't watching her, and she hung herself. And it was really hard; I just felt heartbroken, and I was so pissed at the psychiatrist.

One participant discussed the ongoing stressors that are related to working with chronically ill clients who don't progress:

> . . . depression that doesn't lift. All kinds of interventions; I mean, some people have had therapy for years before they get to me. Some of them have had shock treatment, some of them have had medication, and nothing seems to be helpful. You know, people who have been searching for a long while, and maybe you can help them make some inroads, but there are some people for whom it just feels like we don't have what's needed yet.

Other participants discussed their sense of feeling lost or depleted when working with specific client behaviors:

> And I'm realizing that, for example, I don't work well with addictives, people who are addictive. I find I get sucked into their dynamics, and I can't keep track that these people are also con people because they need to be.
>
> I've had a few men who have been very abusive . . . they're coming to me, and the allegation of physical or sexual abuse may be in the air, but they haven't dealt with it at all, or maybe it hasn't been in the air at all. But I find myself angry at the end of those sessions. Those are the people that I find myself, I feel used up rather than giving 100%; I feel like I've been stolen from; I feel like I've been taken from. It's totally unrewarding, like they don't give anything back.

Sometimes this sense of being tapped out resulted from the level of distress expressed by the client:

> I think it has more to do with when there's been a lot. So, for example, there are some weeks where it feels like you always thought you heard the worst that you could possibly hear and then someone comes in with something worse about what people are able to do to people that causes pain and distress. . . . And sometimes it's just in waves.

Theme 2: A frozen therapy process is highly stressful for participants

Participants reported that they experienced a sense of boredom related to clients who were unmotivated or resistant to treatment. This experience of feeling bored within the therapeutic relationship was reported as a significant stressor. Participants stated:

> For me the issues would be probably somebody is just really without any willingness whatsoever to reflect. It is always something outside of themselves, continuously so . . . mostly I think I lose interest.
> I think what's challenging, frankly, are the boring clients, you know, where it's time after time and very little is happening.

In reflecting on his work with clients who were resistant, one participant spoke about the need to deal with his own defensive response:

> Well, I find I don't mind their resistance; it's when I start getting resistant in the face of their resistance. I mean, they have the right; I expect them to get resistant. But then when they do their resistance in a way that engenders my resistance, then I don't like that.

Theme 3: Breaches in peer relationships are stressful

Participants consistently reported that they derived a beneficial sense of support from their peer relationships, both within the work environment and in the broader professional community. Not surprisingly, breaches in these relationships are especially stressful. One participant stated:

> Some of the most stressful times have been when I've accidentally ended up working with colleagues that I didn't feel compatible with, to come to work every morning and greet a face that you're not happy to see. Someone you don't trust or respect who doesn't seem to trust or respect me, that's very hard, but it's not my situation now.

Another participant discussed his struggle to stay engaged with peers in the broader professional community when discussing issues relevant to professional practice and integrity:

> [Stressful for me are] my own relationships and associations with colleagues where we hit points of important divergence. And my willingness to stay present to those, to stay in a relationship with those colleagues and to stay present to the divergence without favoring a tendency to want to split off or isolate or withdraw.

In a similar way, a participant spoke about her negative response to conflicts between separate divisions in the psychological community:

> They're both really good groups, and I think it's good for our practices and the community and everything else, but there are elements of competition and resentment and politics, I guess is what you'd call it, but I really dislike it, and when I'm caught in the middle of one of those frays, I'm very unhappy.

Theme 4: Intrapersonal crises have a negative impact on the professional role

Participants reported that personal life crises and related problems presented challenging situations in their professional role. Although the participants had developed proactive methods for coping with these issues, they reported a strong sense of discomfort when initially faced with this type of challenge. One participant described the unease that he felt when personal issues created a sense of incongruence in his perception of self:

> When I was experiencing a lot of tearing in relation to my own family, which I did some years ago, a long time ago. That was pretty difficult, and I think the difficulty was having to redo my conception of myself while I was continuing to practice. And you really can't take yourself off line and decide to redo your conception of yourself and come back because that's always so closely integrated to whatever you're doing every place else.

Another participant described the hardship that she encounters when she is in the process of resolving her own crises:

> So then I feel very split in terms of what I need to attend to with clients, and yet knowing this other thing is playing in my own life that is not going to resolve today in a phone call and is not going to resolve in a week, and it's going to be with me for whatever period of time. And so those, frankly, are torture chambers for me. . . . When I'm sitting with clients and they're talking about anything that remotely is similar or identifies with or touches on, the anxiety just shoots up. . . . How do I manage that level of anxiety and at the same time try to be here for my clients?

CATEGORY B: EMERGENCE OF THE EXPERT PRACTITIONER

Category B contains five themes that highlight aspects of the participants' approaches to professional practice. These themes reflect attitudes and techniques that promote wellness and preserve professional vitality.

Theme 1: Participants learned role limits and boundaries

Over time, participants learned the value of establishing clear boundaries and limits in areas that included their role as a helper, the level of responsibility that they assumed, the structure of their practice, the makeup of their caseloads, and their relationships with clients. The establishment of these boundaries and limits enabled the practitioners to maintain a sense of wellness and vitality, to cope more effectively with difficult client behaviors, and to manage their own continuous exposure to suffering. In discussing her evolving role, one participant stated:

> I'm far more wise about all the things that I don't need to know about and don't need to fix, and I think when I started out, like most of us when we start out, feeling a need to have all the answers. My job was to fix this, be helpful. I think with experience and time in the field, you learn that our job is really to relax more and sit back and listen and hear better what it is that the person is trying to sort through.

One participant discussed the establishment of limits and boundaries as a necessary ingredient in both practicing with integrity and fostering a sense of wellness and vitality:

> It is up to me to do everything I can to maintain my own emotional health so that I can actually be available to my patients without needing them. I think one of the ways therapy goes awry is that the therapist starts to use the patient for their own emotional sustenance, regulation of the therapist's self-esteem, all those sorts of things. I think that to be a good therapist, you must be well fed and well loved. Basically, have a life out there that is working.

Participants noted that limits and boundaries played a key role in structuring their actual workday. In discussing the framework of her schedule, one participant stated:

> It's important for me to keep track of the hours I'm putting in because it's very easy to start going over a 40-hour week. And I start to know that something's wrong when I wake up in the morning and I'm not rested or when I'm dreading the day, or I'll find myself sleepy or bored, and this is not boring work, and I start to make mistakes, double schedule people, or there are just certain signs I recognize as that I'm working too hard.

Regarding his ability to implement limits on client behaviors, one participant stated:

> I'm more sure of myself. . . . I can set limits with, you know, the authority of a Dutch uncle, and it can have the subtleties of both nurturance and a stop sign.

Another participant noted the importance of understanding her limitations as a practitioner:

Part of it has been to really advocate for clients where it feels like it's really important; part of it has been to make alternatives available, like sliding fees for people; some of it is just coming to grips with that there are certain agencies that can provide certain things, and that we can't provide everything for everybody. So part of it is accepting limitations.

Theme 2: Over time, participants experienced less performance anxiety

With time, participants became more comfortable in their professional role. With this change, they experienced a decrease in stress and an increase in confidence and ability to handle a variety of difficult therapeutic issues and client behaviors. This shift allowed them to be more open and genuine in their role as a helper. Three practitioners commented:

There's less of a need to prove yourself, and so you can be more open because you don't feel as much that you need to defend anything or protect anything. I think when you first start out sometimes, it feels like you're on the line, you know; no one knows who you are, how you're doing, and so I think there's much more a sense of protection around yourself; seems like as you grow older and more experienced, there's more of a sense of "We all don't know, and we're all learning," so you can be pretty open about hearing feedback, getting information.
  I laugh a lot more, a lot more. I am old. That is one thing that helps. And . . . I am not forever wondering if I am good enough.
  Comfort with coming to work each day and assuming that it would be okay. You know, I'd do all right somehow, or I'd be able to deal with whatever happened that day; I'm just guessing, but I'm thinking maybe 10 years into my practice, I started to have that kind of sense of equilibrium about it.

Theme 3: With experience, participants moved from theory to use of self

Participants noted that, as they accumulated experience, they moved from a reliance on specific techniques and approaches to being more open and genuine. This change occurred as they became increasingly aware of the therapeutic process and how to best use their own self within the relationship. For these participants, the shift from a reliance on specific approaches to the use of self required an element of risk and openness. Once achieved, it felt more like a comfortable professional "fit" that was conducive in creating intimate and intense interactions with clients that enhanced their work. When focusing on the intense and intimate nature of the therapeutic relationship with clients, participants stated:

In a sense it's a joy. . . . It's the fact of working with people and watching them grow and feeling that you have a part in that growth. It's fun.

Well, I get off on it. I mean, honest to God, contact is very exciting. I mean, when two boundaries meet, that's where the energy is.

Well, I think the one thing that has prevented me from burning out . . . is the fact that no two people look alike to me. The people who burn out begin to see everybody as alike; they see people as problems, and they see problems as the things they are working with.

Theme 4: Participants view attachment and separation as a natural process

Participants discussed their belief that attachments and separations in the therapeutic relationship followed a natural course, similar to those experienced in other relationships. This belief appears to fortify the participants through years of fostering attachments and facilitating separations with a multitude of clients. They are committed to engaging in that process, even through times of difficulty, and hold the belief that it is a mutually beneficial process. One participant discussed her belief that the therapeutic process of attachment and separation mimics life:

But it seems to me that all of life is about attachment and separation. You know, even with marriage, there are times when attachment is really important, but there's also times when separation is really important. Where you're individuals and you have different needs and different abilities to be present. So I think that's how I help myself with it, is that it feels part and parcel with just what's true in life . . . I think it's totally important that people are able to attach in order to work through some of what might not have happened for them. But I also think it's important to be able to separate and let go.

Participants also discussed their experience that relationships continue beyond the separation. This continuation may exist on an internal level or, in other cases, actually involve the client returning to therapy. In some cases, work that began with a client eventually extended to the client's children. This belief regarding the ongoing nature of relationships appeared to insulate the participants from the potential distress of repeated attachments and separations:

And then a number of people come back over the years, so I have more and more confidence, sort of like an object constancy, in me at least, that these people remain alive in my psyche. They're out there in the world, and I feel connected to them and believe that they'd return if the situation arose.

I think in a core way, attachment is an internal phenomena rather than external. You can see people for years every day and probably not have that much attachment. So if you stop seeing people, there is some loss, but it doesn't mean that, therefore, something got yanked out.

I feel like I really do give people something, part of myself, and when they leave, I really have an investment. But these days, I almost never say a permanent goodbye to anybody. I'm always having old clients come back; I'm even having the children who were playing on the floor coming in with their spouses at this point.

Theme 5: Participants understand human suffering at a profound level

Through their work, participants developed a profound understanding of suffering. This includes an awareness of the painful elements and the potential for growth. The participants' comments reflected a profound awareness of suffering and the healing process that is part of their role as a helper. Their hopeful outlook toward how suffering can be transformed also seemed to enhance their own lives. One participant talked about how his perspective has been altered through continual exposure to suffering:

I think all in all, it leaves me with a certain kind of enthusiasm because I see people go through extraordinary pain and come out the other side. And so it makes me patient.

Another participant differentiated between the short-term stressors and the long-term benefits continually confronting client suffering:

In visiting the intensity of the private world of several people who are your clients, empathizing with the misery, and it can feel like, at the end of the day, lonely to have been so intensely in all of those places, and nobody had been in all of those places with me. And I couldn't tell anybody where I'd been. . . . The loneliness of that is a big part of the burden, I think. But that's more like the immediate at the end of the day kind of thing. What I think I'm left with is more a sense of the humanity. . . . And I think I'm a lot more comfortable with the topics of grief and sex and life crises. I just think that I just have that settled sense of the humanity of it.

CATEGORY C: CREATING A POSITIVE WORK STRUCTURE

Category C contains four themes that focus on how, over time, the participants created important support that enhanced their sense of wellness in the work environment.

Theme 1: Mentor and peer support was critical at the novice phase

Participants reported that positive mentor and peer relationships had a great impact on the novice phase of their careers. These relationships often developed during long-term first placements that were frequently described as challenging but not overwhelming. The novice setting provided enriching work environments full of learning opportunities and encouragement for responsible autonomy and risk taking. While at these sites, a foundation was built for the participants' future practices. In reflecting on his first placement, one participant stated:

> I remember those as good years. I'm sure they were stressful because a lot was new, but I felt very supported. I had resources about me, and I was valued and also I had a tremendous amount of independence.

Another participant stated:

> [It was] a time of working intensely with colleagues in relation to having lots of feedback, lots of inspection of one's practice. All of that, by and large, was very good. I certainly wouldn't trade those years.

While discussing a supervisor at her first placement following graduate training, one participant stated:

> At my first job, I was fortunate enough to have a really fine supervisor who literally I credit with the major amount of training and experience that I have. And that was totally geared to emotional self-awareness and use of self in ways in which I grew a hell of a lot, but I also learned never to ignore that part. . . . It opened all the doors for me, and it also made what I was doing very vital and real, and I feel real grateful for that.

Another participant discussed her decision to join a group of seasoned clinicians who then became important mentors and teachers:

> I think that I had either the good fortune or the good judgment to join a group of senior clinicians, all people 20 years older than I, very experienced, and I brought them something they needed which was the M.D. I could prescribe medications for their patients, and I could hospitalize their patients, which was fine. But they gave me the depth and breadth of clinical experience and an understanding of how the practice works, and it was very important to me.

Although the need for strong mentor relationships gradually diminished over time for many of the participants, the salience of these early relationships was highlighted in the reflections of one participant:

> It's more in retrospect than I was aware at the time, that there were people along the way who believed in me and kind of engaged with me because

they believed in me. And I really thrived on that, more than I knew, in the moment. I got so much from that in a way that if I hadn't gotten that, my life . . . would have taken a different path.

Theme 2: Participants have ongoing and enriching peer relationships

Participants reported that they initiated and sustained relationships with a variety of peers and coworkers beyond the novice phase. These relationships served a critical role in supporting the participants. One participant described the value of combining ongoing experience with peer relationships in this way:

I don't think years of experience by itself does it, because . . . I might have the same year of experience 20 times, and so I need to put that together with good consultation and a good collegial system around you; that is a part of the therapist's well-being.

When discussing peer relationships specific to the work environment, one participant stated:

I think that it is actually kind of a unique and rare environment that offers a therapist that kind of support for continuing growth. One that says even if you've been in this business for a number of years, you are still allowed to not know, you're still allowed to be afraid of what's happening, you're still allowed to feel like a failure, or whatever the issue is.

Both formal and informal interactions were emphasized as being important components of peer relationships in the work environment. One participant described how she and her coworkers had strategically created a work environment that provided a variety of interactions:

We've made a coffee room so that we run into each other on purpose, and we meet once a week for lunch, and that's very helpful both for relaxation and socializing and for consulting. There's always somebody I can say, "Listen to this situation, tell me what you think," and without naming names, I can describe the problem and get feedback from somebody that I respect.

In reflecting on his peer relationships, one participant highlighted the value of friendship and of sharing life events along with professional concerns:

We sit down for our staff meeting, and before we do anything else, we just sit at the table, take a few minutes, and talk about our lives. It's sort of this is what's happening with my kids; this is what I did last weekend; by the way, I saw a great movie; and just that personal level, before we get into talking about [clients].

Oftentimes, the intimate quality of peer and coworker relationships was an enriching factor in the participants' ability to deepen their level of self-awareness and, in turn, to invest more intensely in the therapeutic process with clients. Two participants described the importance of sustained, close relationships in the actual work environment:

Here, for example, we have a group of six, and some of us have been together for about 14 years, so you really have a chance to deepen the experience with one another and, therefore, I think also be able to deepen your work with clients, because you're better able to know about yourself in relationship to the work, and other people know you well enough to say, "Hey, look at this."

. . . we've been present here in this practice for going on 18 years, and we've always done weekly consultations and the kind that really gets at what might be stopping us, what might be blocking us, what we might be struggling with.

Diverse peer relationships in the broader professional community were also highlighted as vital sources of support. Participants tended to be actively involved in numerous professional activities, organizations, and community groups. One participant discussed the value of serving on a committee with a cross-section of helping professionals:

To have all these people giving time and energy to thinking about what will make our work improve. It's just inspiring, and for me it's invigorating and energizing. Just helpful in that way.

Similarly, another participant stated:

I have a group of colleagues that are very important to me, have been for 10 years now, and we meet in the West Coast every year; we spend a week together; we rent a room together for a week. They're all existentialists, and they're my closest colleagues in terms of tradition, and I see them maybe two, three times a year in groups or individually . . . . And that has been very, very helpful over the years.

Theme 3: Multiple roles are a protective factor

Participants reported that they structured their practices to include multiple tasks and professional involvements. They also exhibit a measure of freedom in choosing the type of clients they work with and how they do their billing. The ability to control the nature of their practice provided the participants with a stimulating balance of professional responsibilities while limiting the stressors that they encounter. In discussing her need for task diversity versus doing only clinical work, one participant stated:

> If I did only this work, I would be bored out of my mind. . . . It has nothing to do with the people I see; it's about having to empty yourself out so constantly and regularly to do that work. And that wouldn't be healthy; it just wouldn't be healthy.

Another participant discussed how involvement in diverse activities improved her professional and clinical work:

> I think there is something really enriching about supervising and teaching. It keeps me interested in my work and feeling alive and motivated to read and to think from some point of view other than just inside my head.

Participants reported that freedom to design one's caseload and control the billing also contributed positively to the professional experience. On client-related stressors, one participant stated:

> I don't think of my clients as impacting me in ways that I would consider stressors; . . . there's been stuff obviously over the years . . . we'll be dealing with suicide or we'll be dealing with this or that. . . . I haven't had much of that for a long time, and it's partly this practice; I mean, it's set up in a way in which I'm not dealing with crisis. I mean I'm dealing with . . . wellness perspectives. So I'm also not in situations at this point that would push that.

One participant discussed the way that she structured her caseload and completed billing:

> I've been very fortunate in two ways. One is that I'm an old-timer, so I've developed my own reputation and my own referral. Most of my patients come referred by other patients. And many pay out of pocket, and I'm willing to make some adjustments; I'd rather give them the money than the insurance company actually in terms of discount.

Theme 4: Participants create health-promoting work environments

Participants said that their work environments were suited to meet specific needs of space, aesthetics, and personal comfort. Equally important, these environments were conducive to facilitating successful therapeutic relationships. One participant outlined the benefits of her work area:

> I really like it here. I like my space. I like being here. I love being here when it's raining or snowing, and it's kind of a cocoon kind of feel to it. I think about the holding environment that helps therapy to work. That is part of what's here, and I like it, and I've heard clients talk about that it's nice to be here.

Other participants also discussed the need to create a comfortable, therapeutic work area:

> Space that allows for both enough distance to accommodate mine but also the other person's personal space requirements. And with clients, that varies actually. So I think sometimes I move forward or backward, depending on what I'm sensing, but also not so big that it feels like you're talking into a room rather than connecting to people. I think something that feels, that gives the sense of privacy and safety. I think it has the sense of being protected but not trapped.
>
> You know, I'm really into friendly textures and colors, and the light is important; the quiet is important. We went to great lengths to soundproof all these offices. The building would think that it was adequately soundproof, but I could still hear what was going on next door. We just kept putting insulation in the walls until it was soundproof. I guess I have to feel generally safe. I know people who work in clinics and kind of dangerous parts of town, and I think that's not conducive to the comfort of therapist or patient.

CATEGORY D: PROTECTIVE FACTORS

Category D contains three themes identifying proactive strategies that participants employ to master stressors.

Theme 1: Participants directly engage highly stressful professional dilemmas

Participants are skilled in their ability to handle ongoing difficult situations and to manage crises in a proactive manner that serves to prevent future incidents. Their strategies reflect an ability to adapt to change, and to bounce about unexpected or shifting events and issues. Participants tended to identify and frame challenges and issues in a hopeful light and to access appropriate resources. In confronting challenges and issues, participants discussed their need to remain receptive to possibilities and approaches on both internal and external levels:

> And then I have to engage [the stressful issue] in myself because there's always the possibility that there's some piece of me working here that would rather not see this, would rather not own the power that I have; I'd rather see that I wasn't that important, diminish my own responsibility in that way, or minimize my responsibility to be a better attender to somebody else's experience.
>
> One of my most profound learning experiences was stimulated by, first of all, working with a couple of therapists who turned out to be highly unethical and abusing their patients, and I had a dear friend of mine exploited by a therapist, and I'm thinking, "I've got to understand this; something really went wrong here." I find myself somewhat of an expert on boundaries and boundary violations because it really challenged my whole self-concept as a therapist or challenged the whole idea of therapy as a healing process. So I wanted to go after that problem.

An appropriate reliance on peer consultation was a critical resource that participants used in their process of exploring important issues and incidents:

> I get lots of consultation, so I'm not by myself with the really hard cases. That's primary for me. If there's anything that feels really important, it's not to be by myself in really hard situations, that I have colleagues with me. So that I feel that kind of a sense that I'm not all alone in this. It's really important to me that I'm seeing things clearly, and I think it's hard sometimes when you're all by yourself. And to have other eyes and ears looking at something with you. So that's one major way [to protect myself].

A key characteristic of the participants' reports was their willingness to remain open and to adapt. In discussing these traits, one participant stated:

> I think sometimes it's caused me not to feel like I know what I know at times, but on the other hand, it also keeps me kind of fresh and open. I'm willing to entertain almost anything, and I'm willing to look at where I could be off base about almost anything.

Another participant described her daily clinical work and provided an example of her ability to adapt from one client to another:

> I think I'm emotionally resilient in the sense of I can be with someone in their pain . . . but then I can in the next session be laughing with somebody about something or celebratory with somebody. So it feels like that's a way that I can move.

Theme 2: Participants confront and resolve personal issues

Participants reported that their own personal life crises and problems were a challenging area for them. They also believed that direct acknowledgment and resolution of these issues allowed for congruence between the personal self and the professional self. One participant explained how her experience in dealing with the unexpected death of a family member challenged her at a profoundly personal level yet allowed her to be more attuned to clients:

> Well, I think the suicide [in the family] made the work very challenging. And yet at the same time, I was fortunate in that I had a very fine therapist. And because I had that therapist, while the work was difficult, I constantly felt like I was being so tended to emotionally . . . I found myself taking from that experience and just automatically moving it into what I was doing with clients. So it's like as the therapist was willing to go with me where I needed to go and that opened up areas or that developed areas inside of me that I didn't even know were there. Then, automatically, I would hear those areas in clients. I would ask the questions because they were coming from where I'd been taken to.

Theme 3: Highly engaged learning is a powerful source of renewal

Participants reported that they had histories of being open to new experiences, seeking out diverse avenues of learning, and synthesizing information from multiple sources. Their lives were marked by an insatiable curiosity, a deep comfort with ambiguity, and constant consumption of knowledge. This ongoing learning process helped them to maintain an energy level necessary to continually engage in the helper role. In discussing a draw toward learning and its effect on her, one participant stated:

> Well, it provides constant energy for one thing, and I think what happens in our field is that we can get tired and exhausted, but I think that's one of the things that keeps me feeling high energy and a lot of interest and love for what we do, and it's exciting.

Some participants described why a tolerance for ambiguity and an openness for learning were critical ingredients in their work:

> I mean, we don't throw away what we know in favor of mystery, but to favor mystery is to prefer it above what we know.
>
> If nothing else, you want to work with these people from all walks of life with various occupations and various interests, and if you don't sustain at least some awareness or at least openness to learn from your patients about their work, then how can you be of any use to them if you stay on the outside? So one has to have the interest and curiosity and some

fondness, I think, for the client. If you're not interested in joining them, then why would they trust you to come and open themselves up.

If you can't work with the unknown and the uncertain, you can't last in this business.

Another participant discussed her efforts to bring new information into her work:

When I read, I always know what I define as active learning, which is trying to take the new information and see how I can incorporate it into what's already there, which means that I'm always modifying existing information too. And adapting it to my needs and integrating what I already know. It can be a negative thing if you go with the approach that everything has to fit to some rigid fixed scheme set already in existence. But I don't think I do that. I think I really constantly modify my schemes by incorporating the new stuff, but it's probably the integration and incorporation that are really important.

One participant discussed how she utilized peers to facilitate her own learning process:

I think being in a group practice has helped because it keeps you kind of interested and hungry for what's available and keeps you open, I think. I've done groups with co-therapists for years upon years. I've done co-therapy, marriage therapy. I think that also helps to stay open because you're constantly getting new information, getting new ways of thinking when working with someone. Getting input about your ways of working, so I think that also helps.

CATEGORY E: NURTURING SELF THROUGH SOLITUDE AND RELATIONSHIPS

Participants clearly identified their need to maintain a strong sense of self. Category E contains four themes that focus on components important to the participants for this need. The themes reflect multiple approaches and a network of internal and external involvements that enable the participants to maintain a personal and professional congruency.

Theme 1: Participants foster professional stability by nurturing a personal life

Participants were aware of the importance of maintaining a balance between their personal and professional lives. They believe that their role as a helper is facilitated by a lifestyle that includes multiple involvements and connections apart from their professional life. One participant verbalized this sentiment when he stated:

What helps me do it well is to give a damn about what I'm doing, but . . . I've got to have a life out of here. This can't be everything. I can't be over-invested in it. There's an appropriate kind of investment in which I care very much about what happens here, and I'm willing to invest myself as fully as I can, and part of what helps me do that is the fact that I've got a very real existence in a lot of ways, not just this.

Another participant succinctly stated:

There's [need for] some kind of larger balance. I don't think anybody could do this work justice and not tip over in some way. The tendency to get off center is too great.

Theme 2: Participants invest in a broad array of restorative activities

Participants cultivate a collection of activities and leisure pursuits. Although the actual involvements are varied, a shared theme that runs through them is their function of providing a diversion from work-related stressors and an avenue for reconnecting with self and others. The function of these activities and pursuits was reflected in one participant's statement:

[Helpful is] doing things personally like physical kinds of things. When we talked about secondary post-trauma, there are some days when I just feel like I need to go out and kick something and just kind of biking real hard or walking real fast; doing things like that can be really helpful I think. I do a lot of going to plays, going to movies, getting together with friends, and just talking about plays we've seen, books we've read.

A similar draw toward multiple involvements was reflected when this participant stated:

I love mystery stories and historical biography; that's where I learn my history, from historical novels. I like movies; I love sports; I'm an avid football fan; I knit; I do a lot of knitting and crocheting.

Other participants discussed the pull that they feel to nature and other creative activities:

I think something happens for me spiritually when I'm doing stuff with flowers and plants. I've got plants all over the place in my home, and it's kind of a ritualistic peace about tending those. I have gardens here and at a cabin up north, and there's, again, sort of a ritualistic peace with tending those. I think that takes me to a place that is real deeply nourishing, and I can get lost in it in a whole different way. I love the creative so the book that I wrote and stuff that I do for school and the papers, I really try to approach those as creative endeavors.

I find that music is a way for me to ground myself in the larger experience of my life and life itself. I suppose that's true for a lot of people . . . but that's certainly true for me, and always has been. And one of the ways, when I find myself feeling deprived of being able to cry, it'll come through that way.

One participant discussed the critical function of travel:

It's very helpful for perspective purposes. Very helpful. The trick is to be gone long enough . . . so you recognize fully your entire replaceability. That you are absolutely replaceable. And there, you talked about freedom and relief; there is real freedom and relief in that.

Theme 3: Participants construct fortifying personal relationships

Participants are highly skilled relationship builders. They establish nurturing and challenging connections with family, friends, and other social groups that are intimate and rich. Among other things, their relationships with others provide consistent, ongoing support and enable a realistic perspective of self. Although these relationships are important on a day-to-day basis, they are especially critical in times of crisis. Some of the participants discussed how a network of supportive relationships fortified their lives and acted as an emotional safety net:

If you have good friends in your life, if you have a good support system, folks will let you know that you're feeling worn out or depleted or whatever and then will support you getting some help.

A lot of close friends and my children are best friends. And they keep me very well balanced and keep my perspective, don't let me get a big head. They're very good, a very supportive bunch.

Having your own family connection solid is, at least for me, pretty important. I think I have a lot of reliance on other people in my life or friends or my wife, catching me in areas where I don't catch myself.

Some participants spoke about the encouragement and comfort they derived from a relationship with a spouse or life partner:

I married the right lady; my wife has a master's level degree in child development. And so we can talk, and she understood what I did. She never worked after we got married because she started having kids right away. But we could communicate and understand each other. And she was always a nice balance when my head started getting too big. She would pop it. . . . And so that was very supportive, still is.

We met actually as classmates. And I'm sure that's probably the most important relationship personally, but also I think probably professionally in some ways. We do talk psychology with each other, have all these years. So I'm sure that's been very important.

One participant highlighted the essential function of children and family:

We do a lot with family celebrations. Socializing, having people over for dinner. My children, now they are out of the home, but when they were younger, I think we did some things that were really helpful. Taking time just to play some games together. Just do something completely separate from work.

Another participant also commented on the very significant role that her friends play:

What I would say is that there are a few close friends, and when I'm in trouble, when they're in trouble, the rules are we get access to each other whenever and however long we need it. And when the trouble's over, we go back to our lives. And those people are very in place, and I think I am for them too.

Participants also fostered an essential relationship with the world at large, and they usually spoke about this in terms of a spiritual awareness or seeking a greater sense of connection with others:

I have a sense of spirit. I have a sense of reverence. I have a sense of place in the universe even though I know it's just a speck; it's a place to participate. I believe that there's benevolence in all that. I believe that warm, gentle breezes blow my way besides the cold, bitter winds.

Theme 4: Participants value an internal focus

Participants reported that they are aware of the significant role that their internal processes play in sustaining their own sense of wellness and in their ability to function effectively as practitioners. They are open to, and willingly engage in, their own personal therapy as a means of enhancing this process of introspection and self-examination. This commitment to understanding self represents an important self-care method that has a positive impact on their sense of resiliency and wellness in the helping role. Statements by the participants reflected the value of being continually self-aware. One said that it was important to attend to:

> what's coming up in my world that needs me to understand what's going on or feel like I get it in terms of whatever's happening internally so that when I'm doing my work, I'm sort of cleared out, and it isn't that the stuff isn't in there, but I'm not obsessing about it; it's not taking me some other place than where I need to be in the room.

Another stated:

> To learn something about vulnerability yourself, I don't know that anybody can really do therapy well until they know vulnerability, unless they are aware of their woundedness. . . . And be able to work from there.

One participant shared her belief that staying attuned to internal processes was, in part, an ethical responsibility:

> I think that's where we need to build this self-monitoring and be self-aware. If I become psychotic, then probably those around me would notice it, but outside of those extremes, if my work fluctuates on life events or whatever like physical health . . . I think to what extent one is ethical in their conduct [relates to] the kind of posture of self-reflection and self-monitoring and judgment.

Other participants discussed their belief that personal therapy was an important vehicle in their quest for self-awareness. One participant stated:

> The other thing I would say is it's important for every therapist to know when it's time to go back for some therapy of your own; personal anxieties or problems are either getting stirred up by the work or are intruding from the outside world.

CONCLUSION

Several pertinent areas were highlighted in this chapter. Participants identified stressors connected to various therapeutic issues and client behaviors, breaches in peer relationships, and the impact of their own personal crises and life changes. The areas of stressors that were reflected in the participants' comments underscore the demanding nature of the helping role and reinforce the value of protective approaches and self-care strategies as a means of ensuring practitioner wellness and professional vitality.

The participants identified important protective factors. These factors ranged from internal coping strategies to variables within the external environment. A commonality that existed among this group of participants was their commitment to self-care and their high-level skill in accessing valuable resources.

This group of practitioners has acute awareness of the internal landscape and maintains a watchful focus on their emotional selves. Their strong commitment to self-observation was frequently combined with a proactive style in directly confronting stressors that emerged both from their work and in their personal lives. When combined, these approaches allowed the participants to maintain a sense of personal congruence and an energy level that are critical components in professional wellness and burnout prevention.

This group of participants was nurtured through multiple avenues and relationships. The role that peers played in providing the participants with a realistic perspective and ongoing professional support was emphasized. While peer support was vital throughout the participants' careers, it played an especially key role during the participants' novice phase of development and also during times of unexpected crisis. In a similar way, participants also noted the importance of immersing themselves in enriching relationships and activities apart from their work environments. It appears that these diverse involvements were essential components to self-care plans that maintained a healthy sense of balance.

There are many practical applications of this chapter. One active practitioner in psychology working in a school setting, and in a private practice too, says she uses these insights *every day* as she works with great vitality to be helpful to those in need. Now that is an example of useful research!

SELF-REFLECTION EXERCISES

1.   What impresses you most about the methods used by experts to maintain professional vitality?

_____

_____

_____

_____

_____

_____

_____

_____

_____

2. What can the experts teach you for your own resiliency development and self-care?

_____

_____

_____

_____

_____

_____

_____

_____

_____

NOTES

* This chapter is based on the work of Mullenbach, M. A. (2000). *Expert therapists: A study of professional resiliency and emotional wellness* (Unpublished doctoral dissertation). University of Minnesota, Minneapolis. Thomas Skovholt was the dissertation advisor. This study also appeared in Skovholt, T. M., & Jennings, L. (Eds.) (2004). *Master therapists: Exploring expertise in therapy and counseling.* Boston, MA: Allyn & Bacon.
** Quotations have been edited with small changes that increase the clarity of the writing.

13
EPILOGUE

Helping others with significant concerns in their lives can be highly effective, satisfying, and meaningful. It can be great work. To do this well, however, we must constantly attach and separate successfully, over and over again, with person after person. We experience ambiguous professional loss, normative failure, secondary trauma, and vicarious traumatization. Yet, we must continually invest positively in others, and this means constant renewal of the self and an ongoing focus on the intricate balance between caring for others versus caring for self.

Our work can be so valuable and so pleasurable. A 68-year-old psychologist said, in reflecting on her work at that age:

> With diminishing anxiety, I became less and less afraid of my clients and with that came an ease for me in using my own wide repertoire of skills and procedures. They became more available to me when I needed them. And during those moments it became remarkable to me that someone would have the willingness to share their private world with me and that my work with them would bring very positive results for them. This brought a sense of intense pleasure to me.
>
> (Skovholt & Rønnestad, 1992a, p. 96)

IMAGERY EXERCISE

Let us suggest that you imagine a favorite tree in front of you. See its beauty, vibrancy, vitality, and strength. Now imagine yourself as the tree – beautiful, vibrant, vital, and strong. As a tree, you take in carbon dioxide and give off oxygen to those you help. Taking in carbon dioxide and giving off oxygen is literally giving life to those you serve. To do so, however, the tree must work hard, and to work hard, it must be healthy. That means it must have ample sunlight, plenty of rain, rich soil, and freedom from dangerous pests – like the insidious larvae of the emerald ash borer that kills trees by cutting off the water supply and nutrients. There are lots of tree pests, both overt and subtle. To grow, the tree must branch out and respond well to pruning. How then can you ensure that you, as a helping professional, will keep away those excessive professional losses – those dangerous pests that might cut off your nutrients and eat your leaves – and that you will have abundant soil, rain, and sunlight? And what for you comprises the sunlight, the rain, and the soil?

What ultimately is a better way to spend one's working days than giving off oxygen to those choking and gasping for air? What is more beautiful than a strong, healthy tree doing its work, or more tragic than a tree that is now dead and devoid of the capacity to give life? How will you remain as the healthy tree and remember the constant need, over 30 to 40 years as a caring professional, to defend against pests and always have rain, soil, and sunlight?

We wish you well.

SELF-REFLECTION EXERCISES

In the epilogue, we suggested that you think of a favorite tree and the way that a tree takes in carbon dioxide and gives off oxygen. Working with people, practitioners do a similar thing. Apply this tree metaphor to your life as a helper of others.

1.   What is your water, your sun, your soil? How adequate are they for you?

_____

_____

_____

_____

_____

_____

_____

_____

2. What are the large pests that can potentially eat away at your vitality? What are the small, invisible, or stealthy pests?

_____

_____

_____

_____

_____

_____

_____

_____

3. What changes, if any, do you need to make to be a healthy tree that can serve others by taking in carbon dioxide and giving off oxygen?

_____

_____

_____

_____

_____

_____

_____

_____

14

SELF-CARE ACTION PLAN

The intent of the first 13 chapters in this book is to engage you, the reader, in topics that are central to your work as a practitioner. In this chapter, the focus is on doing more than reading. We urge you to employ this chapter in a practical way that can be directly applied to your life as a practitioner. This chapter on self-care asks you to respond in writing to ideas in the text and also to additional inventories and charts. Then you are asked to develop a self-care action plan for yourself. The chapter has two parts:

Part 1 – You are to assess your own other-care–self-care balance while finding out what activities other practitioners choose for self-care.

Part 2 – You are to decide if any changes in your behavior, thinking patterns, or feelings are necessary to achieve a healthy other-care–self-care balance. Last, you are asked to make concrete but realistic plans for any change that seems needed.

PART 1: ASSESS YOUR OWN OTHER-CARE VS. SELF-CARE BALANCE

Step 1: Assessing the stress level of your work

A first step is to assess your job stress level. In stressful jobs, individuals often feel high demands and low control. Quadrant four (low control/

high demand) in Figure 14.1 is often thought of as much more stressful than quadrant one (high control/low demand). How would you assess the stress level of your job? The results are helpful in calibrating the other-care versus self-care balance. Next, fill out the short questionnaire in Figure 14.2.

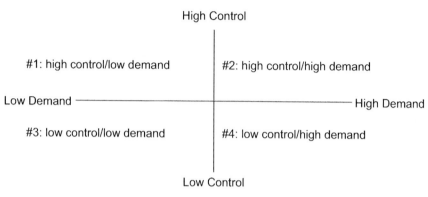

Figure 14.1 Elements of job stress. Adapted from Karasek & Theorell, 1992

Using the four-quadrant chart and the inventory, describe the stress level of your job.

_____

_____

_____

_____

_____

_____

_____

_____

_____

_____

_____

_____

How stressful is your job?

This test can give you a rough indication of how much stress you're under at work. The test was adapted for us by researcher Robert Karasek, Ph.D., of the University of Massachusetts at Lowell, based on a longer questionnaire of his. Answer yes or no:

	Yes	No
Demand		
I have to work very hard	____	____
I am not asked to do an excessive amount of work*	____	____
I have enough time to get my work done*	____	____
Control		
I have to do a lot of repetitive work*	____	____
I have to be creative	____	____
I have to learn new things	____	____
I have a lot of say about what happens	____	____
I have very little freedom to decide how I do my work*	____	____
Social support		
I work with helpful people	____	____
I work with people who take a personal interest in me	____	____
My supervisor is helpful	____	____
My supervisor is concerned about my welfare	____	____

Scoring: Calculate a separate score for each of the three parts—demand, control, and social support. In each part, give yourself one point for every "yes" answer to the questions that don't have an asterisk(*). For those that do have an asterisk, give yourself one point if you answered "no." Jot down your three scores in the spaces below. Then write in the word that describes each of those scores.

Demand score: ☐
   My job demands are _____
   (Write "low" if your score was 0 or 1; "high" if your score was 2 or 3.)

Control score: ☐
   My control at work is _____
   (Write "low" if you scored 0 to 2; "high" if you scored 3 to 5.)

Social-support score: ☐
   My social support at work is _____
   (Write "low" if you scored 0 or 1; "moderate" if 2; "high" if 3 or 4.)

Interpretation: High demand, low control, and low social support all tend to increase job stress. The more of those factors that you face at work—and the more extreme your score on each factor—the greater your stress. Jobs where you experience all three tension-producing features are generally very stressful, while jobs with two such features generate moderately high stress. Those with only one stressful factor may be moderate or moderately low in stress, depending on how much the other two scores offset that factor. The least stressful jobs combine high control and high social support with low demand.

Figure 14.2 Questionnaire: How stressful is your job?

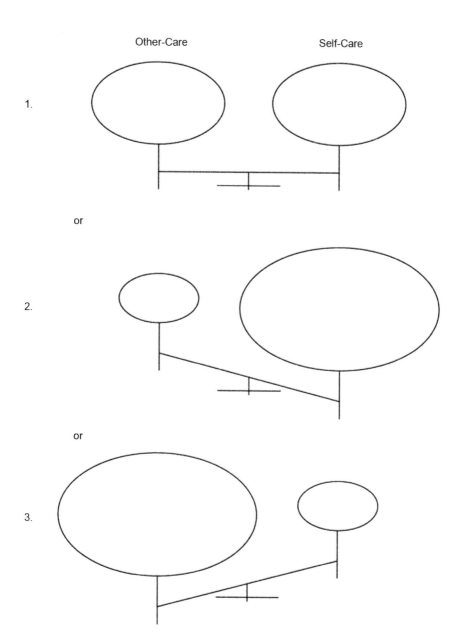

Figure 14.3 Other-care / self-care balance

Step 2: Assessing your other-care–self-care balance

Another step is to assess your other-care–self-care balance. Choose your type in Figure 14.3, and indicate the other-care–self-care balance score. Is it 50–50, 10–90, 90–10, 70–30, or 30–70?

What is your other-care–self-care balance score? _____ – _____

Often, other-care practitioners are more oriented to other-care than self-care. Some imbalance can be fine, but when is this direction excessive for you?

_____

_____

_____

_____

_____

_____

_____

_____

_____

_____

_____

_____

_____

_____

_____

Step 3: Assessing your professional self-care

In Chapter 8, we suggested 13 methods to sustain the professional self. Considering each method, what are you doing to sustain your professional self? How well are you sustaining your professional self? Please realize that we know that not all methods are of equal value for different practitioners in different settings and situations.

1   In the second column of Table 14.1, list example activities that you are doing to sustain your professional self.
2   Assess how well you are sustaining your professional self regarding each factor, and indicate the assessment score of 0 to 6 in the third column.

Table 14.1

0	1	2	3	4	5	6

Not at all ——————————————➤ *Very well*

Factors

Meaningful work

Maximizing the experience of professional success

Avoiding the grandiosity impulse and relishing small "I made a difference" victories

Thinking long-term

Creating and sustaining an active, individually designed development method

Professional self-understanding

Creating a professional greenhouse at work

    a. Learning environment where practitioner growth is encouraged growth is encouraged

    b. Leadership that promotes balance between caring for others and self

    c. Professional social support from peers

    d. Receiving support from mentors, supervisors, or bosses

    e. Being nurtured from your work as mentor, supervisor, or manager

    f. Learning how to be professional and playful

Using professional venting and expressive writing to release distress emotions

Being a "good enough" practitioner

Understanding the reality of pervasive early professional anxiety

Increasing cognitive excitement and decreasing boredom by reinventing yourself

Minimizing ambiguous endings

Learning to set boundaries, create limits, and say no to unreasonable requests

From the preceding assessment, list your three strongest professional self-care areas and your three areas for growth.

Strongest professional self-care areas:

1. _____

_____

2. _____

_____

3. _____

_____

Areas for growth in professional self-care:

1. _____

_____

2. _____

_____

3. _____

_____

Step 4: Assessing your personal self-care

In Chapter 9, parts of the personal self are presented. What are you doing to nurture each part of yourself? How well are you nurturing each part of your self?

1 In the second column of Table 14.2, list specific activities to nurture each part of your self.
2 Assess how well you are nurturing each part of your self, and indicate the assessment score of 0 to 6 in the third column.

Table 14.2

0	1	2	3	4	5	6
Not at all					→	*Very well*

Part of Your Self	*Specific Activities to Nurture This Part of Your Self*	*Assessment*
Emotional self		
Financial self		
Humorous self		
Loving self		
Nutritious self		
Physical self		
Playful self		
Priority-setting self		
Recreational self		
Relaxation and stress-reduction self, including		
a. Mindfulness		
b. Yoga		
Solitary self		
Spiritual or religious self		

From the preceding assessment, list your three strongest personal self-care areas and your three areas for growth.

Strongest personal self-care areas:

1. _____

2. _____

3. _____

Areas for growth in professional self-care:

1. _____

2. _____

3. _____

Step 5: Review positive strategies

Review the positive strategies used by psychologists and other practitioners in Tables 14.3 and 14.4 and in the following list, the Poor Self-Care Deadly Dozen.

Table 14.3 Three studies of therapists' self-care activities

Study 1: Top 10 Helpful Activities[a]	Study 2: Top 10 Career-Sustaining Behaviors[b]	Study 3: 234 Well-Functioning Psychologists' Top 10 Activities Contributing to Well Functioning[c]
Utilize close friends, significant others, or family as a source of support	Spending time with partner/family	Self-awareness and self-monitoring
Seek solutions to difficulties	Maintaining balance between professional and personal lives	Personal values
Use humor	Maintaining a sense of humor	Preserving balance between personal and professional lives
Choose internship activities of interest	Maintaining self-awareness	Relationship with spouse, partner, or family
Maintain self-awareness of the impact my internship experiences has on me and my work	Maintaining professional identity	Personal therapy
Seek out pleasurable diversions outside of internship	Engaging in quiet leisure activities	Relationships with friends
Consult with my fellow interns	Maintaining a sense of control over work responsibilities	Vacations
Set realistic goals for myself regarding internship	Engaging in physical activities	Professional identity
Seek supervision from clinical supervisor	Taking regular vacations	Informal peer support
Work to create a comfortable work environment for myself	Perceiving clients' problems as interesting	Mentor

[a] *Source:* "Intern Self-Care: An Exploratory Study into Strategy Use and Effectiveness," by J. A. Turner, L. M. Edwards, I. M. Eicken, K. Yokoyama, J. R. Castro, A. N. Tran, and K. L. Haggins, 2005, *Professional Psychology: Research and Practice, 36*, pp. 674–680.

[b] *Source:* "Career-Sustaining Behaviors, Satisfactions, and Stresses of Professional Psychologists," by P. Stevanovic and P. A. Rupert, 2004, *Psychotherapy: Theory, Research, Practice, Training, 41*, pp. 301–309.

[c] *Source:* "Well-Functioning in Professional Psychologists," by J. J. Coster and M. Schwebel, 1997, *Professional Psychology: Research and Practice, 28*, pp. 5–13.

Table 14.4 Self-care methods of practitioners

Trauma Therapists' Top 10 Helpful Activities[a]	*Counselors', Teachers', and Health Professionals' 10 Commonly Described Activities*[b]
Discussing cases with colleagues	Being with family
Attending workshops	Education for job skills
Spending time with family or friends	Fun hobby
Travel, vacations, hobbies, movies	Physical activity
Talking with colleagues between sessions	Reading
Socializing	Receiving consultation or supervision
Exercising	Social activity
Limiting case load	Time alone
Developing spiritual life	Time with friends, partner, spouse
Receiving general supervision	Vacation

[a] *Source:* "Vicarious Traumatization: An Empirical Study of the Effects of Trauma Work on Trauma Therapists," by L. A. Pearlman and P. J. MacIan, 1995, *Professional Psychology: Research and Practice, 26*, pp. 558–565.

[b] In alphabetical order. Data from workshops by T. M. Skovholt in 1996.

The Poor Self-Care Deadly Dozen

1 Toxic supervisor and colleague support
2 Little fun (e.g., playfulness, humor, laughing) in life or work
3 Only a fuzzy and unarticulated understanding of one's own needs
4 No professional development process that turns experience into more competence and less anxiety
5 No energy-giving personal life
6 An inability to say no to unreasonable requests
7 Vicarious traumatization that takes an accumulated toll
8 Personal relationships that are predominantly one-way caring relationships with self as giver
9 Constant perfectionism in work tasks
10 Continual unresolved ambiguous professional losses
11 A strong need to be needed
12 Professional success defined solely by client, student, or patient positive change or appreciation

Step 6: Assessing self-care strengths and weaknesses

Using information gathered from Steps 1 to 5, write an assessment of your self-care strengths and areas of growth. As has been noted throughout the preceding chapters, there are joys in the work but also hazards—plenty of them.

The constant giving of the self, a necessity in optimal work by counselors, therapists, teachers, and health professionals, means that practitioners must assertively nurture the wellness of the professional and personal selves. How are you doing with nurturing your own wellness?

_____

_____

_____

_____

_____

_____

_____

_____

PART 2: ACTION PLAN FOR CHANGE

Step 7: Action plan

Now, develop an action plan to work on one or two self-care growth areas. Remember that slower behavioral change usually works best. We suggest that you be modest in your goals and build on attainable change, with reinforcement to maintain the change.

Your general action plan:

_____
_____
_____
_____
_____
_____
_____
_____

Specific Goal 1:

_____
_____
_____
_____
_____
_____
_____

Method for achieving Goal 1:

_____
_____
_____
_____
_____
_____
_____

Reinforcement to maintain new behavior:

_____

_____

_____

_____

_____

_____

_____

Specific Goal 2:

_____

_____

_____

_____

_____

_____

Method for achieving Goal 2:

_____

_____

_____

_____

_____

_____

Reinforcement to maintain new behavior:

_____

_____

_____

_____

_____

_____

_____

ACKNOWLEDGMENTS

As a part of the first edition, Tom acknowledged the following individuals: Lynda Borchers, Dan Detzner, Sally Hage, Len Jennings, Fran LaFave, Susan Lee, Mary Mullenbach, John Romano, Helge Rønnestad, and L. P. Smith. In addition, he noted the sustaining love from his family: his mother and father, Jane and Annie, Glen and Anna, David, Rachel, Hanna, and Cathy. He also appreciated the friendship of Shirley, Rachel, and David. Elisabeth Nealy and Carla Hill were able and patient with word processing through many drafts of the first edition. Thanks to them.

Many people contributed to the second edition. Thank you to Lidan Gu, Ruth Swartwood, and Alexandra Stillman for your work. Tom appreciates the valuable feedback, since the first edition of this book, about professional resiliency from students and participants in workshops. He is thankful for the help, support, and love from his family, friends, and Lisa. Michelle is grateful for the ever-present love and support from friends and family, including her parents, Nick and Judy; her husband, John; wonderful friends Maren, Eli, Julie, Sandy, Andy, Kelly, and Sharmi. We also wish to thank Dana Bliss, Chris Tominich, and Tara Nieuwesteeg at Routledge for their support and guidance as we developed the second edition, as well as Mary Farquhar and Shawn Rutka in the Counseling Program of the Department of Educational Psychology at the University of Minnesota.

As part of rewriting the book for this third edition, Tom and Michelle acknowledge the valuable work of Meredith Martyr and Elise Madden as RAs. Additionally, we would like to thank Anna Moore and Zoey Peresman at Routledge and Sheri Sipka at Apex CoVantage for the many ways they helped bring this book to birth.

Michelle extends her appreciation to her friends, family, and colleagues for the support in completing the third edition of this book. Special thanks to her family, John and Lars, for their encouragement and love throughout this process and always. Michelle is also grateful for the opportunity to present workshops on practitioner resiliency to others in the relationship-intense professions, enhancing her understanding of the complexities of practitioner resilience. Additionally, she is always grateful for the opportunity to do meaningful and fulfilling work with clients in therapy.

Tom expresses appreciation to Jian-Ming Hou for his dissertation work on highly resilient therapists, Len Jennings for his work on master therapists, Helge Rønnestad for his work on counselor and therapist development, Sandra Wick for providing a positive practice setting, and his University of Minnesota graduate students and counseling clients who have taught him so much about the human capacity to be resilient. Joe Johnston, Harry Grater, and Sam Schur have been great mentors through the thickets of career life. Special thanks to Lisa, Rachel YD, and Danny, Hanna, Julius, and Abby.

REFERENCES

Ackerley, G. D., Burnell, J., Holder, D. C., & Kurdek, L. A. (1988). Burnout among licensed psychologists. *Professional Psychology: Research and Practice, 19,* 624–631. doi: 10.1037/0735–7028.19.6.624

Ackerman, D. (1999). *Deep play.* New York: Random House.

Adams, H. (1918). *The education of Henry Adams.* New York: Houghton Mifflin.

Adolson, M. J. (1995). Clinical supervision of therapists with difficult-to-treat patients. *Bulletin of the Menninger Clinic, 59,* 32–52. Retrieved from http://www.unboundmedicine.com/medline/citation/7894380/Clinical_supervision_of_therapists_with_difficult_to_treat_patients_

Ambrose, S. E. (1996). *Undaunted courage.* New York: Touchstone.

Ampel, C. (2013, July 26). Minister connected with everyone. *Minneapolis Star Tribune,* p. B4.

Angus, L., Hayes, J. A., Anderson, T., Ladany, N., Castonguay, L. G., & Muran, J. C. (2010). Future directions: Emerging opportunities and challenges in psychotherapy research. In L. G. Castonguay, J. C. Muran, L. Angus, J. A. Hayes, N. Ladany, & T. Anderson (Eds.), *Bringing psychotherapy research to life: Understanding change through the work of leading clinical researchers* (pp. 353–362). Washington, DC: American Psychological Association.

Anonymous. (Ed.). (1982). *Each day a new beginning.* San Francisco, CA: HarperCollins.

Associated Press. (2012, December 16). Acts of altruism emerge. *Columbia Daily Tribune.* Retrieved from http://www.columbiatribune.com

Ayers, W. (1993). *To teach: The journey of a teacher.* New York: Teachers College Press.

Bachelor, A., & Horvath, A. (1999). The therapeutic relationship. In M. A. Hubble, B. L. Duncan, & S. D. Miller (Eds.), *The heart and soul of change:*

What works in therapy (pp. 133–178). Washington, DC: American Psychological Association.

Bain, K. (2004). *What the best college teachers do.* Cambridge, MA: Harvard University Press.

Baker, E. (2003). *Caring for ourselves: A therapist's guide to personal and professional well-being.* Washington, DC: American Psychological Association.

Balch, J. F., & Balch, P. A. (1997). *Prescription for nutritional healing.* Garden City Park, NY: Avery Publishing Group.

Baltes, P. B., & Smith, J. (1990). Toward a psychology of wisdom and its ontogenesis. In R. E. Sternberg (Ed.), *Wisdom: Its origins and development* (pp. 87–120). Cambridge: Cambridge University Press.

Bandhauer, B. (1997). Waiting for wisdom to arrive. In J. Kottler (Ed.), *Finding your way as a counselor* (pp. 7–9). Alexandria, VA: American Counseling Association.

Barnett, J. E., Baker, E. K., Elman, N. S., & Schoener, G. R. (2007). In pursuit of wellness: The self-care imperative. *Professional Psychology: Research and Practice, 38*(6), 603–612. doi: 10.1037/0735–7028.38.6.603

Barnett, J. E., Johnston, L. C., & Hillard, D. (2006). Psychologist wellness as an ethical imperative. In L. VandeCreek & J. B. Allen (Eds.), *Innovations in clinical practice: Focus on health and wellness* (pp. 257–271). Sarasota, FL: Professional Resources Press.

Beck, H. (2009, December 20). Bowing to body clocks, N.B.A. teams are sleeping in. *New York Times*, pp. SP1, SP3.

Becker, E. (1973). *The denial of death.* New York: Free Press.

Beckett, S. (1997). *Waiting for Godot.* New York: Grove Press.

Belenky, M., Chinchy, B., Goldberger, N., & Tarule, J. (1986). *Women's ways of knowing.* New York: Basic Books.

Benjo, C., & Scotta, C. (Producers), & Cantet, L. (Director). (2009). *The class* [Motion picture]. Paris, France: Sony Pictures Classics.

Benner, P., & Wrubel, J. (1982). Skilled clinical knowledge: The value of perceptual awareness, part 2. *Journal of Nursing Administration, 12,* 28–33. Retrieved from http://journals.lww.com/nurseeducatoronline/Abstract/ 1982/05000/Skilled_Clinical_Knowledge__The_Value_of.3.aspx

Benson, H. (1975). *The relaxation response.* New York: Morrow.

Benson, H. (1999, August). *Power and biology of belief.* Presented at the annual convention of the American Psychological Association, Boston, MA.

Benson-Henry Institute for Mind Body Medicine. (2010). *Eliciting the relaxation response.* Retrieved from http://www.massgeneral.org/bhi/basics/ eliciting_rr.aspx

Berman, P., Heller, R., Prelinger, E., & Munch, E. (2006). *Edvard Munch: The modern life of the soul.* New York: Museum of Modern Art.

Bernard, J. M., & Goodyear, R. K. (2008). *Fundamentals of clinical supervision* (4th ed.). Boston: Allyn & Bacon.

Berry, C. R. (1988). *When helping you is hurting me: Escaping the Messiah trap.* New York: Harper & Row.

Blatt, S. (2008). *A dialectical psychology: Implications for research and practice.* Washington, DC: American Psychological Association.

Bohart, A. C., Elliot, R., Greenberg, L. S., & Watson, J. C. (2002). Empathy. In J. C. Norcross (Ed.), *Psychotherapy relationships that work: Therapist contributions and responsiveness to patients* (pp. 89–108). London: Oxford University Press.

Borders, L. D. (1989). A pragmatic agenda for developmental supervision research. *Counselor Ed & Supervision, 29,* 16–24. doi: 10.1002/j.1556–6978.1989.tb01130.x

Borders, L. D., & Brown, L. L. (2005). *The new handbook of counseling supervision* (5th ed.). Mahwah, NJ: Lawrence Erlbaum Associates.

Boss, P. (1999). *Ambiguous loss: Learning to live with unresolved grief.* Cambridge, MA: Harvard University Press.

Boss, P. (2006). *Loss, trauma, and resilience: Therapeutic work with ambiguous loss.* New York: W.W. Norton.

Boss, P., & Carnes, D. (2012). The myth of closure. *Family Process, 51,* 456–469. doi: 10.1111/famp.12005

Boss, P., Caron, W., Horbal, J., & Mortimer, J. (1990). Predictors of depression in care-givers of dementia patients: Boundary ambiguity and mastery. *Family Process, 29,* 245–254. doi: 10.1111/j.1545–5300.1990.00245.x

Boss, P., & Greenberg, J. (1984). Family boundary ambiguity: A new variable in family stress theory. *Family Process, 23,* 535–546. doi: 10.1111/j.1545–5300.1984.00535.x

Bowlby, J. (1969). *Attachment.* New York: Basic Books.

Bowlby, J. (1973). *Separation: Anxiety and anger.* New York: Basic Books.

Bowlby, J. (1980). *Loss: Sadness and depression.* New York: Basic Books.

Bowlby, J. (1988). *A secure base: Parent–child attachment and healthy human development.* New York: Basic Books.

Brazelton, T. B. (2013). *Learning to listen: A life caring for children.* Boston: DA CAPO Press.

Brinson, J. (1997). Reach out and touch someone. In J. Kottler (Ed.), *Finding your way as a counselor* (pp. 165–167). Alexandria, VA: American Counseling Association.

Brown, B. (2012). *Daring greatly: How the courage to be vulnerable transforms the way we live, love, parent, and lead.* New York, NY: Penguin Random House.

Brown, R. M. (Ed.). (1986). *The essential Reinhold Neibuhr: Selected essays and addresses.* New Haven, CT: Yale University Press.

Buber, M. (1970). *I and thou.* New York: Touchstone.

Campbell, D. P., Hyne, S. A., & Nilsen, D. L. (1992). *Manual for the Campbell Interest and Skill Survey.* Minneapolis, MN: NCS Pearson.

Canfield, J. (2005). Secondary traumatization, burnout, and vicarious traumatization: A review of the literature as it relates to therapists who treat trauma. *Smith College Studies in Social Work, 75*(2), 81–101. doi: 10.1300/ J497v75n02_06

Carey, B., Cave, D., & Alvarez, L. (2009, November 8). A military therapist's world: Long hours, filled with pain. *New York Times*, p. 1.

Carkhuff, R. (1969). *Helping and human relations.* New York: Holt, Rinehart and Winston.

Carvalho, H., & Matos, P. M. (2011a). Ser e tornar-se psicoterapeuta parte I: Diálogo entre experiências pessoais e profissionais. *Psicologia: Ciência e Profissão, 31*(1), 80–95. Retrieved from http://www.redalyc.org/articulo. oa?id=282021809008

Carvalho, H., & Matos, P. M. (2011b). Ser e tornar-se psicoterapeuta parte II: Diálogo entre mudanças pessoais e profissionais. *Psicologia: Ciência e Profissão, 31*(4), 778–799. Retrieved from http://www.redalyc.org/articulo. oa?id=282021813008

Cassidy, J. (1999). No satisfaction: The trial of a shopping nation. *The New Yorker, 129*(43), 88–92.

Castonguay, L. G., Constantino, M. J., & Grosse Holtforth, M. (2006). The working alliance: Where are we and where should we go? *Psychotherapy: Theory, Research, Practice, Training, 43*(3), 271–279. doi: 10.1037/ 0033–3204.43.3.271

Cedoline, A. J. (1982). *Job burnout in public education.* New York: Teachers College Press.

Chang, V. Y., Palesh, O., Caldwell, R., Glasgow, N., Abramson, M., & Luskin, F. (2004). The effects of a mindfulness-based stress reduction program on stress, mindfulness self-efficacy, and positive states of mind. *Stress and Health: Journal of the International Society for the Investigation of Stress, 20*(3), 141–147. doi: 10.1002/smi.1011

Cherniss, C. (1980). *Staff burnout: Job stress in the human services.* Thousand Oaks, CA: Sage.

Cherniss, C. (1995). *Beyond burnout.* New York: Routledge.

Chi, M. T. H., Glaser, R., & Farr, M. J. (Eds.). (1988). *The nature of expertise.* Hillsdale, NJ: Erlbaum.

Chodorow, N. (1978). *The reproduction of mothering.* Berkeley: University of California Press.

Christopher, J. C. (2010). Mindfulness and my search for meaning. In M. Trotter-Mathison, J. M. Koch, S. Sanger, & T. M. Skovholt (Eds.), *Voices from the field: Defining moments in counselor and therapist development* (pp. 37–40). New York: Routledge.

Colvin, G. (2010). *Talent is overrated.* New York: Portfolio Penguin.

Corey, G. (2005). A meaningful life-personal and professional-has many twists and turns. In R. K. Conyne & F. Bemak (Eds.), *Journeys to professional excellence: Lessons from leading counselor educators and practitioners* (pp. 57–72). Alexandria, VA.: American Counseling Association.

Corey, M. S., & Corey, G. (1989). *Becoming a helper.* Pacific Grove, CA: Brooks/Cole.

Corsini, R. J., & Wedding, D. (2010). *Current psychotherapies* (9th ed.). Belmont, CA: Brooks/Cole.

Coster, J. S., & Schwebel, M. (1997). Well-functioning in professional psychologists [Special section]. *Professional Psychology: Research and Practice, 28,* 5–13.doi: 10.1037/0735-7028.28.1.5

Cousins, N. (1979). *Anatomy of an illness as perceived by the patient.* New York: W. W. Norton.

Csikszentmihalyi, M. (2008). *Creativity: Flow and the psychology of discovery and invention.* New York: Harper & Row.

Danby, H. (Trans.). (1933). *The Mishnah, Talmud.* London: Oxford University Press.

David, D. P. (2012). *Resilience as a protective factor against compassion fatigue in trauma therapists* (Order No. 3544932, Walden University). ProQuest Dissertations and Theses, 214. Retrieved from http://login.ezproxy.lib.umn. edu/login?url=http://search.proquest.com/docview/1235717224?accoun tid=14586 (1235717224).

Davis, D. D. (2008). *Terminating therapy.* New York: Wiley.

Davis, M., Eshelman, E. R., & McKay, M. (2008). *The relaxation and stress reduction workbook* (6th ed.). Oakland, CA: New Harbinger Publications.

Didion, J. (2007). *The year of magical thinking.* New York: Vintage.

Diener, E., Suh, E. M., Lucus, R. E., & Smith, H. L. (1999). Subjective well-being: Three decades of progress. *Psychological Bulletin, 125,* 276–302. doi: 10.1037/0033-2909.125.2.276

Dodge, K. A., & Feldman, E. (1990). Issues in social cognition and sociometric status. In S. R. Asher & J. D. Coie (Eds.), *Peer rejection in childhood* (pp. 119–155). New York: Cambridge University Press.

Doehrman, M. J. (1976). Parallel processes in supervision and psychotherapy. *Bulletin of the Menninger Clinic, 40,* 1–104. Retrieved from http://www. ncbi.nlm.nih.gov/pubmed/1252650

Dominguez, J., & Robin, V. (1992). *Your money or your life.* New York: Penguin Books.

Donne, J. (1975). *Devotions: Upon emergent occasions* (A. Raspa, Ed.). Montreal: McGill-Queen's University Press.

Dreyfus, H. L., & Dreyfus, S. E. (1986). *Mind over machine: The power of human intuition and expertise in the era of the computer.* New York: Free Press.

Dubé, V., & Ducharme, F. (2015). Nursing reflective practice: An empirical literature review. *Journal of Nursing Education and Practice, 5*(7), 91. doi: 10.5430/jnep.v5n7p91

Duncan, B. L., & Miller, S. D. (2000). *The heroic client: Doing client-centered, outcome-informed therapy.* San Francisco, CA: Jossey-Bass.

Dupree, P. I., & Day, H. D. (1995). Psychotherapists' job satisfaction and job burnout as a function of work setting and percentage of managed care clients. *Psychotherapy in Private Practice, 14*(2), 77–93. doi: 10.1300/J294v14n02_11

Eison, J. A. (1985, August). *Coming of age in academe: From teaching assistant to faculty member.* Presented at the annual convention of the American Psychological Association, Los Angeles.

Ellwein, M. C., Grace, M. E., & Comfort, R. E. (1990). Talking about instruction: Student teachers' reflections on success and failure in the classroom. *Journal of Teacher Education, 41*(4), 3–14. doi: 10.1177/002248719004100502

Emmons, H., & Kranz, R. (2006). *The chemistry of joy: A three-step program for overcoming depression through western science and eastern wisdom.* New York: Fireside.

Ericsson, K. A. (2007). An expert-performance perspective of research on medical expertise: The study of clinical performance. *Medical Education, 41,* 1124–1130. doi:10.1111/j.1365–2923.2007.02946.x

Ericsson, K. A., Charness, N., Feltovich, P. J., & Hoffman, R. R. (2006). *The Cambridge handbook of expertise and expert performance.* New York: Cambridge University Press.

Ericsson, K. A., Prietula, M. J., & Cokely, E. T. (2007). The making of an expert. *Harvard Business Review, 85*(7–8), 114–121. Retrieved from https://hbr.org/2007/07/the-making-of-an-expert

Erikson, E. (1950). *Childhood and society.* New York: W. W. Norton.

Erikson, E. (1968). *Identity, youth and crisis.* New York: W. W. Norton.

Etringer, B. D., Hillerbrand, E., & Claiborn, C. D. (1995). The transition from novice to expert counselor. *Counselor Education and Supervision, 35,* 4–17. doi: 10.1002/j.1556–6978.1995.tb00205.x

Farber, B. (1983). The effects of psychotherapeutic practice upon the psychotherapists. *Psychotherapy: Theory, Research, and Practice, 20*(2), 174–182. doi: 10.1037/h0088488

Farber, B. (1990). Burnout in psychotherapists: Incidence, types, and trends. *Psychology in Private Practice, 8*(1), 35–44. doi: 10.1300/J294v08n01_07

Farber, B. A., & Heifetz, L. J. (1981). The satisfactions and stresses of psychotherapeutic work: A factor analytic study. *Professional Psychology: Research and Practice, 12,* 621–630. doi.org.ezp2.lib.umn.edu/10.1037/0735–7028.12.5.621

Figley, C. R. (1995). Compassion fatigue: Toward a new understanding of the costs of caring. In B. H. Stamm (Ed.), *Secondary traumatic stress: Self-care issues for clinicians, researchers and educators* (pp. 3–28). Baltimore: Sidran Press.

Figley, C. (2002). Compassion fatigue: Psychotherapists' chronic lack of self-care. *Journal of Clinical Psychology, 58,* 1433–1441. doi: 10.1002/jclp.10090

Firestone, R. W., & Catlett, J. (1999). *Fear of intimacy.* Washington, DC: American Psychological Association.

Fletcher, D., & Sarkar, M. (2013). Psychological resilience: A review and critique of definitions, concepts, and theory. *European Psychologist, 18*(1), 12–23. doi: 10.1027/1016–9040/a000124

Foa, V. G. (1971). Interpersonal and economic resources. *Science, 171,* 345–351. doi: 10.1126/science.171.3969.345

Frank, J. D., & Frank, J. B. (1991). *Persuasion and healing* (3rd ed.). Baltimore: Johns Hopkins University Press.

Frankl, V. (1959). *Man's search for meaning.* Boston: Beacon Press. (Original work published 1946)

Frattaroli, J. (2006). Experimental disclosure and its moderators: A meta-analysis. *Psychological Bulletin, 132,* 823–865. doi: 10.1037/0033–2909.132.6.823

Freudenberger, H. (1974). Staff burnout. *Journal of Social Work, 30,* 159–165. doi: 10.1111/j.1540–4560.1974.tb00706.x

Freudenberger, H. J. (1990). Hazards of psychotherapeutic practice. *Psychotherapy in Private Practice, 8*(1), 31–34. doi: 10.1300/J294v08n01_06

Freudenberger, H. J., & Robbins, A. (1979). The hazards of being a psychoanalyst. *The Psychoanalytic Review, 66*(2), 275–295.

Fromm, E. (1968). *The revolution of hope toward a humanized technology.* New York: Harper & Row.

Galluzzo, G. R., & Kacer, B. A. (1991). *The best and worst of high school student teaching.* Paper presented at the annual meeting of the American Educational Research Association, Chicago, IL.

Garfield, C. (1995). *Sometimes my heart goes numb.* San Francisco, CA: Jossey-Bass.

Garfunkel, G. (1995). Lifeline. In M. R. Sussman (Ed.), *A perilous calling: The hazards of psychotherapy practice* (pp. 148–159). New York: John Wiley & Sons.

Garmazey, N. (1971). Vulnerability research and the issue of primary prevention. *American Journal of Orthopsychiatry, 41,* 101–116. doi: 10.1111/j.1939–0025.1971.tb01111.x

Garmazey, N., & Devine, V. (1984). Project competence: The Minnesota studies of children vulnerable to psychopathology. In N. Watt, E. J. Anthony, L. Wynne, & J. Rolf (Eds.), *Children at risk for schizophrenia* (pp. 289–303). New York: Cambridge University.

Gawande, A. (2007). *Better: A surgeon's notes on performance.* New York: Henry Holt and Co.

Geller, S. M., & Greenberg, L. S. (2012). *Therapeutic presence. A mindful approach to effective therapy.* Washington, DC: American Psychological Association.

Geller, J. D., Norcross, J. C., & Orlinsky, D. E. (Eds.). (2005). *The psychotherapist's own psychotherapy: Patient and clinician perspectives.* New York: Oxford University Press.

Gilligan, C. (1982). *In a different voice.* Cambridge, MA: Harvard University Press.

Gladwell, M. (2008). *Outliers: The story of success.* New York: Little, Brown.

Gladwell, M. (2013). *David and Goliath: Underdogs, misfits, and the art of battling giants.* New York: Little, Brown.

Glaser, R., & Chi, M. T. H. (1988). Overview. In M. T. H. Chi, R. Glaser, & M. J. Farr (Eds.), *The nature of expertise* (pp. xx–xxi). Hillsdale, NJ: Erlbaum.

Goffman, E. (1967). *Interaction ritual.* Garden City, NY: Doubleday Anchor.

Golden, A. (1997). *Memoirs of a geisha.* New York: Vintage.

Goldfried, M. R. (1980). Toward the delineation of therapeutic change principles. *American Psychologist, 35,* 991–999. doi: 10.1037/0003–066X.35.11.991

Goodyear, R. (1981). Termination as a loss experience for the counselor. *Personnel and Guidance Journal, 59,* 347–350. doi: 10.1002/j.2164–4918.1981.tb00565.x

Gray, L. A., Ladany, N., Walker, J. A., & Ancis, J. R. (2001). Psychotherapy trainees' experience of counterproductive events in supervision. *Journal of Counseling Psychology, 48,* 371–383. doi: 10.1037/0022–0167.48.4.371

Grosch, W. N., & Olsen, D. C. (1994). *When helping starts to hurt: A new look at burnout among psychotherapists.* New York: W. W. Norton.

Grotevant, H., & Cooper, C. (1986). Individuation in family relationships: A perspective on individual differences in the development of identity and role-taking skill in adolescence. *Human Development, 29,* 82–100. doi: 10.1159/000273025

Grothe, M. (2008). *I never metaphor I didn't like.* New York: Collins Books.

Guy, J., Brown, K., & Poelstra, P. (1990). Who gets attacked? A national survey of patient violence directed at psychologists in clinical practice. *Professional Psychology: Research and Practice, 21,* 493–495. doi: 10.1037/0735–7028.21.6.493

Guy, J., Brown, K., & Poelstra, P. (1992). Safety concerns and protective measures used by psychotherapists. *Professional Psychology: Research and Practice, 23,* 421–423. doi: 10.1037/0735–7028.23.5.421

Gysbers, N. C., & Henderson, P. (2005). *Developing & managing your school guidance and counseling program* (4th ed.). Alexandria, VA: American Counseling Association.

Gysbers, N. C., & Rønnestad, M. H. (1974). Practicum supervision: Learning theory. In G. F. Farwell, N. R. Gamsky, & P. Mathieu-Coghlan (Eds.), *The counselor's handbook: Essays on preparation* (pp. 133–140). New York: Intext Educational Publishers.

Hage, S. (2010). Caring and letting go: Balancing both sides of the turtle. In M. Trotter-Mathison, J. M. Koch, S. Sanger, & T. M. Skovholt (Eds.), *Voices from the field: Defining moments in counselor and therapist development* (pp. 182–185). New York: Routledge.

Hagstrom, S. J., Skovholt, T. M., & Rivers, D. A. (1997). The advanced undecided college student: A qualitative study. *NACADA Journal, 17*(2), 23–30. doi: 10.12930/0271–9517–17.2.23

Hall, C. W., Row, K. A., Wuensch, K. L., & Godley, K. R. (2013). The role of self-compassion in physical and psychological well-being. *The Journal of psychology, 147*(4), 311–323. doi: 10.1080/00223980.2012.693138

Hampl, P. (1995). *Burning bright: An anthology of sacred poetry.* New York: Ballantine Books.

Harmon, C., Hawkins, E. J., Lambert, M. J., Slade, K., & Whipple, J. (2005). Improving outcomes for poorly responding clients: The use of clinical supports tools and feedback to clients. *Journal of Clinical Psychology, 61*(2), 175–185. doi: 10.1002/jclp.20109

Harrison, R. L., & Westwood (2009). Preventing vicarious traumatization of mental health therapists: identifying protective practices. *Psychotherapy Theory, Research, Practice, Training, 46*(2), 203–219. doi:10.1037/a0016081

Hartmann, P. S. (2001). Women developing wisdom: Antecedents and correlates in a longitudinal sample. *Dissertation Abstracts International, 62*(1), 501B.

Hays, K. F. (1999, August). Nutrition and exercise: Key components of taking care of yourself. In L. T. Pantano (Chair), *Taking care of yourself: The continuing quest.* Symposium conducted at the annual convention of the American Psychological Association, Boston.

Healy, M. (2014, May 2). Study: Laughing puts brain in mock-meditative state. *St. Paul Pioneer Press*, p. 12A.

Help for helpers: Daily meditations for counselors. (1989). Center City, MN: Hazelden Foundation.

Henry, W. E. (1966). Some observations on the lives of healers. *Human Development, 9*, 47–56.

Heppner, P. P. (1989). Chance and choices in becoming a therapist. In W. Dryden & L. Spurling (Eds.), *On becoming a therapist* (pp. 69–86). New York: Routledge.

Hernández, P., Engstrom, D., & Gangsei, D. (2010). Exploring the impact of trauma on therapists: Vicarious resilience and related concepts in training. *Journal of Systemic Therapies, 29*(1), 67–83. doi: 10.1521/jsyt.2010.29.1.67

Hill, L. (1988). From chaos to organization. *Journal of Counseling and Development, 67*, 105. doi: 10.1002/j.1556–6676.1988.tb02049.x

Hillenbrand, L. (2010). *Unbroken: A world war II story of survival, resilience, and redemption.* New York: Random House.

Hirai, T. (2010). *Personal and professional characteristics of Japanese master therapists: A qualitative investigation on expertise in psychotherapy and counseling in Japan* (Unpublished doctoral dissertation). University of Minnesota.

Hoffer, E. (1951). *The true believer.* New York: Harper & Row.

Holland, J. L. (1997). *Making vocational choices: A theory of vocational personalities and work environments* (3rd ed.). Odessa, FL: Psychological Assessment Resources.

Hou, J. M. (2015). *Characteristics of highly resilient counselors* (Unpublished doctoral dissertation). University of Minnesota, Minneapolis, MN.

Howard, E. E., Inman, A. G., & Altman, A. N. (2006). Critical incidents among novice counselor trainees. *Counselor Education & Supervision, 46*, 88–102. doi: 10.1002/j.1556–6978.2006.tb00015.x

Jenkins, S. R., & Baird, S. (2002). Secondary traumatic stress and vicarious trauma: A validational study. *Journal of traumatic stress, 15*, 423–432. doi: 10.1023/A:1020193526843

Jennings, L., D'Rozario, V., Goh, M., Sovereign, A., Brogger, M., & Skovholt, T. (2008). Psychotherapy expertise in Singapore: A qualitative investigation. Psychotherapy Research, 18(5), 508–522. doi: 10.1080/10503300802189782

Jennings, L., & Skovholt, T. M. (1999). The cognitive, emotional and relational characteristics of master therapists [Special section]. *Journal of Counseling Psychology, 46*(1), 3–11. doi: 10.1037/0022–0167.46.1.3

Jennings, L., & Skovholt, T. M. (Eds.). (in press). *Expertise in counseling and therapy: Master therapist studies from around the world.* New York: Oxford University.

Jennings, L., Soverign, A., Renninger, S., Goh, M., Skovholt, T. M., Lakhani, S., & Hessel, H. (in press). Bringing it all together: A qualitative meta-analysis of seven master therapists studies from around the world. In L. Jennings & T. M. Skovholt (Eds.), *Expertise in counseling and therapy: Master therapist studies from around the world.* New York: Oxford University Press.

Johnson, T. H., & Ward, T. (Eds.). (1958). *The letters of Emily Dickinson* (Vol. 2). Cambridge, MA: Belknop Press of Harvard University.

Jordan, K. (2010). Vicarious trauma: Proposed factors that impact clinicians. *Journal of Family Psychotherapy, 21*, 225–237. doi: 10.1080/08975 353.2010.529003

Kabat-Zinn, J. (2003). Mindfulness-based interventions in context: Past, present, and future. *Clinical Psychology: Science and Practice, 10*(2), 144–156. doi: 10.1093/clipsy/bpg016

Kabat-Zinn, J., Lipworth, L., & Burney, R. (1985). The clinical use of mindfulness meditation for the self-regulation of chronic pain. *Journal of Behavioral Medicine, 8*, 163–190. doi: 10.1007/BF00845519

Karasek, R., & Theorell, T. (1992). *Healthy work: Stress, productivity and the restructuring of working life.* New York: Basic Books.

Kaslow, N. J., Keilin, W. G., & Hsu, J. (2010). Internship and postdoctoral programs in professional–Psychology. *Corsini Encyclopedia of Psychology*, 1–3. Association of Psychology Postdoctoral and Internship Centers. New York: Wiley.

Kassam-Adams, N. (1995). The risks of treating sexual trauma: Stress and secondary trauma in psychotherapists. In B. H. Stamm (Ed.), *Secondary traumatic stress: Self-care issues for clinicians, researchers, and educators* (pp. 37–48). Lutherville, MD: Sidran Press.

Kierkegaard, S., Hong, E., & Hong, H. (1983). *Fear and trembling/repetition: Kierkegaard's writings* (Vol. 6). Princeton, NJ: Princeton University.

Kinnetz, P. L. (1988). Saving myself vs. serving clients. *Journal of Counseling and Development, 67,* 87. doi: 10.1002/j.1556–6676.1988.tb02031.x

Klem, A. M., & Connell, J. P. (2004). Relationships matter: Linking teacher support to student engagement and achievement. *Journal of School Health, 74*(7), 262–273. doi: 10.1111/j.1746–1561.2004.tb08283.x

Kohlberg, L. (1979). *Measuring moral judgment.* Worcester, MA: Clark University Press.

Kottler, J. A., & Carlson, J. (2014). *On being a master therapist: Practicing what you preach.* New York: Wiley.

Kram, K. (1985). *Mentoring at work: Developmental relationships in organizational life.* Glenview, IL: Scott, Foresman.

Kramer, K. P. (2004). *Martin Buber's I and thou: Practicing living dialogue.* Mahwah, NJ: Paulist Press.

Kristof, N. D. (2009, February 16). Week in review: Our greatest national shame. *New York Times,* p. 11.

Kushner, H. S. (1996). *How good do we have to be? A new understanding of guilt and forgiveness.* Boston: Little, Brown.

Kwon, K., & Kim, C. (2007). Analysis of the characteristics of Korean master group counselors. *The Korean Journal of Counseling, 8*(3), 979–1010.

Ladany, N., Hill, C. E., Corbett, M. M., & Nutt, E. A. (1996). Nature, extent, and importance of what psychotherapy trainees do not disclose to their supervisors. *Journal of Counseling Psychology, 43,* 10–24.

Lambert, M. J., Garfield, S. L., & Bergin, A. E. (2004). Overview, trends, and future issues. In M. J. Lambert (Eds.), *Handbook of psychotherapy and behavior change* (pp. 805–821). New York: John Wiley & Sons.

Lange, S. (1988). Critical incidents aren't accidents. *Journal of Counseling and Development, 67,* 109.

Larson, D. G. (1993). *The helper's journey.* Champaign, IL: Research Press.

Leiter, M. P., & Maslach, C. (2005). *Banishing burnout: Six strategies for improving your relationship with work.* San Francisco, CA: Jossey-Bass.

Levine, H. (1996). *In search of Sugihara: The elusive Japanese diplomat who risked his life to rescue 10, 000 Jews from the Holocaust.* New York: Free Press.

Levinson, D., Darrow, D., Klein, E., Levinson, M., & McKee, R. (1978). *The seasons of a man's life.* New York: Ballantine Books.

Lieberman, M. A., Yalom, I. D., & Miles, M. B. (1973). *Encounter groups: First facts.* New York: Basic Books.

Lief, H. I., & Fox, R. C. (1963). Training for "detached concern" in medical students. In H. I. Leif, V. I. Lief, & N. R. Leif (Eds.), *The psychological basis of medical practice* (pp. 12–35). New York: Harper & Row.

Lindbergh, A. M. (1975). *Gift from the sea.* New York: Pantheon Books.

Linley, A., & Joseph, S. (2007). Therapy work and therapists' positive and negative well-being. *Journal of Social and Clinical Psychology, 26*(3), 385–403. doi: 10.1521/jscp.2007.26.3.385

Linville, M. (1988). The long afternoon. *Journal of Counseling and Development, 67,* 101. doi: 10.1002/j.1556–6676.1988.tb02045.x

Lisle, L. (1987). *Portrait of an artist: A biography of Georgia O'Keeffe.* Albuquerque: University of New Mexico Press.

Lopez, S., & Edwards, E. M. (2008). The interface of counseling psychology and positive psychology: Assessing and promoting strengths. In S.D. Brown & R.W. Lent (Eds.), *Handbook of counseling psychology* (pp. 86–102). New York: Wiley.

Luthar, S. S., Cicchatti, D., & Becker, B. (2000). The construct of resilience: A critical evaluation and guidelines for future work. *Child Development, 71*(3), 543–563. doi: 10.1111/1467–8624.00164

Maas, H. S. (1963). Long term effects of early childhood separation and group care. *Vita Humana, 6*(1–2), 34–56. doi: 10.1159/000269669

Maclay, E. (1977). *Green winter: Celebrations of later life.* New York: Readers Digest Press.

Maggio, R. (1997). *Quotations from women on life.* Paramus, NJ: Prentice Hall.

Mahoney, M. J. (1997). Psychotherapists' personal problems and self-care patterns. *Professional Psychology: Research and Practice, 28*(1), 14–16. doi: 10.1037/0735–7028.28.1.14

Majeski, T. (1996, August 6). Hospital turns a corner. *St. Paul Pioneer Press,* pp. 1A, 5A.

Mallinckrodt, B., & Wei, M. (2005). Attachment, social competencies, social support, and psychological distress. *Journal of Counseling Psychology, 52,* 358–367. Doi: 10.1037/0022–0167.52.3.358

Mann, K., Gordon, J., & MacLeod, A. (2009). Reflection and reflective practice in health professions education: A systematic review. *Advances in Health Sciences Education, 14*(4), 595–621. doi: 10.1007/s10459–007–9090–2

Mann, T., Tomiyama, A. J., Westling, E., Lew, A., Samuels, B., & Chatman, J. (2007). Diets are not the answer. *American Psychologist, 62*(3), 220–233. doi: 10.1037/0003–066X.62.3.220

Martin, J., Slemon, A. G., Hiebert, B., Halberg, E. T., & Cummings, A. L. (1989). Conceptualizations of novice and experienced counselors. *Journal of Counseling Psychology, 36,* 395–400. doi: 10.1037/0022–0167.36.4.395

Maslach, C. (1982). *Burnout: The cost of caring.* Englewood Cliffs, NJ: Prentice-Hall.

Maslach, C. (2003). *Burnout: The cost of caring.* Cambridge, MA: Malor Books.

Maslach, C., & Jackson, S. E. (1981). *The Maslach Burnout Inventory.* Palo Alto, CA: Consulting Psychologists Press.

Maslach, C., & Leiter, M. P. (1997). *The truth about burnout.* San Francisco, CA: Jossey-Bass.

Maslach, C. & Leiter, M. P. (2008). Early predictors of job burnout and engagement. *Journal of Applied Psychology, 93*(3), 498–512. doi: 10.1037/0021–9010.93.3.498

Maslow, A. H. (1968). *Toward a psychology of being.* New York: Van Nostrand Reinhold.

Masten, A. S. (2014). *Ordinary magic: Resilience in development.* New York: Wiley.

Mathieu, F. (2012). *The compassion fatigue workbook.* New York: Routledge.

May, R. (1969). *Love and will.* New York: W. W. Norton.

Mayeroff, M. (1990). *On caring.* New York: Harper Perennial.

McAslan, A. (2010, March 14). Re: *The concept of resilience: Understanding its origins, meaning and utility* [Web blog message]. Retrieved from http://www.torrensresilience.org/origins-of-the-term

McCann, I. L., & Pearlman, L. A. (1990). Vicarious traumatization: A framework for understanding the psychological effects of working with victims. *Journal of traumatic stress, 3,* 131–149. doi: 10.1007/BF00975140

McConnell, E. A. (Ed.). (1982). *Burnout in the nursing profession.* St. Louis, MO: Mosby.

McCourt, F. (2005). *Teacher man: A memoir.* New York: Scribner.

McRae, C. (2010). One hour of career counseling and 30 years of influence. In M. Trotter-Mathison, J. M. Koch, S. Sanger, & T. M. Skovholt (Eds.), *Voices from the field: Defining moments in counselor and therapist development* (pp. 32–34). New York: Routledge.

Milbouer, S. (1999, August 21). Social worker slain outside client's home. *Boston Globe,* pp. B1–B2.

Miller, W. R., & Rollnick, S. (2002). *Motivational interviewing: Preparing people for change* (2nd ed.). New York: Guilford.

Mitchell, K. R., & Anderson, H. (1983). *All our losses, all our griefs: Resources for pastoral care.* Louisville, KY: Westminster, John Knox.

Molassiotis, A., & Haberman, M. (1996). Evaluation of burnout and job satisfaction in marrow and transplant nurses. *Cancer Nursing, 19,* 360–367. Retrieved from http://journals.lww.com/cancernursingonline/Abstract/1996/10000/Evaluation_of_burnout_and_job_satisfaction_in.5.aspx

Montagu, A. (1974). *The natural superiority of women.* New York: Collier Books.

Moreland, L. (1993). Learning cycle. *Family Therapy Networker,* May/June, 13.

Morton, L. L., Vesco, R., Williams, N. H., & Awender, M. A. (1997). Student teacher anxieties related to class management, pedagogy, evaluation and staff relations. *British Journal of Educational Psychology, 67,* 69–89. doi: 10.1111/j.2044–8279.1997.tb01228.x

Moskowitz, S. A., & Rupert, P. A. (1983). Conflict resolution within the supervisory relationship. *Professional Psychology: Research and Practice, 14,* 632–641. doi: 10.1037/0735–7028.14.5.632

Mullenbach, M. (2000). *Expert therapists: A study of professional resiliency and emotional wellness* (Unpublished doctoral dissertation). University of Minnesota, Minneapolis, MN.

National Mental Health Survey of Doctors and Medical Students in Australia. (2013, October 8). Retrieved from https://www.beyondblue.org.au/docs/default-source/research-project-files/bl1132-report—nmhdmss-full-report_web.pdf?sfvrsn=4

National Sleep Foundation. (2006). *Sleep–wake cycle: Its physiology and impact on health.* Retrieved from http://www.sleepfoundation.org

Neff, K. D. (2003). Development and validation of a scale to measure self-compassion. *Self and Identity, 2,* 223–250. doi: 10.1080/15298860390209035

Neff, K. D., Kirkpatrick, K. L., & Rude, S. S. (2007). Self-compassion and adaptive psychological functioning. *Journal of Research in Personality, 41,* 139–154. doi: 10.1016/j.jrp.2006.03.004

Neufeldt, S. A. (2007). *Supervision strategies for the first practicum* (3rd ed.). Alexandria, VA: American Counseling Association.

Neufeldt, S. A., Karno, M. P., & Nelson, M. L. (1996). A qualitative study of experts' conceptualization of supervisee reflectivity. *Journal of Counseling Psychology, 43*(1), 3–9. doi: 10.1037/0022–0167.43.1.3

Neusner, J. (Trans.). (1984). *Torah from our sages.* Dallas: Rossel Books. (Original work approximately 900 A.D.)

Newell, J. M., & MacNeil, G. A. (2010). Professional Burnout, Vicarious Trauma, Secondary Traumatic Stress, and Compassion Fatigue. *Best Practices in Mental Health, 6*(2), 57–68.

Nissen-Lie, H. A., Havik, O. E., Høglend, P. A., Monsen, J. T., & Rønnestad, M. H. (2013). The contribution of the quality of therapists' personal lives to the development of the working alliance. *Journal of Counseling Psychology, 60*, 483–495. doi:10.1037/a0033643

Nissen-Lie, H.A., Rønnestad, M.H., Høglend, P.A., Havik, O.E., Solbakken, O.A., Stiles, T.C., & Monsen, J.T. (2015). Love yourself as a person, doubt yourself as a therapist?. *Clinical Psychology & Psychotherapy*. doi: 10.1002/cpp.1977

Norcross, J. C. (2010). The therapeutic relationship. In B. L. Duncan, S. D. Miller, B. E. Wampold, & M. A. Hubble (Eds.), *The heart and soul of change: Delivering what works in therapy* (pp. 133–178). Washington, DC: American Psychological Association.

Norcross. J. C., & Guy, J. D. (2007). *Leaving it at the office: A guide to psychotherapist self-care.* New York: Guilford.

Ogles, B. M., & Hayes, J. A. (2010). Michael J. Lambert: Building confidence in psychotherapy. In L. G. Castonguay, C. J. Muran, L. Angus, J. A. Hayes, N. Ladany, & T. Anderson (Eds.), *Bringing psychotherapy research to life: Understanding change through the work of leading clinical researchers* (pp. 141–151). Washington, DC: American Psychological Association.

Okun, B. F., & Kantrowitz, R. E. (2008). *Effective helping: Interviewing and counseling techniques* (7th ed.). Belmont, CA: Brooks/Cole.

Oliner, S. P. (2003). *Do unto others: Extraordinary acts of ordinary people.* Boulder, CO: Westview Press.

Olson, D. H. (2000). Circumplex model of marital and family functioning. Journal of Family Therapy, 22(2), 144–167. doi: 10.1111/1467–6427.00144

Olson, S. (1997). *The singing wilderness.* Minneapolis: University of Minnesota Press.

Orlinsky, D. E., Botermans, J.-F., & Rønnestad, M. H. (2001). Toward an empirically grounded model of psychotherapy training: 5000 therapists rate influences on their development. *Australian Psychologist, 36*, 139–148. doi: 10.1080/00050060108259646

Orlinsky, D. E., & Rønnestad, M. H. (2005). *How psychotherapists develop: A study of therapeutic work and professional growth.* Washington, DC: American Psychological Association.

Orlinsky, D., & Rønnestad, M. H. (2013). Positive and negative cycles of practitioner\development: Evidence, concepts and implications from a collaborative quantitative study of psychotherapists. In M. H. Rønnestad & T. M. Skovholt (Eds.), *The developing practitioner: Growth and stagnation of therapists and counselors* (pp. 265–290). New York: Routledge.

Orlinsky, D. E., Rønnestad, M. H., Ambuhl, H., Willutzki, U., Botermans, J.-F., Cierpka, M., Davis, J., & Davis, M. (1999). Psychotherapists' assessment of their development of their development at different career levels. *Psychotherapy, 35,* 203–215. doi: 10.1037/h0087772

Osachuk, T. A. G. (2010). The transforming moment with David. In M. Trotter-Mathison, J. M., Koch, S. Sanger, & T. M. Skovholt (Eds.), *Voices from the field: Defining moments in counselor and therapist development* (pp. 64–66). New York: Routledge.

Palmer, P. J. (1998). *The courage to teach: Exploring the inner landscape of a teacher's life.* San Francisco, CA: Jossey-Bass.

Palmer, P. J. (2004). *A hidden wholeness: The journey toward an undivided life.* San Francisco, CA: John Wiley & Sons.

Papastylianou, A., Kaila, M., & Polychronopoulos, M. (2009). Teachers' burnout, depression, role ambiguity and conflict. *Social Psychology of Education, 12*(3), 295–314. doi: 10.1007/s11218–008–9086–7

Pearlman, L. A. (1995). Self-care for trauma therapists: Ameliorating vicarious traumatization. In B. H. Stamm (Ed.), *Secondary traumatic stress: Self-care issues for clinicians, researchers, and educators* (pp. 51–64). Lutherville, MD: Sidran Press.

Pearlman, L. A., & MacIan, P. S. (1995). Vicarious traumatization: An empirical study of the effects of trauma work on trauma therapists. *Professional Psychology: Research and Practice, 26,* 558–565. doi: 10.1037/0735–7028.26. 6.558

Peck, M. S. (1978). *The road less traveled: A new psychology of love, traditional values and spiritual growth.* New York: Simon & Schuster.

Penedo, F. J., & Dahn, J. R. (2005). Exercise and well-being: A review of mental and physical health benefits associated with physical activity. *Current Opinion in Psychiatry, 18,* 189–193. doi: 10.1097/00001504–200503000–00013

Perry, W. G. (1981). Cognitive and ethical growth: The making of meaning. In W. Chickering & Associates (Eds.), *The modern American college* (pp. 76–116). San Francisco: Jossey-Boss.

Piaget, J. (1972). Intellectual evolution from adolescence to adulthood. *Human Development, 15,* 1–12. doi: 10.1159/000271225

Pica, M. (1998). The ambiguous nature of clinical training and its impact on the development of student clinicians. *Psychotherapy, 35,* 361–365. doi: 10.1037/h0087840

Pilpay. (1872). *The fables of Pilpay.* New York: Hurd and Houghton.

Pincus, S. (1997). Recognizing your emotional vulnerabilities. In J. Kottler (Ed.), *Finding your way as a counselor* (pp. 59–61). Alexandria, VA: American Counseling Association.

Piper, M. (2003). *Letters to a young therapist.* New York: Basic Books.

Pistole, M. C. (2003). Linking work, love, individual, and family issues in counseling: An attachment theory perspective. In P. Erdman & T. Caffery

(Eds.), *Attachment and family systems: Conceptual, empirical, and therapeutic relatedness* (pp. 117–137). New York: Brunner-Routledge.

Pistole, M. C., & Fitch, J. C. (2008). Attachment theory in supervision: A critical incident experience. *Counselor Education and Supervision, 47,* 193–205. doi: 10.1002/j.1556–6978.2008.tb00049.x

Plante, T. G. (1993). Aerobic exercise in prevention and treatment of psychopathology. In P. Seraganian (Ed.), *Exercise psychology: The influence of physical exercise on psychological processes* (pp. 358–379). New York: John Wiley & Sons.

Pollack, S. K. (1988). Grieving and growing. *Journal of Counseling and Development, 67,* 117.

Pope, K. S., & Tabachnick, B. G. (1994). Therapists as patients: A national survey of psychologists' experiences, problems and beliefs. *Professional Psychology: Research and Practice, 25,* 247–258. doi: 10.1037//0735–7028. 25.3.247

Pope, K., & Vasquez, M. (1991). *Ethics in psychotherapy and counseling.* San Francisco, CA: Jossey-Bass.

Prochaska, J. O., DiClemente, C. C., & Norcross, J. C. (1992). In search of how people change: Applications to addictive behavior. *American Psychologist, 47*(9), 1102–1114. doi: 10.1037/0003–066x.47.9.1102

Prochaska, J. O., & Norcross, J. C. (2001). Stages of change. *Psychotherapy, 38*(4), 443–448. doi: 10.1037//0033–3204.38.4.443

Radeke, J. T., & Mahoney, M. J. (2000). Comparing the personal lives of psychotherapists and research psychologists. *Professional Psychology: Research and Practice, 31,* 82–84. doi: 10.1037//0735–7028.31.1.82

Raimy, V. C. (Ed.). (1950). *Training in clinical psychology.* Upper Saddle River, NJ: Prentice Hall.

Reibel, D. K., Greeson, J. M., Brainard, G. C., & Rosenzweig, S. (2001). Mindfulness-based stress reduction and health-related quality of life in a heterogeneous patient population. *General Hospital Psychiatry, 23*(4), 183–192. doi: 10.1016/S0163–8343(01)00149–9

Reissman, F. (1965). The "helper" therapy principle. *Social Work, 10,* 27–32. Retrieved from http://www.jstor.org/stable/23708219

Rilke, R. M. (2000). *Letters to a young poet.* Novato, CA: New World Library.

Roberts, C. A. (1986). Burnout: Psychobabble, or a valuable concept? *British Journal of Hospital Medicine, 36,* 194–197.

Robiner, W. N., Fuhrman, M., & Ristvedt, S. (1993). Evaluation difficulties in supervising psychology interns. *Clinical Psychologist, 46,* 3–13.

Robinson, B. E. (1992). *Overdoing it: How to slow down and take care of yourself.* Deerfield Beach, FL: Health Communications.

Rodolfa, E. R., Kraft, W. A., & Reilley, R. R. (1988). Stressors of professionals and trainees at APA-approved counseling and VA Medical Center internship sites. *Professional Psychology: Research and Practice, 19,* 43–49. doi: 10.1037/0735–7028.19.1.43

Rogers, C. R. (1957). The necessary and sufficient conditions of therapeutic personality change. *Journal of Consulting Psychology, 21*(2), 95–103. doi: 10.1037/h0045357

Rogers, C. R. (1961). *On becoming a person.* Boston: Houghton Mifflin.

Rogers, C. R. (1995). *A way of being.* Boston: Houghton Mifflin.

Rønnestad, M.H. (1985). A developmental model of supervision in clinical work [English abstract of Norwegian journal]. *Journal of the Norwegian Psychological Association, 22,* 175–181.

Rønnestad, M. H. (2008). Profesjonell utvikling [Professional development]. In A. Molander & L. I. Terum (Eds.), *Profesjonsstudier* [*Professional studies*] (pp. 279–294). Oslo: Universitetsforlaget.

Rønnestad, M. H., Gullestad, S. E., Halvorsen, M. S., Haavind, H., Lippe, A. L. von der, Nissen-Lie, H. A., & Reichelt, S. (2014, June). *The outcomes of therapies conducted by highly experienced therapists.* Paper presented at Society for Psychotherapy Research; International meeting, Copenhagen, Denmark.

Rønnestad, M. H., & Lippe, A. L. von der. (2002). *Det kliniske intervjuet* [*The clinical interview*]. Oslo: Gyldendal Akademisk.

Rønnestad, M. H., & Skovholt, T. M. (2001). Learning arenas for professional development: Retrospective accounts of senior psychotherapists. *Professional Psychology: Research and Practice, 32,* 181–187. doi: 10.1037/0735-7028. 32.2.181

Rønnestad, M. H., & Skovholt, T. M. (2003). The journey of the counselor and therapist: Research findings and perspectives development. *Journal of Career Development, 30*(1), 5–44. doi: 10.1023/A:1025173508081

Rønnestad, M. H., & Skovholt, T. M. (2013). *The developing practitioner: Growth and stagnation of therapists and counselors.* New York: Routledge.

Roth, A. L. (2014). *Yoga as a psychological intervention: Conceptualizations and practice integration of psychologists-yoga teachers* (Unpublished doctoral dissertation). University of Minnesota, Minneapolis, MN.

Rothschild, B., with M. Rand (2006). *Help for the helper: The psychophysiology of compassion fatigue and vicarious trauma.* New York: W. W. Norton.

Ruddick, S. (1989). *Maternal thinking: Toward a politics of peace.* Boston: Beacon Press.

Rupert, P. A., Stevanovic, P., & Hunley, H. A. (2009). Work-family conflict and burnout among practicing psychologists. *Professional Psychology: Research and Practice, 40,* 54–61. doi: 10.1037/a0012538

Rupp, J. (1994). *Little pieces of light.* Mahwah, NJ: Paulist Press.

Rutter, M. (1985). Resilience in the face of adversity: Protective factors and resistance to psychiatric disorders. *The British Journal of Psychiatry, 147,* 598–611.

Sanger, S. (2010). How to fail. In M. Trotter-Mathison, J. M. Koch, S. Sanger, & T. M. Skovholt (Eds.), *Voices from the field: Defining moments in counselor and therapist development* (pp. 72–75). New York: Routledge.

Schafer, W. (1996). *Stress management for wellness.* Fort Worth, TX: Harcourt Brace.

Schaufeli, W. B., Leiter, M. P., & Maslach, C. (2009). Burnout: 35 years of research and practice. *Career Development International, 14*(3), 204–220. doi: 10.1108/13620430910966406

Schelske, M. T., & Romano, J. L. (1994). Coping skills and classroom management training for student teachers. *The Teacher Educator, 29,* 21–33. doi: 10.1080/08878739409555059

Schlossberg, N. K. (1984). *Counseling adults in transition: Linking practice with theory.* New York: Springer Publishing Company.

Schoefield, W. (1974). *Psychotherapy: The purchase of friendship.* Englewood Cliffs, NJ: Prentice-Hall.

Schön, D. A., (1987). *Educating the reflective practitioner.* San Francisco: Jossey-Bass.

Schor, J. (1998). *The overspent American.* New York: Basic Books.

Schorr, M. (1997). On being a wounded healer. In J. Kottler (Ed.), *Finding your way as a counselor* (pp. 55–58). Alexandria, VA: American Counseling Association.

Schweitzer, A. (1975). In *The Reader's Digest Treasury of Modern Quotations.* New York: Readers Digest Press.

Selye, H. (1974). *Stress without distress.* New York: Signet.

Sexton, T. L., & Whiston, S. C. (1994). The status of the counseling relationship: An empirical review, theoretical implications, and research directions. *The Counseling Psychologist, 22*(1), 6–78. doi: 10.1177/0011000094221002

Shirom, A., Oliver, A., & Stein, E. (2009). Teachers' stressors and strains: A longitudinal study of their relationships. *International Journal of Stress Management, 16*(4), 312–332. doi: 10.1037/a0016842

Skinner, B. F. (1953). *Science and human behavior.* New York: Macmillan.

Skovholt, T. M. (1974). The client as helper: A means to promote personal growth. *The Counseling Psychologist, 4*(3), 56–64. doi: 10.1177/001100007 400400308

Skovholt, T. M. (1986, Spring). Learning to teach. In *Focus: On teaching and learning,* (p. 8). Minneapolis, MN: Office of Educational Development, University of Minnesota.

Skovholt, T. M. (1988). Searching for reality. *The Counseling Psychologist, 16,* 282–287. doi: 10.1177/0011000088162010

Skovholt, T. M. (2001). *The resilient practitioner: Burnout prevention and self-care strategies for counselors, therapists, teaches and health professionals.* Needham Heights, MA: Allyn & Bacon.

Skovholt, T. M. (2005). The cycle of caring: A model of expertise in the helping professions. *Journal of Mental Health Counseling, 27,* 82–93. doi: 10.17744/ mehc.27.1.mj5rcvy6c713tafw

Skovholt, T. M. (2008). Two versions of erosion in the helping professions: Caring burnout and meaning burnout. *New Therapist, 52,* 28–29.

Skovholt, T. M. (2012a). *Becoming a therapist: On the path to mastery.* New York: John Wiley and Sons.

Skovholt, T. M. (2012b). The counselor's resilient self. *Turkish Journal of Counseling and Guidance, 4,* 137–146.

Skovholt, T. M. (2014). Searching for certainty. In D. Salvador & R. Collins (Eds.), *Mentoring doctors: How to design and implement a junior doctor mentoring program in Australia* (pp. 8–10). Queensland, Australia: Dianne Salvador Publisher.

Skovholt, T. M., & D'Rozario, V. (2000). Portraits of outstanding and inadequate teachers in Singapore: The impact of emotional intelligence. *Teaching & Learning, 40*(1), 9–17. Retrieved from http://hdl.handle.net/10497/342

Skovholt, T. M., & Jennings, L. (2004). *Master therapists.* Boston: Pearson.

Skovholt, T. M., Jennings, L., & Mullenbach, M. (2004). Portrait of the master therapist: Developmental model of the highly functioning self. In T. M. Skovholt & L. Jennings. (Eds.), *Master therapists: Exploring expertise in therapy and counseling* (pp. 125–146). Boston: Allyn and Bacon.

Skovholt, T. M., & McCarthy, P. R. (Eds.). (1988). Critical incidents in counselor development [Special issue]. *Journal of Counseling and Development, 67,* 69–135. doi: 10.1002/j.1556–6676.1988.tb02016.x

Skovholt, T. M., Morgan, J., & Cunningham, H. N. (1989). Mental imagery in career counseling and life planning: A review of research and intervention methods. *Journal of Counseling and Development, 67,* 287–291. doi: 10.1002/j.1556–6676.1989.tb02604.x

Skovholt, T. M., & Rønnestad, M. H. (1992a). *The evolving professional self.* John Wiley and Sons.

Skovholt, T. M., & Rønnestad, M. H. (1992b). Themes in therapist and counselor development. *Journal of Counseling & Development, 70,* 505–515. doi: 10.1002/j.1556–6676.1992.tb01646.x

Skovholt, T. M., Rønnestad, M. H., & Jennings, L. (1997). Searching for expertise in counseling, psychotherapy, and professional psychology. *Educational Psychology Review, 9*(4), 361–369. doi: 10.1023/A:1024798723295

Skovholt, T. M., & Starkey, M. T. (2012). The practitioner's intense search for knowing in a sea of ambiguity: Answers from the learning triangle of practice, academic research and personal life. In G. Neimeier & J. Taylor (Eds.), *Continuing professional development and lifelong learning: Issues, impacts and outcomes* (pp. 229–247). Hauppauge, NY: Nova Science.

Skovholt, T. M., & Trotter-Mathison, M. (2011). *The resilient practitioner* (2nd ed.). New York, NY: Routledge.

Skovholt, T. M., Vaughan, M., & Jennings, L. (2012). Practitioner mastery and expertise. In T. M. Skovholt (Ed.), *Becoming a therapist: On the path to mastery* (pp. 203–242). New York: Wiley.

Smetanka, M. J. (1992, November 6). Burnout vaccine: Institute gives teachers a shot of enthusiasm. *Minneapolis Star Tribune,* p. 1B.

Smiley, J. (1991). *A thousand acres.* New York: Ivy Books.

Smith, A. (2008). *Personal characteristics of master couple therapists* (Unpublished doctoral dissertation thesis). University of Alberta, Canada.

Smith, P. L., & Moss, S. B. (2009). Psychologist impairment: What is it, how can it be prevented and what can be done to address it? *Clinical Psychology: Science and Practice, 16,* 1–15. doi: 10.1111/j.1468–2850.2009. 01137.x

Smith, T., & Hawks, S. R. (2006). Intuitive easting, diet composition, and the meaning of food in healthy weight promotion. *American Journal of Health Education, 37*(3), 130–136. doi: 10.1080/19325037.2006.10598892

Söderfeldt, M., Söderfeldt, B., & Warg, L. E. (1995). Burnout in social work. *Social Work, 40,* 638–646. Retrieved from http://www.jstor.org/stable/23718210

Stamm, B. H. (1995). Preface. In B. H. Stamm (Ed.), *Secondary traumatic stress: Self-care issues for clinicians, researchers, and educators* (pp. ix–xii). Lutherville, MD: Sidran Press.

Stanley, T. J., & Danko, W. D. (1996). *The millionaire next door.* New York: Pocket Books.

Stevanovic, P., & Rupert, P. A. (2004). Career-sustaining behaviors, satisfactions, and stresses of professional psychologists. *Psychotherapy: Theory, Research, Practice, Training, 41*(3), 301–309. doi: 10.1037/0033–3204.41.3.301

Stevens, W. (1923). *Harmonium.* New York: Alfred A. Knopf.

Stiles, W. (1997). Multiple voices in psychotherapy clients. *Journal of Psychotherapy Integration, 7,* 177–180. doi: 10.1037/h0101121

Stone, G. L. (1988). The heroic syndrome. *Journal of Counseling and Development, 67,* 108. doi: 10.1002/j.1556–6676.1988.tb02052.x

Strauss, J. L., Hayes, A. M., Johnson, S. L., Newman, C. F., Brown, G. K., Barber, J. P., . . . A. T. Beck. (2006). Early alliance, alliance ruptures, and symptom change in a nonrandomized trial of cognitive therapy for avoidant and obsessive-compulsive personality disorders. *Journal of Consulting and Clinical Psychology, 74*(2), 337–345. doi: 10.1037/0022–006X.74. 2.337

Strupp, H. H., & Hadley, S. W. (1978). Specific vs. non-specific factors in psychotherapy: A controlled study of outcomes. *Archives of General Psychiatry, 36,* 1125–1136. doi:10.1001/archpsyc.1979.01780100095009

Sussman, M. B. (Ed.). (1995). *A perilous calling: The hazards of psychotherapy practice.* New York: John Wiley & Sons.

Swanson, K. W. (2010). Constructing a learning partnership in transformative teacher development. *Reflective Practice, 11,* 259–269. doi: 10.1080/14623941003672428

Tarasoff v. Regents of the University of California. 118 Cal. Rptr. 129, 529 P 2d 533 (1974).

Teater, M., & Ludgate, J. (2014). *Overcoming compassion fatigue.* Eau Claire, WI: PESI Publishing & Media.

Thoits, P. A. (2011). Mechanisms linking social ties and support to physical and mental health. *Journal of Health and Social Behavior, 52,* 145–161. doi: 10.1177/0022146510395592

Thorson, T. (1994). *Reflections on practice*. Unpublished manuscript, Minneapolis, MN.

Tippett, K. (2007). *Speaking of faith*. New York: Viking.

Torrence, P. (1996). The culture and mentoring series. In A. M. Soliman (Ed.), *Mentoring relationships in the Arab culture* (pp. 2–7). Athens, GA: Georgia Studies of Creative Behavior.

Tracey, T. J. G., Wampold, B. E., Lichtenberg, J. W., & Goodyear, R. K. (2014). Expertise in psychotherapy: An elusive goal? *American Psychologist, 69,* 218–229. doi: 10.1037/a0035099

Tredgold, T. (1818). On the transverse strength of timber. *Philosophical Magazine: A Journal of Theoretical, Experimental and Applied Science,* Chapter XXXXVII. London: Taylor and Francis.

Trotter, M. J. (2009). *Effects of participation in a mindfulness-based stress reduction program on college students' psychological well-being.* Unpublished doctoral dissertation, University of Minnesota, Minneapolis, MN.

Trotter-Mathison, M., Koch, J., Sanger, S., & Skovholt, T. M. (2010). *Voices from the field: Defining moments in counselor and therapist development.* New York: Routledge.

Turner, J. A., Edwards, L. M., Eicken, I. M., Yokoyama, K., Castro, J. R., Tran, A. N-T., & Haggins, K. L. (2005). Self-care: An exploratory study into strategy use and effectiveness. *Professional Psychology: Research and Practice, 36,* 674–680. doi: 10.1037/0735–7028.36.6.674

U.S. Census Bureau. (2014). *US and world population clocks.* Retrieved from www.census.gov/main/www/popclock.html

van Dernoot Lipsky, L., & Burk, C. (2009). *Trauma stewardship: An everyday guide to caring for self while caring for others.* San Francisco, CA: Berrett-Koehler.

Vitaliano, P. P., Zhang, J., & Scanlan, J. M. (2003). Is caregiving hazardous to one's physical health? A metaanalysis. *Psychological Bulletin, 129*(6), 946–972. doi: 10.1037/0033–2909.129.6.946

Vygotsky, L. S. (1962). *Thought and language.* Cambridge: MIT Press.

Wampold, B. E., & Weinberger, J. (2010). Jerome Frank: Psychotherapy researcher and humanitarian. In L. G. Castonguay, J. C. Muran, L. Angus, J. A. Hayes, N. Ladany, & T. Anderson (Eds.), *Bringing psychotherapy research to life: Understanding change through the work of leading clinical researchers* (pp. 29–38). Washington, DC: American Psychological Association.

Ward, C. C., & House, R. M. (1998). Counseling supervision: A reflective model. *Counselor Education and Supervision, 38,* 23–33. doi: 10.1002/j.1556–6978.1998.tb00554.x

Warner, C. (1992). Chinese proverb. In *Dictionary of women's quotations.* Englewood Cliffs, NJ: Prentice Hall.

Weis, A. C. (2010). Growing my perspective beyond the "secret knowledge" mindset. In M. Trotter-Mathison, J. M. Koch, S. Sanger, & T. M. Skovholt

(Eds.), *Voices from the field: Defining moments in counselor and therapist development* (pp. 52–54). New York: Routledge.

Werner, E. E. (1992). The children of Kauai: Resiliency and recovery in adolescence and adulthood. *Journal of Adolescent Health, 13,* 262–268. doi: 10.1016/1054–139X(92)90157-7

Werner, E. E., Bierman, J. M., & French, F. E. (1971). *The children of Kauai: A longitudinal study from the prenatal period to age ten.* Honolulu: University of Hawaii.

Werner, E. E., & Smith, R. (1992). *Overcoming the odds: High risk children from birth to adulthood.* Ithaca, NY: Cornell University Press.

Wessells, D. T., Kutscher, A. H., Seeland, I. B., Selder, F. E., Cherico, D. J., & Clark, E. J. (Eds.). (1989). *Professional burnout in medicine and the helping professions.* New York: Haworth Press.

White, E. C. (2004). *Alice Walker: A life.* New York: W. W. Norton.

Wicks, R. J. (2008). *The resilient clinician.* New York: Oxford University Press.

Winnicott, D. W. (1965). *The maturational processes and the facilitating environment.* New York: International Universities Press.

Wood, D. J., Bruner, J. S., & Ross, G. (1976). The role of tutoring in problems solving. *Journal of Child Psychology and Psychiatry, 17,* 89–100. doi: 10.1111/j.1469–7610.1976.tb00381.x

Woolf, V. (1990). *A moment's liberty: The short diary* (A. O. Bell, Ed.). San Diego, CA: Harcourt Brace Jovanovich.

Yalom, I. D. (1985). *The theory and practice of group psychotherapy* (3rd ed.). New York: Basic Books.

Yalom, I. D. (1989). *Love's executioner.* New York: Basic Books.

Yalom, I. D. (1995). *The theory and practice of group psychotherapy* (4th ed.). New York, NY: Basic Books.

Yalom, I. D. (2002). *The gift of therapy: An open letter to a new generation of therapists and their patients.* New York: HarperCollins.

Yalom, I. D., & Leszcz, M. (2005). *The theory and practice of group psychotherapy* (5th ed.). New York: Basic Books.

Young, M. E. (1997). How to avoid becoming a zombie. In J. Kottler (Ed.), *Finding your way as a counselor* (pp. 45–48). Alexandria, VA: American Counseling Association.

Zeh, J. B. (1988). Counseling behind closed doors: How safe? *Journal of Counseling and Development, 67,* 89. doi: 10.1002/j.1556–6676.1988.tb02033.x

Zeigler, J. N., Kanas, N., Strull, W. M., & Bennet, N. E. (1984). A stress discussion group for medical interns. *Journal of Medical Education, 59,* 205–207.

INDEX

Note: Page numbers in *italics* indicate figures and tables.

cynicism of colleagues and managers
90–1
Czeisler, Charles 170

Darrow, D. 150
data, keeping up with 143–4
David, D. P. 185
Davis, D. D. 33, 34
Davis, M. 174–5
death, denial of 181
demoralized hopelessness 79
detached concern 28
Developing Practitioner, The (Rønnestad
and Skovholt) 193
development method, creating and
sustaining active, individually
designed 143–5
Dickinson, Emily 40
DiClemente, C. C. 69, *69*
Didion, Joan 224
dieting 169
direct engagement of stressful dilemmas
245–6
disillusionment with training 43,
220
distress emotions *see* stress emotions
Dominguez, J. 165
Dreyfus, H. L. 200
Dreyfus, S. E. 200
D'Rozario, V. 20, 65
Dubé, V. 144
Ducharme, F. 144

egotism, altruistic 128
Eison, J. A. 47
elders, professional: affective reactions
to 205–6; development of 227–30; as
models 214
Ellwein, M. C. 61
Elman, N. S. 133
Emmons, Henry 169
emotional boundaries: of experienced
professionals 226–7; of novice
practitioner 56–8; optimal level of
attachment and 27–8; setting 158,
237–8
emotional self-care 162–3
emotional trauma of practitioner 91–3

emotions *see* emotional boundaries;
negative feelings; stress emotions
Empathetic Attachment phase of Cycle
of Caring: difficulty in attaching
28–30; nature of attachment process
25–7; optimal attachment 27–8;
overview 24–5, 188
empathy: constant need for 81–3;
defined 22; sympathy compared
to 210–11; *see also* Empathetic
Attachment phase of Cycle of
Caring; vicarious traumatization
endings, ambiguous 112–16, 156–8
Engstrom, D. 111–12
Ericsson, K. A. 54, 142
Erikson, E. 207, 227
Eshelman, E. R. 174–5
ethical fears 91
ethics: novice practitioner and 58–9;
professional 186
Etringer, B. D. 154
evaluation: by professional gatekeepers
55–6; self-evaluation of practitioner
52–3
Evolving Professional Self, The (Skovholt
and Rønnestad) 193
excess baggage 74
exercise 169–70
expectations: glamorized, as core novice
stressor 51–5; monitoring and
reducing 142; of practitioner related
to success 84–5, 226
experienced professional phase 220–7
expertise: emergence of 233, 236–40;
internalization of 228; professional
140; shift from external to internal
43–7, 153–5, 199–200
expressive writing to release distress
emotions 151–2
external expertise, shift to internal expertise
from 43–7, 153–5, 196–7, 199–200
Eye of the Storm model: Expertise in
Cycle of Caring 187–9; High Vitality
Index 186–7; Intense Will to Learn and
Grow 189–91; overview 184–6, 191

Farber, B. 232
Farr, M. J. 142

Olsen, D. C. 145–6
Olson, D. H. 28
one-way caring relationships, danger of 162
openness to experience 143
optimal level of attachment 27–8
Orlinsky, D. E. 44, 163, 189, 190, 193, 217
orphan distress 48
Osachuk, T. A. G. 50–1
Other: in Eye of the Storm model 185; as hero 207–8; I-Thou relationships with 65; resources of 72; right practitioner for 67–8; as source of influence and teacher 202–3; stress emotions of 78–80; as wanting quick solution 65–6
Other-care, balancing with self-care 4–7, 126–7, 128–9
overarousal 173–4
overconsumption 164–5
overinvolvement 57–8, 69, 80

patient *see* Other
Pearlman, L. A. 58, 112
Peck, Scott 21
peer nomination methodology 231
peer relationships 235–6, 241–4
performance anxiety 60, 238
Perry, W. G. 200
personal self, integration of professional self and 195–6, 203–4, 223–5
personal self, sustaining: be avoiding one-way caring 162; with mindfulness 175–6; overview 161, 182, *182*; with renewal process 161–2; with yoga 176–9; *see also* nurturing self
perspective taking 5–6
phases of practitioner development: advanced student 216–18; beginning student 211–16; experienced professional 220–7; lay helper 210–11; novice professional 218–20; overview 195, 209–10; senior professional 227–30
physical self-care 169–70
physical trauma of practitioner 93–6
Pica, M. 38, 39

Pincus, S. 53
Pistole, M. C. 24, 29
playful self-care 171
Poelstra, P. 93
Pollack, S. K. 130–1
Pope, K. S. 163
positive adaption and resilience 126
positive emotions at work 150–1
positive psychology, shift toward 123–4
positive work structure, creating 233, 240–5
practice: gap between theory and 42–3, 206–7; gifts of 14–15; joys of 10–12; rewards of 12–14, *13*; *see also* hazards of practice
practitioners: emotional trauma of 91–3; physical trauma of 93–6; *see also* phases of practitioner development; stressors, of novice practitioners
practitioner self, as fragile and incomplete 60–2
premature closure 208–9
Prietula, M. J. 142
primary trauma experience 93–6
priorities, setting 172
privacy: ambiguous endings and 113–14; covert nature of work and 80–1
Prochaska, J. O. 68–9, *69*
professional development: cyclical/trajectories model of *209*; importance of 247–8; Intense Will to Learn and Grow 189–91; metaphor for 194; *see also* phases of practitioner development; themes of professional development
professional self, integration of personal self and 195–6, 203–4, 223–5
professional self, sustaining: by avoiding grandiosity impulse 142; by creating greenhouse 148–51; with development method 143–5; factors in *159*; with "Good Enough Practitioner" idea 152–3; by maximizing experience of success 138–42, *139*; with meaningful work 136–8; by minimizing ambiguity 156–8; overview 135–6; by reinventing oneself 155–6, *156*; by

releasing distress emotions 151–2; with self-understanding 145–8, *147*; by setting boundaries and limits, and saying no 158; by thinking long term 142–3; by understanding early anxiety 153–5

progressive relaxation 174

projection of negative feelings 74–5

prospective termination 33

protective factors *233*, 245–8, *253*

psychological wellness 133

quick solutions, desire for 65–6

Radeke, J. T. 12, *13*

Raimy, V. C. 56

readiness gap *69*

readiness of Other 54, 68–71, *69*

recreational self-care 172–3

Re-creation phase of Cycle of Caring 35, 189

reflection, professional 144–5, 197–8, 208–9

regulation oversight and control 83

reinforcement, direct 14

reinventing oneself 155–6, *156*

Reissman, F. 13

relationship-intense professions 12, 22, 33, 90–1, 186

relationship of helping *see* helping relationship

relationships, personal 250–1; *see also* peer relationships

relaxation and stress reduction 173–9

religious self-care 181–2

renewal 155, 161, 247–8

Renninger, S. 32, 150–1

resilience: defined 3–4; as demand on helping professionals 4; ingredients for 125–6; research on 124–5; use of term *123*, 123–4

resources: of Other 72; Other need for 75

respect 186

rewards: insufficient, and burnout 106; of practice 12–14, *13*

Rilke, R. M. 112–13

rituals of separation 34–5

Rivers, D. A. 73

Robin, V. 165

Robinson, B. E. 128

Rogers, C. 143, 178, 195

role limits 237–8

Rollick, S. 71

Rønnestad 117

Rønnestad, M. H. 44, 189, 190, 192–3, 194, 212, 217

Roth, Anna 176, 177, 178, 179

Rothschild, B. 78

Row, K. A. 163

Ruddick, S. 132

Rude, S. S. 163

Rupert, P. A. 13, 128–9, 216

Rupp, J. 12

Rutter, M. 125–6, 185

Salvador, Dianne 51

Sanger, S. 44–6

Sarkar, M. 126, 185

Schaufeli, W. B. 103

Schoefield, W. 72

Schoener, G. R. 133

Schön, D. A. 198

Schor, J. 164

Schorr, M. 129–30

Schwebel, M. 185

scrutiny by professional gatekeepers 55–6

secondary gains 72–3

secondary trauma experience 91–3, 110–11

self: practitioner self, as fragile and incomplete 60–2; use of in therapy 238–9 *see also* nurturing self; personal self, integration of professional self and; personal self, sustaining; professional self, integration of personal self and; professional self, sustaining

self-blame 43

self-care: action plan for 258–68; assertive need for 127–9; balancing with Other-care 4–7, 126–7, 128–9; codependency and 132–3; as ethical imperative 133; methods of *266, 267*; at times of crisis or stress 129–31; *see also* nurturing self

self-compassion 163, 178